WHAT BLACK LIBRARIANS ARE SAYING

Edited
with an Introduction by
E. J. JOSEY

The Scarecrow Press, Inc.
Metuchen, N.J.   1972

Library of Congress Cataloging in Publication Data

Josey, E   J   1924-
  What Black librarians are saying.

  1. Negro librarians. 2. Libraries and Negroes.
I. Title.
Z711.9.J65   021   72-5372
ISBN 0-8108-0530-8

Copyright 1972 by E. J. Josey

Dedicated
With Love and Affection
to my
Mother
Frances Bailey Josey
and
to my
Sister
Melba Josey Epps

CONTENTS

	Page
INTRODUCTION by E. J. Josey	1

PART I: A THEORETICAL BUT A PRAGMATICAL PROBLEM

Professionalism Versus Advocacy: The Black
Librarian's Dilemma, by Walter J. Fraser ... 12

PART II: BLACK COMMUNITIES AND INFORMATIONAL NEEDS

The Information Potential in the Liberation of
Black People, by James C. Welbourne, Jr. ... 50

Rat Race, by Binnie L. Tate ... 60

Vignettes and Designs: Schools and School
Librarians, by Ann Stewart Watt ... 65

Black Pride Grows in Brooklyn,
by Edward C. Mapp ... 79

PART III: ON ACADEMIC LIBRARIES

The Democratization of the Urban University
Library, by Etta Stanton Bullock ... 90

A Black Library in a White University,
by Mary D. Walters ... 96

Black Rage and Black Academic Libraries,
by Casper LeRoy Jordan ... 107

Pinhead Libraries and Librarians, In Praise of,
by Margaret Perry ... 113

Black Materials: Time for a National Plan,
by William D. Cunningham ... 120

PART IV: AN INTELLECTUAL FREEDOM QUESTION

    What Price Freedom, Angela Davis?
    by Jeanne English   132

PART V: CRITICAL ISSUES IN LIBRARY EDUCATION

    Against All Odds, We Have Been Believers,
    by Mohammed M. Aman   150

    Library Education and Non-Print Media: The
    State of the Art, by Herman L. Totten   163

    Library Schools and Black People,
    by Robert L. Wright   183

PART VI: ORGANIZING FOR PROFESSIONAL ACTION

    The Professional Librarian As Unionist,
    by Oliver Kirkpatrick   192

    As a Black Librarian, I Am Asking What's Next?
    by James E. Crayton   202

    The Black Caucus--A Meaningful Course of Action,
    by John A. Axam   208

PART VII: TOWARD BETTER PUBLIC LIBRARY SERVICE FOR BLACK PEOPLE

    The Public Library and the Black Experience,
    by James R. Wright   220

    Thinking Out Loud, by Doreitha R. Madden   227

    Thoughts on Public Libraries and Librarianship,
    by Thomas Alford   231

    Community and Out-Reach Librarians: Challenge
    and Change, by Ella Gaines Yates   241

    Farewell Traditionalism: A Perspective of the
    Inner City Library, by Robert B. Ford, Jr.   249

PART VIII: LIBRARIANS AS PERPETRATORS OF CHANGE

    The Black Librarian as Change Agent,
    by Louise Giles   256

Special Libraries, Librarians and the Continuing
Education of Black People, by Vivian D. Hewitt 268

A Black Librarian's Challenge to the Publisher's
World, by Bessie R. Grayson 275

Culture Shock, The Third World, Soul Power
and Other Thoughts, by Miles M. Jackson 283

Dreams, Reality, and Tailor-Made Service,
by Ann Knight Randall 288

Notes on Contributors 303

Index 309

INTRODUCTION

The struggle of black people in the United States is at an historical crossroad. For the last twenty years, black people in this country pursued a program of integration but their heroic attempts to participate in the larger society on an integrated basis were blocked by a recalcitrant white racist society. When it became evident that black people were still facing the most blatant and humiliating forms of discrimination and oppression from the larger society in general, and indifference, disinterest, and outright bigotry from the government, specifically, black people adopted the slogan, "Black Power."

This slogan sent chills up and down the spines of white Americans. The term was denounced by some black moderates and white liberals. In the midst of the debate regarding the new rhetoric that black Americans seized from the freedom cry of Stokely Carmichael, a National Committee of Negro Churchmen in July, 1966 issued a manifesto which put the slogan in a realistic perspective.

Commenting on the substantive aspects of the expression, these distinguished black clergymen stated that,

> The fundamental distortion facing us in the controversy about <u>black power</u> is rooted in a gross imbalance of power and conscience between Negroes and White Americans. It is this distortion, mainly, which is responsible for the widespread, though often inarticulate, assumption that white people are justified in getting what they want through the use of power, but that Negro Americans must ... make their appeal only through conscience. As a result, the power of white men and the conscience of black men have both been corrupted. The power of white men is corrupted because it meets little meaningful resistance from Negroes to temper it and keep white men from aping God. The conscience of black men is corrupted because having no power to implement the demands of conscience,

the concern for justice is transmuted into a distorted form of love, which, in the absence of justice, becomes chaotic self-surrender. Powerlessness breeds a race of beggars. We are faced now with a situation where conscienceless power meets powerless conscience, threatening the very foundation of our nation.

And this is really the fundamental question to which these gentlemen addressed themselves: is it possible for meaningful relationships to develop between black and white people as long as there is an imbalance of power? Six years ago these men reached the conclusion that "American democratic power with a small d" could not be acquired under such circumstances. Furthermore, and with an historical perspective, they declared that it was the "same old problem of power and race which has faced our beloved country since 1619."

The plight of the black man in America has changed very little since 1966. There is little progress to report at the national level. President Nixon has "made one thing perfectly clear": that he has no genuine interest in the predicament of blacks in this country. This is his record: the nomination and the appointment of a man to the Supreme Court who personally prevented black citizens from voting; his refusal for one year to meet with black members of Congress--and he only met with them after they dramatized their plight by boycotting his 1971 State of the Union Address; the Justice Department supported the Attorney General of Mississippi by opposing the NAACP Legal Defense and Educational Fund in school desegregation cases; the president introduced and obtained no-knock and preventive detention legislation (a law which applied nowhere else in the country) for Washington, D.C., a city that has a 71 per cent black population; he vetoed legislation which would have established child care centers that would have benefited thousands of youngsters under the age of six whose black mothers would have been free to obtain employment; he fought against giving strong enforcement legislation to the Equal Employment Opportunity Commission; he has used the prestige of his office to oppose busing, thus eroding meaningful integration of the schools. This act alone has given hope to the George Wallaces of the country and now has even stampeded so-called liberals in the Congress into voting with racist reactionaries to prohibit the use of emergency desegregation funds for busing programs. Nixon has made the busing of

Introduction

school children, an American phenomenon which has prevailed for many years, a political scare word. The United States Civil Rights Commission reported in 1971 that the Federal Government's civil rights enforcement improved only from "poor to marginal" during the year. The foregoing list of problems is prima facie evidence that black people in this country have had an Administration in Washington that has trampled on their rights as American citizens.

As we turn to other recent events, the most dehumanizing and brutalizing single event was the terrible tragedy at Attica. This was a massacre of blacks and Puerto Rican prisoners and hostages that The New York Times in an editorial described as follows: "The death of these persons ... reflects a barbarism wholly alien to civilized society." Black Americans viewed the holocaust at Attica as a savage retaliation against black people, who comprise the largest majority of the prison population, and as a reinforcement of the dictum that a black man has no rights that a white man should respect. The blood spilled in Attica will have been spilled in vain, if it does not lead to a state and national program of prison reform.

A grim reminder of the man in the White House was the congratulatory message sent to Governor Rockefeller by President Nixon after the storming of Attica and before the evidence had been judiciously examined. The tragedy of Attica was further compounded by releases of "incorrect" news from Attica, wittingly or unwittingly designed to degrade the inmates who were seeking redress of just grievances.

The denial of bail to Angela Davis for almost two years, and the President's castigation of her in the most vicious of terms, and contrasted with his appearance on nationwide television with a promise to review the case of Lt. Calley, a convicted murderer of innocent civilians at Mylai--such events make black people wonder if they have a President. If the President were seriously concerned about justice, he would review the hundreds of cases involving black and poor people in America and the hundreds of cases of black servicemen in the Armed Forces who suffer from blatant discrimination in Germany and even in the war zone of Vietnam.

An analysis of the 1970 census figures shows that minority living areas are growing rapidly as non-Puerto

Rican whites are fleeing from the City of New York. Affluent whites in the Forest Hills section of the Borough of Queens oppose scattered housing in their area of New York City, for it would bring, in their opinion, undesirable poor blacks and Puerto Ricans into their neighborhood. It is difficult to understand why black people and poor people should not have the opportunity to live in Forest Hills or any community they wish. This attempt to deny decent housing to black and poor people is happening in New York, not in Mississippi.

The specter of white women attempting to block busing in Pontiac, Michigan is a frightening reminder of Bull Connor's dogs and George Wallace standing in the schoolhouse door. Black people are wondering about this spectacle. When black children were bused from their neighborhoods past lily-white schools to attend black segregated schools no one complained about busing. If busing could be used as a mechanism to circumvent the law, black people are questioning why it can't be used as a device to comply with the law.

As we move into the 1972 presidential elections, one aspirant has candidly indicated that a black person as a vice presidential running mate would be a liability to the party ticket. This is an open admission of the extent to which black people are subject to racism in America. It is quite obvious that candidates of this ilk for the highest office in the land will not be concerned about the basic issues facing blacks: jobs, housing, real welfare reform, federal health insurance, equal opportunity in employment, and quality education. The black clergymen reminded us that it is the "same old problem of power and race." It follows, then, that if black people are to have justice and an effective response from American society, they must organize into enclaves of black strength, e.g., caucuses and other organizations similar to the National Black Political Convention which met in Gary, Indiana in March of 1972.

An ominous and disturbing question forces itself upon me: Is it possible for black people to love the United States in view of their second class citizenship status? Confronting their conscience with this critical question, most black people, including my fellow black librarians who have made contributions to this book, would probably answer: Yes, I love my country, but not the injustice that I have had to suffer. The great French writer, Albert Camus, prob-

Introduction

ably put it more tellingly: "I should like to be able to love my country and still love justice."

The twenty-seven distinguished black librarians whose essays make up this volume, in my opinion, and as reflected in their essays, still love this country and still love justice. However, as the reader begins to savor their concerns, it will become apparent that they are foes of injustice and inequity.

The foregoing portrait of the plight of black people in America sets the stage for What Black Librarians Are Saying. Black librarians are inextricably tied to the problems that affect the larger black community. They have suffered the same hurts, humiliations, discrimination in employment opportunity, lack of promotion on the job, denial of decent housing, and the whole panorama of what it means to be black in a racist society.

On another level they have become aware of the fact, just as their fellow black citizens have, that the history books, by and large, have ignored the ideas and contributions of black people. They have heard the story of Professor Gregory Willis Hayes, a black educator at Virginia State College, during the early years of this century, who told his class one day: "This history you study is supposed to be the history of the United States. It is incorrect. It does not include the record of the black man." Continuing, he said, "if a true history of the United States is written, a history that will include the records of the black man, a Negro will have to write it."

There is a scarcity of information on black librarians' views about society in general and about librarianship in particular. Like their fellow black professionals in other disciplines, they have, for too long, been invisible. Not only have black librarians been invisible in key leadership positions in the field of librarianship; they have also been scarcely visible in the chronicling of burning issues in the field which affect them as professionals. In too many instances their opinions are not sought. Evidence of this fact may be seen in a recently published book of interviews with university librarians: the author did not invite one black librarian to participate. This overlooking of black librarians has happened in other publishing ventures. To paraphrase Professor Hayes, if a history that will include the record of the black librarian is written, the black librarian will have to write it.

What Black Librarians Are Saying is divided into eight parts. In part one, the focus is on a theoretical but a pragmatical problem, in a provocative essay "Professionalism versus Advocacy: The Black Librarian's Dilemma" by Walter J. Fraser. He defines the black librarian and delineates the difference between his role as a professional and his role as an advocate. Fraser reminds us that "the black librarian, committed simultaneously to excellence in his craft and the improvement of conditions in which his people live, has twin demands on his time, intellect and energies. Never, never for an instant, can he be sure that he has not devoted too much time to one at the expense of the other."

Part two deals with black communities and their informational needs. Welbourne warns that "the deliberate withholding of information as a way to maintain white control over black efforts towards self-determination is not only a dangerous practice, but one certain to bring about the forceful seizure by blacks of their information rights." To this group belong essays also by Tate, Watt and Mapp. Tate indicates that "much has been said but little done to change the structure of libraries to meet the needs of the disenfranchised."

Academic libraries are the subject of part three. Bullock declares: "there is little in the atmosphere of most university libraries that would encourage librarians into activity in keeping with social change." Walters calls attention to the fact that when the black faculty and black students of Ohio State University petitioned the University for the establishment of a departmental library to support the Black Studies Program, "they found that, historically, Ohio State University Libraries had never hired a black professional librarian to head a department library; that only one black professional librarian serves in the public service area of the entire university library system; and that there has never been a black male professional librarian on the staff of the Ohio State University Libraries." Cunningham sounds the alarm for a union catalog of printed materials on Afro-Americana and establishes a model for a national informational, storage and retrieval system for black materials. Penetrating essays by Perry and Jordan complete this section.

Part four is concerned with an intellectual freedom question. English, in "What Price Freedom, Angela Davis?"

Introduction

explores in precise and logical language the many ramifications of the Angela Davis case, and its implications to her personally as a librarian and to all librarians. She writes: "in order, therefore, for the people to exercise intellectual freedom, realize the political and physical freedom which accrue from it, and as a consequence, emerge both as individuals and as a nation from the present impasse of outmoded forms and rituals, it is necessary to increase infinitely the range of sources from which we seek information. We need to delve into political and social viewpoints of a far wider range than provided by the customary conservative, liberal, moderately left and right vehicles of information resting on our library stacks."

A fearless and implacable foe of the curtailment of intellectual freedom, Miss English was requested to dismantle her exhibit on Angela Davis in the Evanston Township High School Library by her high school principal, who viewed Angela's case "as merely a criminal case, very much like the Manson case...." This distinguished librarian stood firm and was supported by her colleagues and students--a good lesson for timid librarians.

Part five presents three views on library education. Aman confronts the problems of libraries and library education in his declaration that "as an American institution, libraries and the library profession cannot claim the distinction of being free from hypocrisy, and racist policies and practices. Libraries and the library profession have consistently ignored the needs of black people." Continuing, he states, "the library profession, as the rest of the professions, has failed to recruit actively, train and employ blacks and other minority groups into the full range of the library profession." In a brilliant argument, he indicts the profession: "if black visibility in the library profession and in its program can be viewed as an indicator of the institutions' intent to reform and reflect the existence, needs and contributions of blacks, then the library profession must be charged with the insidious crime of racism."

The other two essays in this group are by Totten, who presents a state-of-the-art paper dealing with library education and non-print media, and by Wright, who discusses the "Library Schools and Black People."

Organizing for professional action is the subject of part six. Kirkpatrick examines "The Professional Librarian as Unionist." Chastising librarians for being anti-unionist, Kirkpatrick exhorts: "there is the mistaken notion that social cachet is derived from, and some status acquired by, being a librarian. Nothing could be further from the truth. Professionals in other fields regard us with amused tolerance, and the public by and large thinks of us as 'people who stamp out books'."

Crayton discusses the problems that black professionals encountered at the Los Angeles County Public Library, and what steps were taken to right employment and promotional inequities. Axam deals with the Black Caucus as a viable vehicle to give black librarians power, and suggests strategies to accomplish goals.

Black librarians have developed a distinctive consciousness about the failure of public libraries to meet the needs of black people, and part seven includes proposals and suggestions for better library service. Wright demands that we "overhaul the entire public library structure and redesign it to meet present day needs." Yates makes a strong case for innovative community outreach programs by public libraries and suggests the establishment of "new structures in accordance with new times." Ford deplores the fact that inner-city libraries "as they are currently managed and operated, are 'over-institutionalized'." Other essays in this group are by Madden and Alford.

The last section attempts to assess critically librarians as perpetrators of change. Giles examines "The Black Librarian as Change Agent," and challenges librarians "to re-examine the role of the profession." She argues cogently that "self-renewal at this time within the library field could mean self-preservation. For, I submit that librarians have not done anything to make themselves indispensable to society." As a warning to black librarians she advises, "forward-thinking black librarians, who are now more aggressively seeking to make library service more adequate to the needs of black people and to make the library profession more responsive to the talents of black librarians, can take note: if society finds the library profession irrelevant, even obsolete, for its needs, what advantage will it be for blacks to have found a place in a dying profession?"

Hewitt reports on the role of special librarians in aiding students in non-traditional academic programs. Grayson challenges publishers to issue more relevant material.

Introduction

Miles Jackson discusses culture shock abroad and raises this serious question: "Is there something in the Black Experience in this country that prepares a black person to approach an assignment in Africa, Asia or Latin America with more compassion than that of his white colleagues?"

Randall's positive appraisal of the librarian as a perpetrator of change is the final essay in the volume. While Mrs. Randall ranges over a number of serious topics in her stimulating essay, she concludes with the belief that "black librarians, regardless of their position and professional interest, can exercise a viable role in bringing their insight and educational training to the solution of common problems."

While these twenty-seven essays have been grouped under eight rubrics and may claim to have a leitmotiv, the truth of the matter is that all of the authors grapple with various aspects of librarianship in terms of problem areas impinging upon the black community, and of issues facing them as librarians. More importantly, most of the essays reflect something of the anguish of black Americans locked, seemingly interminably, into a racist society. However, there is no wallowing in hopelessness and despair; there, rather, is a clarion call to American society in general and to librarianship in particular to eradicate the inequities of library service to the black community, to ensure equal opportunity for black librarians in every field of librarianship, and to effect the total destruction of racism in American society.

It is our hope that this volume places some of the key issues and their possible consequences in perspective.

E. J. Josey

Albany, New York
March, 1972

PART I

A Theoretical But a Pragmatical Problem

PROFESSIONALISM VERSUS ADVOCACY:
THE BLACK LIBRARIAN'S DILEMMA

by Walter J. Fraser

In discussing the subject matter of this essay it will be very difficult to avoid asking the reader to make several gestalt shifts. Primarily, this requirement for shifting from one Weltanschauung to another is rooted in the fact that the essay is intended to outline one man's impression of the collision of two such world views. The professional and the advocate not only look at the world in very different ways, they have usually fashioned or chosen their world views as much as a function of their training or personality as a response to the pressures and/or opportunities which the environment seems to offer them. Perhaps this short a statement serves more to obfuscate than clarify; if that is the case, I will have to ask the reader's temporary indulgence while I attend to some other matters before returning to a detailed exposition of my perceptions of the world view of the professional and the advocate.

First among these other matters is the requirement to make it clear that this essay is about a serious matter. If the reader is black, he may at first wonder about the need to assert that blacks' dilemmas in American society are really serious; but the printed word's audience defies prediction and some readers may not consider such problems as real. All of which brings us back to the sort of gestalt switches which are required in dealing with the topic of this essay. Caucasians, encountered socially and professionally in recent years, have been continually talking about the preferential treatment which this society accords to blacks. The litany runs--and if one doesn't believe that people really think this way he should tune in to any local radio program which encourages telephone comments from the listening audience--the litany runs that blacks, whatever injuries they may have suffered in the past, are now given first chance at any available job, easier treatment in the courts, preferential treatment by welfare authorities, faster advancement for less work and ability in the military, more scholarship

A Theoretical But A Pragmatical Problem

aid, etc. The fact that such opinions are not only held but widely voiced is one of the reasons that gestalt switches are required in any consideration of race relations today. Those members of the society who perceive it to be functioning in the manner just described are in a very different intellectual world from that of most blacks. Viewed from the position just expressed, any problem which a black man or woman has in this society is a self-made problem and ultimately trivial. It is, in part, the existence of such a world view that prompts the assertion that this essay is in fact dealing with a serious problem.

While presuming on the indulgence of the reader who perceived the seriousness of the subject all the time, it is necessary to try to offer other readers something. Since it is probably impossible to convince or convert, those who view black problems as self-made or trivial are asked to suspend disbelief for the rest of the essay and consider the viewpoint of this particular black author and realize that this essay is written out of his perceptions. I regard the black problem as a serious one because blacks in this society die earlier than Caucasians. Some years ago it was on the average ten years earlier. Recently the difference in life expectancy has narrowed somewhat, but it still exists. Many poignant things have been written about the position of the black in American life, but it seems to me that all of those things can be subsumed in the disheartening reflection that, due to the conditions in which American blacks are forced to live, they die earlier. They die earlier in great numbers, because where there is a population of 22 million quite a few people have to die quite a bit earlier to cause the average age of death to change. As has been said, for the person who seriously believes that blacks are getting preferred treatment in society, reading the rest of this essay will require a gestalt switch. It is not required that such a reader concur with my perception that the early death rate among American blacks is caused by the structure of the society. All that is required to perceive the reality of the dilemma to the black professional is to remember that many black professionals, and particularly this author, do in fact believe that the society and its institutions cause many of his people to die at much earlier ages than their fellow citizens. If, for the time it takes to read this essay, it can be remembered that the black professional perceives the problem as a life and death matter, then the subsequent discussion can be seen to be clearly non-trivial from the black professional's point of view.

Before leaving the question of whether or not this article is non-trivial, one other group of readers may have to be asked to make a gestalt switch. In part because of the internalization of modern social criticism, some young blacks, with the intellectual capacity to function as say a doctor or a physicist or a chemist, have questioned whether or not it was relevant to prepare for and practice any profession that did not <u>directly</u> contribute to changing the execrable conditions in which the great mass of blacks live. While I am old enough to have made my initial professional choice before such views were as widespread as they have since become, the question of whether being a librarian is "relevant" is one which must be answered affirmatively or, again, the dilemma posed by this essay does not exist.

To say it another way: any reader who believes that the only relevant occupation for any black is as an activist devoting his whole time to the movement will also have to make a gestalt switch to perceive that this essay is about a serious matter. While conversion may be no more possible here than with those who think all black problems trivial, it seems appropriate to try. If every black is an activist whose entire working day is devoted to the problem of race relations, then there will be no one to take advantage of any new opportunities in a desegregated society or no one to do the work of a separated society of blacks. It is given to very few, as this world goes, to live solely by the profession of principles. Babies must be fed, clothes must be bought, housing secured and, in addition, money must be found to support those in the community who do make it a profession to work for the rest of the community. The priesthood is always small. Obviously there are some who say the society is bad and work to tear it down stick by stick, and for them the problem of occupation is settled. Just as obviously, no racial group in this country lives that way, by and large, or the society would already be torn down. Blacks alone, while perhaps causing their own destruction, could stop the society in its tracks for a time and leave it scarred forever, given unanimity of will and purpose and effective communications with one another. Those who have not been converted by these remarks will have to make their own gestalt switch and see the problem through the eyes of this author or they might as well not read further. It will have to be assumed as a given fact that there is a good reason for blacks to educate themselves conventionally and practice the professions of this society--in particular the profession of librarianship. If, for the time it takes to read this essay, it can be assumed that it is worthwhile to the black community and to the larger community for people to be professional librarians, with all that that entails, then another group of readers will be able to perceive that the dilemma being sketched is a real one indeed.

Before going on, although this has turned into a long introduction, there are a few other introductory matters which should be taken into account. This is an essay. It is not intended to be a scholarly paper. The volume in which it is to be printed is concerned with the thoughts and feelings of black librarians, not necessarily with their scholarly activity. If it has an academic odor, then I must simply plead guilty to being an academic type. The statements which will be made below are frequently couched as though they were truths, self-evident and not requiring proof; for stylistic reasons qualifying locutions have been avoided in many cases, and it will be left to the reader to determine whether or not his Weltanschauung and mine have any meaningful points of contact.

One last comment of a stylistic nature is required. While I have protested that this is an essay on a serious matter, seriousness contains no requirement for solemnity and no deliberate effort will be expended to try to make the essay any more dull than any other essay by an academic type.

Professionalism

When the trophy-winning, college athlete signs the half-million dollar contract, it is said that he has turned professional. While the designation usually implies that the person so designated is paid for his activities, some individuals are described as professionals due to the avidity with which they indulge in some activity; the professional gossip springs to mind along with others who perform some function because of their avidity. (Both aspects, reward and avidity, may reasonably prompt reflection on the applicability of this entire section to practitioners of the oldest profession. While not intentionally solemn, as was promised, this essay does not seem the place, and I am unwilling to admit the possession of the expertise necessary to pursue such matters.) Others are called professionals because of the frequency with which they practice their art; the professional troublemaker or agitator is not always paid. Almost always the designation implies great skill and competence in a specialty when used as an adjective, but when used as a noun in the phrase "a real professional" the emphasis is on the skill, devotion, and dependability of the individual so described. Indeed, where the professional practices his skill or art in concert with others, he is the leader and takes day-to-day direction only from other professionals; the doctor is king over the para-professionals in the hospital.

When a professional works at his profession the product of his labor is often intangible. Certainly the professional artist offers a concrete object as the result of his labor, but in this case the aspect which gives the artist's work value, the essence of quality for which he is paid, is quite unstable and may congeal or evaporate, causing the physical object to appreciate or be devalued in a wink of the purchaser's anxious eye.

Finally, the professional's work situation is unique. The professional works for many employers but is responsible, ultimately, to none. Access to professional status and continued permission to practice is determined by his peers. The doctors and lawyers, professionals par excellence, have embedded into the civil, if not the criminal, law of most modern societies mechanisms which enable representatives of the profession to control who (and how many) shall practice their profession. In addition, both of those professions have established, legally, the principle that only professional peers may determine the competence of the individual practitioner.

This legally buttressed professional independence means that doctors, who have systematically ensured a chronic shortage in their profession, may practice their skills with lordly indifference to the wishes of the people who pay them. In a society which generally allows the payer of the piper to determine the tune, doctors keep those who pay them waiting for hours and dictate to their clients more often than advising them. The indifference mentioned above also extends to the outcome of professional activity. The lawyer, whose client suffers great loss after having followed his advice, usually requires the client to pay his fee nonetheless. The bereaved family of the deceased is always expected to ante up for services which, even in a gross, nonprofessional view, have demonstrably failed to produce the intended result. Furthermore, when the soul of the corpse who had a heart attack because of his lawyer's ex-

A Theoretical But A Pragmatical Problem

pensive, bad advice and died because of his doctor's even more expensive clumsiness--when that soul arrives in hell, there is no record of his contributions to any church having been refunded. Here again, as in a parenthetical note above, I must deny the possession of perfect information. But the fact remains that, although his clergyman's advice may have been literally as bad as sin, and his lawyer's advice of equal quality, and even if both together reduced him to a state of coma similar to the helpless state he was in when his doctor made the final professional mistake of the client's life, the professional's advice is considered sound and the client's misfortune in all cases is his own responsibility. For the doctor, financially, the operation is always a success whether the patient dies or not. Obviously, there are exceptions; physicians to the wealthy and powerful may occasionally function as employees seeking, above all, to gratify the wishes of their employers, but this is not the norm. It is certainly true that in the long run the determination of whether this or that occupation is a profession, as well as the conditions of practice of all professions, will be decided by the lay or nonprofessional society at large; but few of us live in the long run, and in day-to-day activity the doctors and lawyers and clergymen are responsible only to each other. The professional is allowed to practice and is judged in the efficacy of that practice principally by other members of his own profession.

One of the reasons for this professional independence is related to the nature of the problems with which the professional deals. Typically the professional practices his art or skill in relation to problems which the mathematician or the scientist would consider badly defined. (As an interesting digression it may be pertinent to mention that the phrase "professional scientist," while sometimes used, has a rather uncomfortable, if not deprecatory, ring to it. This may be one of the last remnants of the amateur origins of modern science which bequeathed to posterity the unreal but pervasive view of the scientist as a basically unwordly seeker of truth, disinterested in either remuneration or temporal honors. On the contemporary scene most scientists, even more than many other professionals, are really only subject to peer evaluation and also quite immune to any vital responsibility for socially costly failures. W. H. Auden was not speaking about dedicated, disinterested seekers after truth when he said that in the company of scientists he felt, "like a shabby curate who has wandered by mistake into a drawing room full of dukes." The scientific dukes are professionals and very successful ones at that.) Mathematical and scientific workers may work with well defined problems, but even here the most respected and emulated practitioners of these professions deal with matters which are considerably less clear-cut and therefore require a much larger component of judgment in practicing their profession. Including many mathematicians and scientists then, the professional deals with badly defined problems. In response to the amorphous nature of the problems with which he deals the professional usually offers something like a diagnosis. There is usually a body of knowledge which he seeks to master and a traditional way of applying that knowledge to the problem at hand; but, unless the professional is indeed functioning as a low level worker, each specific application of the profession's corporate experience requires the exercise of that mysterious amalgam of qualities called judgment. The possession of such judgment is what the professionals "profess." From the sanitation engineer to the clergyman, the professional knows the secrets of everything from cleanliness to godliness. No matter how detailed his statement of judgment, however, following his advice is, as noted above, usually the responsibility of the client.

Not only the nature of the problems but the advance of knowledge itself may profit from the professional's privileged freedom from personal and immediate responsibility. Few indeed would be the civil engineers who would dare to build a bridge if they were personally to be held responsible for the safety of all who used the bridge till the end of time. Frank Lloyd Wright, responding to a question on how he knew a tower would stand, proposed that he build a bit, see if it fell, and then build more; then reminded his gasping audience of architects that cathedral walls had many times been constructed only to fall before the flying buttress was discovered. Lest this be considered an isolated instance, it is well to remember that few women died from child-bed fever before they started having babies in hospitals, where the doctors (professional health workers) could rush to the bedside of the mother in labor straight from handling a cadaver or some pathological exudate of another human body and infect the mother and child with unclean hands. Semmelweiss asked contemporaries to wash their hands and got fired more than once, but in the long run the medical profession, in part through its own corporate error, learned more about the spread of disease--knowledge which has saved many in succeeding generations even without direct professional assistance.

A Theoretical But A Pragmatical Problem

Though the temptation is strong, no attempt will be made to encapsulate the definition of the professional in a few short, pithy sentences. This temptation is resisted precisely because the word will have to be interpreted broadly to encompass those who function in the library, and also because the penumbra of meanings which are associated with the word are all pertinent to our subject.

Librarians have for some time been seeking to establish that their craft is a profession. They have sought to establish that only individuals with certain types of academic credentials could practice and then have sought to free those practitioners, in certain vital areas, from any nonprofessional control. It is not difficult to make a case for a librarian as a professional. He or she advises communities or institutions on the type of materials which should be collected to meet their needs, how to store and arrange those materials, and how to promote and control the dissemination of such materials. In addition, librarians advise individuals on the best path to pursue in seeking information without taking any responsibility to that individual should that advice cause delay or loss of resources. In his dealings with patrons across the desk the librarian is no more responsible as an individual for bad advice than is the doctor or lawyer, and--unfortunately--he can sometimes be as indifferently imperious to his clients as either of the others just named. In his more impersonal functions, advising on the acquisition, housing, arrangement, preservation, control, and dissemination of materials, the librarian is even less responsible to the individual patron. There is no one to whom the uninformed user may protest should the information he is seeking on 35mm slide projectors be concealed under the heading LANTERN SLIDES, and scant attention indeed will be given to the more informed user who does find someone to listen to his protest. Clearly, the arrangement of materials in a library is a professional matter.

The pretensions of librarians to professional status and its comfortable tradition of independence from client or employer control are in great part embedded in the librarian's intimate connection with issues of free speech and repression. If free speech is a value, then the librarian should be free to collect for the community any materials which seem appropriate on any basis. If the journalist is accorded professional status to ensure that the community will find out what it needs to know today, then the librarian could logically claim the same freedom to ensure that society will have available the journalist's offerings of both today and tomorrow and the offerings of all society's yesterdays, collected with independence from temporary fanaticisms or aberrations on the part of his employers. Where the <u>Index</u> or the teachings of Mao are important selection tools, it may be more difficult to defend the assertion that the librarian (or the journalist) is a real professional without distorting the traditional, western view of the professional.

Presumably because it is perceived on some level to be in the interests of society, professionals are permitted, even encouraged, and sometimes protected in the maintenance of a type of independence which should be considered a morally neutral stance. In societies where such values are accepted, professionalism means that the practitioner ought to be able to give his advice without fear of reprisal. It is always assumed, in this context, that this will encourage the practitioner to give advice honestly and with all the knowledge, experience, and judgment of which he is capable. Professionalism in our society thus implies that the practitioners, while functioning as professionals, are morally neutral; i.e., the doctor treats the bandit as well as the head of state, the lawyer is not attainted with treason even if his client is guilty of it; and neither the librarian nor the journalist loses his position or his freedom over articles on how to construct bombs or for collecting materials on or describing the activities of the Black Panthers. As the discerning reader has already noted, social decisions are neither discrete nor unchanging. A society which makes a decision to protect the professional's neutrality may simultaneously make other social decisions which turn that morally neutral professional into an enemy of the people. By and large, however, in the democratic west, moral neutrality is a hallmark of the professional because society perceives, occasionally, that the truths of any given day are not written on stone or in the clouds. Moral neutrality is permitted where the conviction exists that not all the answers are known.

The moral neutrality of professionalism has been emphasized here because it is a determining hallmark of the breed and because it is precisely in this aspect that professionalism differs most from advocacy.

<u>Advocacy</u>

Before proceeding too deeply into an examination of

A Theoretical But A Pragmatical Problem

advocacy it is necessary that one possible meaning of the term be excluded quite explicitly. Whatever else is meant by the word in this paper, it will never be used in any sense so that it could cover the activities of the professional advocate, i.e., the lawyer. While sometimes called an advocate, the lawyer, as a professional, is capable of impassioned defense of one side of an issue today and impassioned attack on that very position tomorrow. He is, viewed as a professional, an advocate of his client's cause, not his own. Some lawyers occasionally develop certain interests which they seek to advance in their practice, but most attorneys would agree that the man who has himself for a client has a fool for a lawyer and a fool for a client too. The advocate we seek to describe here is someone who rarely if ever sees the other fellow's point of view; someone who believes that he does indeed have a piece of the truth and seeks to proselytize and promote the spread of his view and, where conversion is impossible, uses any available means to further his goals.

Advocates would be difficult to understand if one did not take into consideration the intensity with which they are oriented toward some goal. The goal, then, overshadows all other considerations and, for the most extreme advocates, no individual is as important as the goals to which the advocate is committed. Eric Hoffer, in his book the *True Believer*, describes the mentality and orientation of the more extreme advocate (for this essay the term true believer may be substituted for the term advocate despite some loss of generality). Hoffer, who considered revolutionary communists and revolutionary Christians as equally valid exemplars of true believers, points out that Jesus said that his follower should not attend to the burial of a relative but let the dead bury their dead and follow him. Hoffer also quotes both Jesus and Lenin as deprecating the family. For Lenin, it was the indestructible cell opposing his utopian plans, and Jesus predicted that he would come to the family not with peace but with a sword to set mother against daughter and brother against brother. For the advocate, the opposition has become the enemy. No person, not father or mother or sister or brother, not one of the millions of kulaks, not a single victim of holy war and inquisition, not even self is as important as the goals of the true believer. With his firmly ordered priorities, the true believer has little trouble with truth or knowledge. The Islamic general who burned the library at Alexandria was a true believer in whose opinion all knowledge was to be found in the Koran. Any lie, any action which serves the greater goal is permissible as the true believer seeks his objectives.

Obviously, as with professionals--and here it is much more important--there are advocates and advocates. Not all advocates take positions as extreme as those outlined in the True Believer. Some, like that much maligned Harriet Beecher Stowe, just write a book that causes a great big war. Neither she nor Julia Ward Howe seem to this writer to have been ruthless sacrificers of all that stood in their way, but advocates they certainly were. They were advocates because advocates, and this is one of their most significant traits, seek to polarize. They seek to ensure that the opposition is pictured, not only as their own personal enemy but, like the pirates of old, as hostis humani generis, or enemies of all mankind. Any move in the direction of recognizing the civil rights of blacks means, to one sort of advocate, either a threat to his daughter's chastity or an attempt to establish black rule. To another sort of advocate any course other than the one he advocates today is racist and a form of genocide. (And--another interesting, or rather sad, digression--one can hear both white and black advocates accuse one another of genocide in this land of ours.) The gentlemen who penned and approved the Declaration of Independence were seeking converts and pledged their sacred honor to a rather ahistorical account of their treatment by the mother country which laid at the door of a supposedly despotic monarch the doings of an elected parliament which was certainly not under the king's absolute control. Nor did those desperate men, who determined to hang together but were concerned that they might have to hang separately, give much space in their Declaration to the services the British lion had offered them in the past. The advocate's memory is selective, his heart is hard, and his hearing defective. Those not with him are not only against him, they are malevolent beasts. Those seeking compromise are often excoriated more viciously than the frankly opposed, because the opposition can, at the very worst, only seduce away part of the advocate's clientele; but the compromisers may not only steal his followers but also negotiate away the basis for controversy, and with it all chance of victory for the advocate's cause.

Polarization, when carried on by advocates, may be as much a tactic as a sign of their status as true believers. You get very few converts by describing accurately the major virtues of the opposition and then indicating the minor instances in which they have erred. But the tendency to polarize is so much a part of the advocate's bag of tricks that some care must be exercised to avoid a definition of

A Theoretical But A Pragmatical Problem 23

advocacy which itself deals only in extremes. Nat Turner and John Brown were advocates, as was DuBois, and the contemporary tendency is to accord them some kind of respect; but Booker T. Washington, who took council of the times, is accused of being an "Uncle Tom" simply because he had a different view of what was really possible in the situation in which he and his people found themselves at a given instant. Those who might disapprove of his insights and reject his example should remember that he too was an advocate. Advocacy need not be violent or seemingly extreme to accomplish its goals. Semmelweiss and Newton were both advocates but neither seems violent or extreme today. Semmelweiss sacrificed a career and Newton, despite his greatness, sacrificed a little of the truth and character to advance himself, if not his ideas. Even as late as 1953, the NAACP members were the principal organized advocates for blacks in the U.S. and while their selfrighteous successors as advocates scorn the past, it might be well to remember that NAACP members have lost livelihood, home, limb, and life itself fighting lynch law in a time when seeking compensatory employment would have caused black and white alike to certify a man as a lunatic. It is important to note here that certification to the status of advocate does not require a molotov cocktail in either hand and the rhetoric of confrontation in one's mouth. The black, little, old lady librarian with the mink on her shoulders and the silver frost in her wig may in fact be doing all that she perceives that she can to change a world that seems to her intolerable.

Here again, it is necessary to remind any readers who may have forgotten that the black professional librarian may see the world in the same way that the author does. And, viewing the present society as one possessed of institutions which systematically, although possibly as much out of indifference as intent, cause the deaths of many other blacks at an early age--with this Weltanschauung, the black librarian may see himself committed to trying to change that society. Obviously, the black professional could seek those changes as a citizen and function in his non-working hours to change things; but just as obviously the pressure to function during the day as a morally neutral professional must be productive of emotional and intellectual tension in the individual who feels himself called upon to be some sort of an advocate against a society in which early death is a socially determined consequence of being born black.

Facets of Dilemma

In a sense, trying to describe the details of the black librarian's dilemma is something like trying to describe the air one breathes. Humans long ago decided that air is odorless, colorless, and tasteless, but this is perhaps more a comment on their adaptation to their environment than a description of that environment. If they could perceive the odor, color, or taste of the pervasive medium in which they are immersed they would be able to perceive little else, since the air which sustains their lives surrounds them enough to crowd out all other sensations. Having been black for a long time, I have grown accustomed to my situation; and, while the odor of that situation is high and offensive, I find it hard to isolate experiences which will be at once meaningful and significant. The attempt made here is very personal and may leave out things central to another's perceptions and include things which others may consider trivial, but some attempt to do this sort of thing is central to the essay.

One experience is that of amazement. Sometimes, having approached a problem on a strictly technical and professional level, I have been amazed when my white co-workers have attributed my intellectual efforts to my racial background. On other occasions when I have become convinced that the issue is racial, I have been amazed at the astonished and disbelieving reaction of my peers who assert that they can see no racial component in the situation. Perhaps this is a demonstration that a man's Weltanschauung determines not only his approach to problems but his ability to detect their very existence.

In addition to amazement there are two other situations which crop up repeatedly. Black professionals are frequently asked to comment on problems from "the" black point of view. Despite the existence of a rich literature indicating the lack of unanimity with which blacks have sought to solve their problems, whites seem to expect that each black is a competent expert on all aspects of the problem. There may, of course, be blacks who deliberately seek such expert status, but this pretention to expertise is dangerous in a day when the black community is very vocal and has many spokesmen who, while they might agree on a critique of the society, offer very different plans for change. Even if he successfully rejects the role of expert, the black librarian is not necessarily home free because he is then

A Theoretical But A Pragmatical Problem

often asked to somehow morally validate the position of the institution. Again and again he is asked, not only to explain to "those people" that the institution is in fact seeking to function on their behalf, but also to reassure his professional colleagues that they are in fact doing the "right thing." It sometimes seems impossible to convince colleagues that there is no black priesthood whose absolution will protect the institution and its program from criticism by other blacks. Frustratingly enough, those who ask, "Well what do you people really want?" and wait impatiently for an answer, are perfectly aware that not all Caucasians will approve of any of their plans. Somehow, even his white peers expect the black professional to be a "representative of his race" while simultaneously functioning as a morally neutral professional.

The facets of the dilemma dealt with thus far are somewhat general and now it is necessary to consider details. For the reasons advanced above, this attempt to list detailed problems will probably be the weakest part of the essay. No listing could be complete enough for some, and any listing will contain matters considered non-racial by others. The listing which follows, then, is intended to be selective and illustrative since I lack the space, the craft, and, again, the knowledge to make it exhaustive. In an effort to make the list as complete as possible it will be helpful to review systematically the major problems of the library profession: i.e., goals, programs, evaluation, recruitment, and professional organizations.

Goals

Until recently it was not usually the fashion for social agencies consciously and explicitly to describe goals, activities, or evaluative methodology. The social acceptability and propriety of the goals, activities, and worth of many agencies were assumed, both by their operating personnel and by that portion of the society at large which counted, to be both obvious and "good." The times they have a-changed. With other portions of the society at large now being heard from, the situation has changed radically. Today it is much more likely that institutions will explicitly state their goals, defend the organization's program for achieving those goals, and evaluate their success or have such evaluation done for them. In this new environment each step is fraught with potential dilemmas for the black professional.

The problems involved in fashioning a coherent, reasonable, and defensible set of goals for the library--for any library--are many, and involve agony for all professionals regardless of color. For years we have assumed that libraries were educational institutions and that we should therefore busy ourselves in acquiring enough material at a relatively low intellectual level to entice those who were uneducated, and then encourage the enticed to read more and progressively to read better materials. There is much evidence that this hasn't worked. There are many librarians, white and black, who assert that we should not be seeking to convert every user into something like a middle class college-educated reader, and many other librarians assert that, whether we should do this or not, we cannot. In the discussion of the goals of a library the black professional is as much involved with the regular knotty problems as any other professional, but he has two extra ones. The two problems relate to: 1) whether the institution intends to serve the blacks in its constituency; and 2) how it intends to serve the blacks in its constituency, and how it intends to serve both blacks and whites in relation to racial matters.

The first problem is perhaps the easiest to deal with. If the institution does not intend to serve blacks within its area, then it should be challenged and help should be sought, because by any canons of professionalism this would be an inappropriate course. Despite the furor in many grant-seeking circles about service to the unserved, let no one assume that every public and private library in this country that hires a black is vitally committed to service to blacks in the community. Although a decision to influence institutional goals in this area is an easy decision for any professional and should not involve much soul-searching for the professional of any color, converting such a decision into agitation might involve loss of position and, what is worse, a hardening of institutional policy. So much for the easy one.

The more difficult of the two problems involves the question of how the institution intends to serve its entire community in areas of race relations. It is possible to devise institutional goals which recognize the existence of both a black community and racial problems, and then to set other goals which commit the institution to seek to mollify the blacks on the one hand and encourage the racist whites on the other. Whatever the color of the society, it is difficult to convince the power brokers in the community that existing

A Theoretical But A Pragmatical Problem 27

institutions and practices need change, and even more difficult to secure funding for such change. Machiavelli asked us to remember "That there is nothing more difficult to plan, more doubtful of success, nor more dangerous to manage than the creation of a new system. For the initiator has the enmity of all who would profit by the preservation of the old institutions and merely lukewarm defenders in those who would gain by the new ones." The times have not changed enough so that that sentence lacks today the validity it had centuries ago when it was written.

Even among professionals it is difficult to gain acceptance of the idea that goals and methods of service which may have had relevance for much of the past, and may still have relevance today, are not, in fact, universals. On the other hand, it is also frequently difficult to convince the professional who has recently gotten religion that not all blacks want to read Tan Confessions, and that some of them are interested in the sort of upgrading which captured the interest of white immigrants years ago. Programs are frequently proposed which embody the use of such pap that any community would be offended. In dealing with questions of how best to serve black communities and the larger community in the area of race relations, it is still difficult to convince many white professionals that there is no way to approach this subject without the investment of institutional resources in long, careful, sensitive, and intelligent study.

Evaluation

The things which can be said about institutional approaches to goals are so germane to matters of evaluation that this subject will be mentioned here rather than, logically, after a consideration of the programs planned to achieve the goals. As with goals, the profession is in the process of coming to grips with matters of evaluation for almost the first time in its history. Of course, some libraries have attempted to evaluate their programs in the past but the pressure on all to evaluate has never been quite as pervasive or quite as threatening in terms of budget. Here, one of the most obvious approaches, a search for consensus among the served, can present rather large problems and undermine the very basis of professional status. If the librarian has to ask the community how his programs are working, it may be more difficult for him to ignore community pressure for the removal of a particular title or for other changes which his professional wisdom tells him are wrong. Nevertheless, the community, black and white, does evaluate the program by using the library or refusing to use it. The black professional, however, should be genuinely concerned by evaluative techniques which ignore the black community or operate on the unreasonable assumption that it functions in the same manner as the white communities which border it.

Program

After a decision--and let it be noted, decision, not agreement--after a decision has been reached on goals, modern institutions grapple with questions of program or services, and much that has been said of goals and evaluation could be trotted out again in relation to the planning of institutional activities designed to achieve the goals decided upon. Rare indeed is the social institution today that can produce a plan for action which will elicit broad agreement that it does in fact provide for the needs targeted in the institution's statement of goals. Again, not all the dilemmas are the exclusive property of the black professional; but, as usual, where there are problems in this society there are some special ones left over for the blacks. Among the latter are some aspects of: the location of branches, the selection of materials, and the cataloging of those materials.

Program--services

The location of branches in many cities is a matter of real concern. In my experience with several city library systems on both coasts and in the midwest, library management has found it impossible to locate branches conveniently for black borrowers. Professional, or supposedly professional, criteria are used by one library administration after another to justify building new branches or expanding old branches in affluent or semi-affluent neighborhoods and closing or reducing the hours of service in branches which serve either economic or racial ghettos. One major midwestern city refused to build a branch in the ghetto because the bookmobile which was sent to the area was not heavily used. Other librarians justify the construction of branches in white areas because they expect that use will be high. A dear friend, now deceased, who worked in public health, once pointed out that wherever publicly supported mental hospitals were constructed the number of certifications of lunacy rose; repeated research with highly literate scientists indicates

A Theoretical But A Pragmatical Problem

that they choose the closest and most convenient information source. If we don't build the asylum, if we make access to information difficult, then it would seem to follow that we will have fewer lunatics and fewer readers. Whatever value such logic has, it is my impression that in most cities in this country, densely populated ghettos are much less well served than sparsely populated higher income areas. But the professional, black or white, who expends community funds and finds it difficult to produce evidence of increased utilization to justify such expenditures is likely to be in hot water. The trouble may be that the services offered the ghetto community lack relevance to the lives of the citizens of those communities; but that, admittedly, is another subject. Few indeed are the communities which plan the dispersion of their services in relation to population rather than usage, and even fewer would be the number of libraries which seek to find out why their services are not being used and establish programs which would lead the poor and the black to use their institutions. Instead, we expect the poorest and most despised among us to come to the one of the society's most forbidding institutions and ask for their services before any need is recognized. The black professional who is concerned both about serving those who already wish to use the library, and also about providing locally available service centers for all citizens, faces dilemmas of major proportion.

Program--selection

Selection in any library presents problems unless the institution's budget is unrestricted; and the day of unrestricted budgets, if it ever existed, has certainly passed. Here again the black librarian is turned to by his professional peers as an expert. Much material has been offered in recent years by unscrupulous reprint publishers, ostensibly for use in relation to black studies, which should never have been reprinted. Much of it is little used by young, black militants or the black community as a whole, and will never be used by most scholars. No librarian, simply by virtue of his race, is competent to decide on the acquisition of new materials without some study and experience. But every black involved faces questions about materials greedily fabricated to take advantage of government funding and the half-awakened conscience of the larger society.

In no other aspect of the profession is the vaunted

neutrality of the professional more defended than in selection activities. The professional is expected to resist, even to the loss of his job, any attempt to censor from any source. The black librarian, as a dispassionate professional, is expected to purchase the works of Carleton C. Coon, the Harvard anthropologist, whose last name may have prompted him to write materials, supposedly academic anthropology, which give aid and comfort to the most racist elements in the society. Jensen, "the educator," who believes that blacks are inherently inferior, is also expected to be represented in the collection because he works at a reputable university and published in reputable journals. Dispassion, however difficult, is much easier to achieve if descriptions of inherently inferior beings do not include your children and do not advocate different education and social situations for them based on their anthropological inferiority. While I am possibly in error, it does seem to me that the urge to censor is more often loudly directed at materials which favor blacks than at materials which insult them. While possibly still in error, it does seem that more energy is expended to prevent the purchase of the writings of young blacks who do, admittedly, use street language than in efforts to keep off the shelves the modern crime novel using the same sort of language. It is difficult to believe that the foul language is in fact the target of those who seek to censor the writings of many blacks; if foul language were their only concern they would have to cast a much wider net than any now being used. Despite these factors, the black professional, according to the tenets of professionalism, is expected to buy materials which proclaim his inferiority and suggest the perpetuation or intensification of social practices designed to prevent him and his inferior children from competing in anything approaching equality with the superior beings who dominate his society. No professional training or experience has provided me with the insight necessary to regard <u>Little Black Sambo</u> as anything other than a disaster, but libraries all over this country still purchase the evidence that Mrs. Bannerman could only see the Indians through lenses refracted for derogatory stereotype; meanwhile, racists battle the picture book which allows the white and black rabbits to marry.

Program--cataloging

After the materials have been purchased the dispassionate, neutral, black professional is expected to catalog them using such headings as MAMMIES and NEGROES <u>AS</u>

A Theoretical But A Pragmatical Problem 31

BUSINESSMEN (and here the patronizing implications if not the italics are in the original). Obviously, it would cost too much for every library in the country to devise its own subject headings and the professionally correct decision is to prefer those headings used by L. C. or Sears. But many of those headings, such as the two above, leave the black librarian considering the possibilities of some unprofessional solution.

Recruitment

As a former library educator who also happened to be black, I have many times been asked how library schools might recruit black students as though there was a special black road for recruitment which baffled the white administrator. Since most library school students are recruited from among people who have worked in libraries, it seems logical that it might be possible, where administrators are serious, to recruit blacks in the same way. It should not be difficult to inform the librarians of colleges with large black enrollments that places are available. In addition, since football teams and Ph.D. candidates in library science have been successfully recruited with money, that approach might also be tried where there are serious intentions to increase the number of blacks in library schools.

There is one other road to recruitment of blacks which has received little if any serious consideration. I have lived in Massachusetts, California, Illinois, Kansas, and Minnesota without encountering one night school program which leads to an accredited master's degree in library science. Blacks, according to all statistics, are not the most wealthy individuals in the society and poor people frequently seek to better their earning power by attendance at night school. Some such programs may exist somewhere in the country but, at least in the states I have mentioned, the accredited library schools, when last heard from, did not offer enough night courses to allow a resident of those states an opportunity to get his master's without going to school during the day. If law schools can prepare students to pass the bar at night, library educators ought to be able to provide professional training on a similar basis. The cost of a library education is further increased in many states where the only, or the only state-supported and therefore inexpensive, library education available is located in rural communities which, in addition to their hostility to blacks, offer little chance for any student to support himself while matriculating. It seems likely that night programs in urban centers, publicized in black communities and colleges, would be able to recruit and prepare more blacks. Since such an approach has had little if any trial this must be regarded as speculation. Even granting that not all the decisions required to implement any of the three proposals above are the responsibility of the same administrator, it is difficult, though perhaps unprofessional, to give full faith and credit to fellow professionals who indicate concern about the situation and leave such simple remedies untested and even unsuggested. And, regardless of the responsibility for the situation, few blacks seem to find their way to library schools.

Once having become a professional and having also been placed in a position where he or she is responsible for hiring other ranks, the black professional has another dilemma. As an officer of a library hiring a truck driver, aware of the hard depression in the black community, I checked with acquaintances and contacted a wide range of agencies with a request for black applicants. The two most qualified black applicants for the position of library truck driver included one who literally could not read well enough to distinguish one book from another, and one whose license to drive had been suspended for six months. When no possible stretching of the obvious requirements of the job will allow one to fill it with a black depression victim there really is a dilemma for the black professional. As a professional, I believe that compensatory employment has only limited utility. If a person receiving the same pay as others on the job does not perform at roughly the same level of efficiency, sooner or later there will be a problem. As an advocate, I would shout that the solution to this problem is worth any cost since human life is involved, and the institution's view of its total social efficiency should be broad enough to include whatever cost is involved in compensatory hiring and retraining. In a country where it has taken until 1970 for the society to find one black capable of running a large city library, most blacks are aware of the vagaries of employment and advancement. While a few blacks direct college libraries, the situation of blacks in libraries, by and large, is similar to their situation in organized sports: they may block and catch passes but seldom if ever quarterback; they may pitch, hit, even play shortstop but never, never manage. As a morally neutral professional, I would say no preferential treatment for any applicant or any employee; as an advocate, I would say, if not now, when? And the dilemma of whom to hire during long continued economic

A Theoretical But A Pragmatical Problem   33

depression for blacks in this country impales the black professional on its horns.

Organizational Activities

The ALA, so they say, is trying. And it is trying for black professionals to realize that the NEA has had a black president but that the next black who becomes president of ALA will be the first. It is trying to note that the Association was able to close the sixtieth decade of the twentieth century without ever having found a black professional worthy of representing the association at a meeting of the International Federation of Library Associations. Every black professional, whatever his professional background and interests, must decide whether to vote for white candidates who agree with him about intellectual interests in the Association or to search the list for blacks to ensure that his other constituency is represented. Each vote and every committee choice presents the same boring dilemma. Each vote requires the black professional to weigh anew his intellectual and professional interests against responsibilities to other black professionals and marginally served black users or potential users of library services.

More on Professionalism

What has been written up to now has only partially described the problems involved. It is somewhat disheartening to reflect that the most forceful comments above seem to be those supporting advocacy, while the benefits to be derived from a professional approach to problems seem, when stated, to stand more politely and therefore more quietly on the page. The difficulties involved in selecting meaningful aspects of black professional experience should not overshadow the fact that complaining about black treatment in this society is easy; only sorting out the significant from the rest is difficult. One of the difficulties may be that I am, as was admitted earlier, an academic type. Before the correct emphasis can be established, it will have to be noted that there is little difference between an academic and a professional type but quite a bit of difference between either of those and the advocate. It is, perhaps, a penchant of the academic or professional type to qualify each statement (viz the "perhaps" in this sentence); it is, perhaps, an academic failing to qualify each statement either to death or, what may be worse, to the point of insipidity. Add to this academic-professional use of language a slight middle-class veneer and the door to insipidity yawns. Speaking of insipidity, there is a story of a college-educated young lady who, having stepped in the leavings of an ill-trained puppy, announced her misfortune with the words, "Oh shit! I stepped in the doo-doo!" The middle-class out of some curious sense of propriety, and the academic professional out of an attempt to be judicious, can allow their language to wander from the basic, real meaning of words.

It is possible--it's very hard to stop using qualifying locutions--that communication on social issues is made more difficult when attempted in keeping with middle class propriety or academic-professional linguistic techniques. The academic professional's urge to qualify, his striving for the most judicious evaluation of the situation, may even stimulate his listener's antagonism as the listener seeks to find out for certain which side this guy is really on. The redeeming virtue of the academic and the best professional approach is precisely involved in the fact that the guy is not on any side when considering issues central to his profession. Not all advocates would agree, since it would seem that where a cause is as just as that of the American black, even dispassionate professional analysis would come to the sort of just solutions which they have in the main missed. That most American professionals never seem to get there is another evidence of social sickness. The correct prescription might be more neutrality on the part of white professionals, not the abandonment of professional neutrality on anyone's part. It may be that the academic, professional types are seeking to understand in terms clear enough to facilitate communication of the situation and forceful enough to prompt action. That's what this essay has been attempting. While some of the material in the last two paragraphs has been a defense of the language of the academic professional, much of it is still a worried digression by an author concerned about having obscured worthwhile insights with some linguistic doo-doo.

No academic type professional, however, could let the last paragraph stand without some judicious balancing. The language of the academic may disturb because of its retreat from simplicity; but the language of confrontation, while clear at times, may also inhibit communication. The language of confrontation, while clear, is intended to polarize. It does polarize. It does inform the listener where the advocate stands. It does tell the listener where the advocate thinks he stands and what the advocate thinks the listener should do. It does promise the listener the advocate's undying enmity should the listener choose any other course than that being advocated here and now. But communication involves listening as well as speaking and the rhetoric of confrontation seldom is couched in terms which encourage dialog.

The advocate describing the pondering professional as an enemy may create an enemy where none previously existed. But many blacks would reject the last sentence. Having lived in a society where black advocates were polite for a long time to no effect, black advocates have noted that more militant language and advocacy seem to have reaped benefits, slim as they are, which were never forthcoming in the days of more restrained rhetoric. While all this is very debatable, the confrontation view of recent changes in race relations is, at best, only a part of the truth. The good clean advocates of the present did not bear or nurture themselves. In the decades before the Supreme Court struck down the "separate but equal" fiction, legions of quiet, polite academics were teaching a generation of black and white college students that this position was morally and intellectually untenable, and equally reserved professionals were constructing the arguments which were later to be used in attacking the "separate but equal" nonsense. (If I may be pardoned for yet another digression, it is sad and strange that the rabid conservatives of this country seem to be almost the only ones who remember that Warren, in the Brown decision, cited Myrdal's American Dilemma and other findings of academics to buttress the case against segregated schools. It is also sad and strange that those rabid conservatives see the academic professional as one of the greatest enemies to "America as our fathers knew it," and as one of the principal agents for non-conservative change in the society, while advocates who would change the society frequently seem to regard the same professionals as moral cowards.)

But there is still one more important consideration: the black professional must deal with other professionals as a member of the craft. It will profit him little, and his race less, if the black professional so completely polarizes his working situation that his insights come to be viewed only as special pleading. There are other realities than the street; and there may even be other ways to accomplish worthwhile goals than by confrontation. At any rate, even the advocate, if he wishes to be successful, should not become so completely enamored of a tactic that the tactic becomes more important than the goal. The successful advocate is always willing to shift the basis and the manner of his attack when necessary, and neither history nor movements in general are kind to leaders who do not shift to the methods appropriate in new or evolving situations. But, and this last one is the terribly important "but" with which this paragraph began, the black professional, to be personally or racially effective, must keep his professional credentials valid in the eyes of his peers. The black professional must use the language of confrontation as judiciously as any professional uses any language.

Much more than the language of the professional, both the movement and the world need the undramatic skills of the academic professionals. It is always easy to criticize the society; it is similarly easy, as demonstrated above, to ridicule the professions and their practitioners; and this is certainly not the first instance in which either thing has been done. However, the professionals have acquired their status, their rewards, their independence, not by conferring these things on themselves but as a grant from the rest of us, as a grant from society at large. Each of the occupations seeking various types of status in the community has had to make a case for structuring the practice of its craft in this or that manner. The librarian's marginal professional status is almost certainly a result of the inability of librarians to convince the society at large that they do in fact preside over the application of worthwhile, difficult to acquire knowledge in areas vital to the continued, effective existence of the society. While most librarians probably believe that the society is mistaken in their case, the last sentence gives the game away. The professions in this society are occupations which the rest of us believe to do exactly what was stated, i.e., preside over the hard business of applying knowledge which is both worthwhile and difficult to acquire in areas perceived as vital to the continued existence of the society. This is what professionalism is all about; and every one of the prerequisites of professionalism has been wrested from the society at large in the interests of furthering that sort of activity.

Collegiality--i.e., the legal or social assignment of control of access to occupations and policing the continued effectiveness of practitioners--was not granted by society to doctors to enable them to demand fatter fees, regardless of

A Theoretical But A Pragmatical Problem 37

contemporary impressions. A collegial form of control in medicine was a direct result of the evils of allowing incompetent people to decide who should be doctors. Whatever the latest positions of the AMA, it and other medical associations earned the gratitude of the entire society in their campaign against quackery. The librarian's claim to professionalism must be supported by convincing the society that there is harmful quackery in libraries too. It is there. One midwestern state with a small population and a large number of independent library districts has nice ladies with little else to do, staffing store front libraries with 50 or so books, and they call that sort of set-up a library. This kind of quackery stifles needed community action to establish worthwhile facilities and deprives all colors of citizens of effective library service. Librarians' claims to professional status, to be effective, will have to involve the exposure of frauds, such as the one described above, as well as successful campaigns which convince the rest of the society that such service is in fact a fraud. The librarians who seek legislative support for professional status will not fare well if their only observed interest is in better working conditions and higher pay, unless they have enough votes to make appeals to reason unnecessary. The argument that collegiality is important is based on the assumption that only professionals are capable of judging other professionals. The man who has passed the bar, the doctor, the pharmacist, etc. are all given a stamp of approval by being permitted to practice. The society has delegated control of the stamp of approval to members of the professions on the assumption that only they are competent to do the job for the rest of us.

Collegiality has led to what was earlier called independence, but most of the recognized professions have managed to make some sort of case for that independence based on the importance and the complexity of the matters with which they deal. In addition, that independence is severely limited in its scope; except perhaps when some profession momentarily captures the public fancy, this is nowhere a plenary grant of independence. As was said above, it would truly be difficult to find civil engineers if each one were personally responsible for all the lives and property carried over his bridge. Instead, each engineer is responsible, not that the bridge never fail but that he has done as good a job as most other engineers would. The standard against which the professional is judged is the current level of professional practice, and this is because the knowledge he is seeking to apply is difficult both to acquire and to apply.

The standard is very hospitable to change since frequently the professional must apply the knowledge of the craft in situations never before faced by any member of the society. Society expects that in such a situation the professional does the best he can with the knowledge available; and our society has embedded this sort of limitation on professional responsibility into the law. Incompetence is not just building a bridge that breaks; incompetence is building a bridge that breaks when the knowledge necessary to build a good one is, or could easily be, the common possession of every marginally competent engineer.

The professional is necessary to the society at large insofar as he does deal with the application of knowledge to the problems of society. Some professionals may specialize in the development of new knowledge, and earn the respect of their peers by so doing, but the professions as a whole are really privileged because they are perceived to be involved with the application of formal knowledge to the problems of the individual and the society at large. The standard, while hospitable to change, is hostile to vagrant innovation and eccentric rigidity alike. We expect the systematic application of the professional's knowledge to the problems he faces, we permit educated guesses but, legally and socially, frown on radical departures which lack sufficient acceptance within the particular professional community. We do not expect a professional to become so enamored of a technique or process that he continues to use it after its abandonment by the rest of his peers. We expect the professional to apply conventional wisdom in a conventional manner. We expect professional communities to insist on reasonable tests of new theories; and we expect the individual practitioner to put them into practice after they have been systematically evaluated by other competent professionals.

There are at least two important consequences of the type of work which professionals do and the sort of training they undergo. First, for a variety of reasons, access to most of the professions has been, if not easier, at least relatively little encumbered with difficulties for blacks in the recent past. It is still easier in most communities in the nation for a black to become a teacher, even a college professor, than to enter most of the trades. In addition, while promotion of blacks is seldom as rapid as promotion of whites, there have again been greater opportunities for advancement in the professions than in the trades or in business at large. It would be absurd, of course, to say that

A Theoretical But A Pragmatical Problem

the commitment of the professional to dispassionate rationality in his work and his status as a guardian of social knowledge have been the only or the determining factors in this situation but, nonetheless, easier access is still the case. Even after one has acknowledged that the professions, like the more remote suburbs, have less to fear from blacks, since the normal restrictions on access to these favored spots which prevent masses of whites from entering also filter out most aspiring blacks; even discounting the fact that few blacks for one reason or another take advantage of apparently easier access to the professional world than to the business community or to the modern trades, the fact remains that access is possible and that direct, overt harassment tends to be lower in the professions.

The second important consequence flows from the fact that, as they are now constituted, the professions are the socially appointed custodians of knowledge. They may qualify, hesitate, temporize and vacillate but, ultimately, like water, the intellectual structures developed and refined within the professions envelop and drown competing ideas and become socially accepted as knowledge; indeed, it is hard to think of any alternate source of technical knowledge that is nearly as good. This is not a discussion of money or power, but of knowledge. Professionals are not the best paid workers in the society. This society, it has been said, supports ten thousand astrologers and only two thousand astronomers. Obviously there is money in the stars, but just as obviously, when the society as a corporate body decided to go to the moon the astrologers were not consulted. The society as a corporate entity was clearly indicating that it believed that the description of reality offered by the astronomers was superior to that offered by the astrologers. And that is what knowledge is; a description of reality. The quiet academic professionals of today are, as the conservatives believe them to be, corrosive agents of change. The laboratory and the study contain the seeds of the future and those who believe otherwise should reflect on the fate of Adolf Hitler after he successfully "cleansed" Europe of the non-Aryan science which contributed greatly to his downfall. The dictator on the white horse, the man of action, may seem to be in control but the laboratory and the typewriter speak to the future in imperative tones.

If professionals are the custodians, not only of current applications of knowledge but also of future truth, then their work is hard to over-value. At this time many young

people reject rationality and assert that the whole society
is too logical, too machinelike, too computerized. Rejecting
rationality, they ask instead that institutions have heart. No
one, least of all a black American, should cavil against an
appeal that social institutions construct their goals and policies with more sensitivity and regard for moral issues; but
those who blame repressive, immoral institutions on rational
actions are far from the mark. Most of the ills of the
society are compounded more from stupidity and irrationality
than from mean spirit. No one, least of all a black American, would deny the existence and the power of mean-spirited
individuals; but it is hard to regard our institutions and not
come to the conclusion that stupidity is more often at work
than purposive malevolence. Race baiting has for years
been the stock in trade of southern and other politicians
seeking to divert white voters from the fact that those politicians were themselves robbing the commonwealth blind.
That such tactics have succeeded to the detriment of the
whites as well as the blacks seems to indicate that stupidity
or irrationality is, and long has been, in the saddle. It
is hard not to agree with the Swedish scientist Stevan Dedijer
who urged that, "We must devote ourselves to reducing irrationality in human behavior from 99 to 97 percent; it could
be the difference between catastrophe and survival."

If black and white radicals don't know the score, the
conservatives do; and George Wallace cheerfully told the
national press club that he was poor, born poor and lived
poor, without feeling badly about it because there were no
sociologists to tell him that he was not happy. Wallace's
solution to the problems of the day is for the social scientists to stop telling people how badly off they are. He and
other conservatives realize that the exposure, the rational
exposure of reality, will eventually fuel a strong movement
for change in the institutions of the society. Ralph Nader's
successes as a consumer advocate are based on the hard
intellectual work of a professionally competent social critic
directed by a sensitive conscience. When men first flew
planes through the air, they flew by the seat of their pants
because they had no instruments to help them orient themselves in mid-air; the contemporary instrument-aided pilot
may be seeking the same city but would be a fool to reject
the collective experience of the profession. Changing and
reforming society can be done with just heart, by the seat
of one's pants, or it can be done following the promptings
of the same heart informed with the cumulated knowledge of
the society. If the society needs more heart, it also needs

A Theoretical But A Pragmatical Problem 41

more head; and, as the body of the society is now constructed, the functions of the head are the responsibility of the professions. The application of study and intelligence to the problems of society is an activity worthy of any man's time, black or white.

Before leaving the subject of middle-class, academic, professional ways versus the manners of the advocate, one other matter should be discussed. This essay has been, and is, an attempt to try to understand some problems and communicate that understanding. The description of the confusion embodied in it should not be interpreted as moral weakness. The problem is that there are two moral courses of action possible. It is moral to function as an advocate for black Americans. It is moral for a black American to function as a professional in this society. The essay has sought to picture vividly how the two moral possibilities conflict. The essay is primarily academic and professional in tone because this is the nature both of the author and the audience for which it is intended. Blacks know that they have dilemmas. Unfortunately, too few outside the profession are interested in libraries. This essay has been written for the library professional. Converting and proselytizing must be carried on in the language of the unconverted and pitched to their understanding. This essay is not an apology. It is not a confession of an inability to make a personal decision. Those who presume that it is and wish to offer advice are politely reminded that in matters of morality no one, no matter how much he respects fellow professionals or fellow blacks, can substitute their consciences for his own. And, if that statement is too polite and academic to be clear, I can, on demand, find phrases from the rhetoric of confrontation to respond to those presumptuous enough to assume that they can tell someone else what his moral duty should be. Each must decide that for himself.

Reconsidering Advocacy

In the introduction to this essay it was mentioned that the discussion would, of necessity, have to deal with the collision of two views of the world. The Weltanschauung of the advocate and that of the professional librarian do collide. If the subsequent discussion has seemed to make a good intellectual case for professionalism, and especially professional neutrality, a better case has been made on an operational level for some sort of advocacy. Where a good case exists on an operational level, a close look should be taken to ensure that a good intellectual case has not been missed. There is a good intellectual case for revision of the definitions of professional neutrality and advocacy but it involves the revision of some even more fundamental world views than any yet discussed. In writing this essay, as a convinced democrat I have been concerned about the broad justification which I could honestly see for advocacy rather than professional neutrality. One basis for this concern is that where all are vitally committed advocates of one kind or another, there is little room for the give and take which is part of a democratic society. Another basis of this concern is that where all are polarized, all are committed to a win-only posture and there is little hope for compromise and less hope for the minorities of the society. Blacks committed to a win-only policy should threaten no one in a society where there is only one of them for every nine others, and the black ten percent is utterly powerless as long as one discounts the blind and fettered power in a Sampson-like surge which can destroy the oppressor only at the cost of self-destruction. Blacks are committed to a win-only posture because their situation is so bad that they have little to lose; they must win something or they will lose life itself. Nonetheless, a defense of advocacy does involve some collision with the historical idea of democracy and should be explored further.

It is appropriate to note that a commitment to democracy is another commitment which can be divided into operational and theoretic aspects. Winston Churchill expressed what might be considered the clearest statement of an operational commitment to democracy when he called that form of government, "The worst of all possible forms of government except for all those other forms of government with which mankind has from time to time experimented." Democracy has some rather untenable philosophic underpinnings, but it certainly does look better, as Churchill says, than any of the other forms of government with which it might be compared. Clearly, this sort of position is an operational rather than a theoretic commitment. But, whether or not one supports the theoretical constructs associated with democracy, it is disconcerting to note that in recent times the theoretic framework of democracy has had some painful body blows with rather fundamental implications.

To begin with, it is necessary to describe a theoretical construct which has seemed fundamental to democracy

A Theoretical But A Pragmatical Problem

in general and certainly basic to the American brand. This is that the free, independent actions of free men will over a period of time redound to the common good. As an explicit corollary, Americans have believed that each individual is and ought to be free to conduct himself and dispose of his property in any idiosyncratic manner he pleases, unless he specifically and directly interferes with another's right to do the same. Colloquially, we have long maintained in this country that one man's right to swing ended only at another man's nose. Corporately, on a social level that is, it has been part of the American faith in democracy until recently that there existed somehow, somewhere, a social version of the "invisible hand" long revered by laissez-faire economists. Because of this faith in an "invisible hand," we, as a society, have been loath to interfere with any human activity which could not be shown to have directly injured some person. Unfortunately, both events and scholarship have conspired to convince many of us that the social version of the "invisible hand" is just as spurious as the economic one is now believed to be by most of the world.

It is hard to maintain one's innocent view of the "invisible hand" of social justice after considering the Nazi experience. That experience and the trials which succeeded it have profoundly altered the way western man now faces the corporate state. Until the Nazi experience one could, perhaps, not be blamed for leaving morality to the government and God; but, whatever the guilt of those who were hung at Nuremberg, what honest man could now claim orders of state as a defense for the commission of heinous crimes? Whatever Lt. Calley did or claimed, the rest of the individuals, officer and enlisted man alike, have not sought to defend themselves by asserting that they were ordered to do things; they have, on the contrary, asserted that they did not do those things or did not know that anything amiss was being done. Even in the army, even as a matter of official policy, each buck private is now considered personally responsible for his actions regardless of any orders he may have received.

In a society where no army private may evade responsibility for his own acts by citing a superior officer's orders it is hardly surprising that the last few years have seen professionals of all stripes taking positions on matters of social justice and public policy. The feeling has spread that these matters are the immediate and personal responsibilities of each individual throughout his working day. Chemists still work for Dow but there were some napalm-based recruiting problems. In the century of the Nazi holocaust it is impossible to ignore the lesson of that society in which individuals avoided moral responsibility or considered such matters the exclusive province of the state. Pastor Niemöller, speaking about German reaction to government persecution, admitted that:

> First they put the Communists and Jehovah's Witnesses in the concentration camps--but I was not a Communist or a Jehovah's Witness, so I did nothing. Then they came for the Social Democrats--but I was not a Social Democrat, and I did nothing. Then they arrested the trade-unionists-- and I did nothing, because I was not one. Then they arrested the Jews and again I did nothing because I was not a Jew. Then they came for the Catholics, but I was not a Catholic and I did nothing. At last they came and arrested me--but then it was too late already.

The United States Army has embedded a response to moral indifference in the rules of conduct for soldiers. The U.S. Army has said that it is the duty of every private to complain when injustice is being done; and who would assert that any army is a model of social responsibility? Other individuals, professionals as well as non-professionals, increasingly see their social responsibilities to be such that they may not be neutral on matters of social justice. Events have contributed to an enlargement of the concept of social responsibility for each individual. Those same events have led many to consider the activist stance of advocacy as the only moral position.

Just as events have undermined the laissez-faire political concepts, so has scholarship. It has been said that while the hard sciences are primarily a search for patterns and constructs to enhance understanding, the social sciences, in addition to seeking laws and rules for understanding, also seek to provide a rationale for intervention in the social processes they describe. (If this idea is any good, Manfred Kochen should get the credit for it, since he mentioned this general concept in some extemporaneous remarks while participating in a panel at the 1971 Denver meeting of the American Society for Information Science; if the author has mutilated a fine idea caught on the fly, then the fault is his.) While it is not hard to concur with

A Theoretical But A Pragmatical Problem 45

that statement it is perhaps germane to point out that in the recent past the hard sciences have been very generous in providing moral and intellectual justification for intervention in many social processes. This fall, for the first time in my life, I was denied the somber joy of smelling burning autumn leaves, since even the suburban bowed to the new regulations designed to reduce air pollution. The hard sciences, while professionally neutral, facilitated the development of techniques, artifacts, and organizations which spew toxins in the air we breathe, degrade arable land, and threaten to destroy every life-sustaining body of water on the planet. Those same sciences, still neutral, have begun to measure the damage we are doing to ourselves and our environment and to predict the consequences of a continuation of that damage; and suddenly, many of the previously neutral scientists have become loud advocates for types of intervention in social processes which would have been unthinkable a decade or two ago.

In addition to the activity in the hard sciences, the social sciences have continued, Governor Wallace notwithstanding, to describe a world which is quite different from that imagined in the naive view of our forefathers. Of special interest to blacks, the social scientists have increasingly advanced the view that racial prejudice, far from being natural, is learned from and buttressed by the institutions of the society. When one reads learned treatises which assert that the fables of the Grimm brothers contributed to the establishment of an authoritarian mentality in Germany, it is even more difficult to view <u>Little Black Sambo</u> and the white world of the easy-to-read book with indifference. In the light of such research it is necessary to regard professional neutrality in a new way. Given new insights about the connectedness of social phenomena, what may have appeared as advocacy in a simpler context may simply be responsible conduct when viewed from a position of greater sophistication. If the world of social phenomena is in fact connected, then the black professional getting himself together is in fact functioning responsibly. When the "invisible hand" can be seen to be a chimera, there is little justification for the sort of neutrality which has been the hallmark of the professional, and the day of the advocate is upon us. If the totalitarian view of man accurately describes reality--i.e., if each individual really impinges on his neighbor and the world in myriad subtle but vital ways, day in and day out--then democrats are between a rock and a hard place; the claims of radicals at either end of the political spectrum that the whole society is out of joint must be given credence; and many more social redefinitions are required in addition to those affecting professionalism and advocacy.

Summary

Basking in the warm glow of massive, but plausible, revision of our view of the society, it is possible to believe for a brief instant that our dilemma can be explained away. Professional neutrality has always been of primary importance in the individual professional's approach to his craft and in the social commitment of the various professional communities to provide service for all individuals. No rational requirement could be made that each professional as an individual had to be personally neutral on all the issues of his society; indeed, when any individual, like Machiavelli or Herman Kahn, does analyze the issues of his profession with more attention to the details of his craft than to the moral ends of human enterprises, the society at large is usually repulsed. Furthermore, no social norm described in this paper enjoins neutrality except in the face of uncertainty. As the medical community has become increasingly convinced of the dangers involved in the use of tobacco, the profession as a whole has placed itself in a position curiously resembling advocacy. Having re-examined the position of the professional in a modern world we may be home free after all. In a world where institutions, once believed to be natural phenomena, can be correctly viewed as social constructs; in a world where the attitudes and ideas which lead to the establishment, continuation, or modification of social institutions are learned; in the reassessed world of today, black professionals are justified in practicing all professions. They are not only justified in practicing the various professions but are responsible, as they do, for enlarging the understanding of their fellow professionals and the society at large. But on sober reflection, the last statement, indeed the whole essay, describes rather than banishes the dilemma. We have not been considering a paradox which could be made to disappear with an intellectual shift. Unlike paradoxes, which are things of the mind and understanding only, dilemmas are the personal property of humans who have strong but conflicting commitments. The black librarian, committed simultaneously to excellence in his craft and to the improvement of conditions in which his people live, has twin demands on his time, intellect, and energies. Never

A Theoretical But A Pragmatical Problem

for an instant can he be sure that he has not devoted too much time to one at the expense of the other. Never can he be sure that the real solution of the problems of his people or of society in general would not be enhanced by his exclusive choice of one role or the other, rather than persistence in attempting both. That his agony may be, and certainly ought to be, shared by his non-black, fellow professionals does not clarify the proper course in making the choices which these conflicting commitments force on him. The pervasiveness of the dilemma simply demonstrates once more the essential commonality of human experience.

Whatever intellectual justifications one may be able to construct, the dilemma persists. In the midst of a search for an honestly tenable position, the black librarian who, like me, enjoys working with computers, studying library systems, teaching in library schools, and working in libraries staffed with polite, literate professionals, is tormented by doubts that he has invented elaborate rationalizations to avoid his real responsibilities for immediate activity to improve the conditions of blacks in this society. In the midst of his advocacy the black librarian is nagged by the possibility that he might be making a greater contribution to his people by deepening his understanding and increasing the value of the contribution which his craft could make to his people and the society at large. As an advocate trying to function professionally he is torn by his concern about the short range effect of <u>Little Black Sambo</u> and Jensen; as a concerned human he is torn by his professional realization that blacks need to read all their enemies to avoid becoming their victims. Dilemmas do not ever exist in naked space; they take root and fester inside the minds and hearts of individuals. It signifies little indeed if there are in fact two equally moral courses of action; until some individuals seek to take both courses simultaneously there is no dilemma. What makes for the agony is when the individual has made commitments to both of those morally respectable courses of action simultaneously.

Only those who choose one course or another with religious fervor can hope to avoid the lure of the other. Most of us have a radicalization point whether we know it or not. Few of us know where that point is. But still fewer of us are willing to wait any longer with Pastor Niemöller until the gauleiter knocks at our own door. Such a course is not only immoral but unwise. For most black Americans the question is how determined is the gauleiter's step; his voice has long been audible. A decision to become an activist is compounded confusedly of despair and hope. As Hoffer points out, few start rebellions unless the present situation leaves them little opportunity for amelioration of their situation, and few join them unless they are convinced that there is some chance of success. In a country where one is a member of a small and essentially powerless minority, radicalization depends in large part on the actions of the powerful majority. The dilemma of all blacks, professional and advocate alike, is how best to move that powerful majority in a sane direction. And that dilemma cannot be made to disappear by black action alone, since it is a dilemma externally imposed on blacks by members of the majority, who through indifference or malice, have constructed and maintained social attitudes and institutions that limit the scope and threaten the survival of every black American.

What has been attempted here is to describe the dilemma. Its internal resolution is a matter of personal conscience. It is not within the scope of the essay nor within my power to do any more than attempt to provide a model which may lead to understanding of the facets of the dilemma. Neither in this essay nor in my own life have I been able to devise a model or provide an insight which would eliminate the dilemma or soften the impact of its horns on myself or any other black librarian.

PART II

Black Communities and Informational Needs

THE INFORMATION POTENTIAL IN THE
LIBERATION OF BLACK PEOPLE

by James C. Welbourne, Jr.

The 1970's began with librarianship, like other professions, being challenged on the ground of non-relevance to the times. It is true that the response of librarians to today's social and political imperatives has been weak and ineffectual. In the inner-city ghetto, the most troubled area of this nation's great cities, the library and its information potential is neither understood nor utilized. More importantly, the information requirements of inner-city residents are largely unmet and have resulted in the presence of serious information imbalances. An "information imbalance" is created when the information pool from which a given client group must draw has been shaped and pre-determined by the habits and preferences of so-called professionals, largely drawn from the white American middle-class, or else in accordance to the dictates of white racist institutional mores and demands.

Information Situation

In the inner-city, the black urban poor find themselves daily surrounded by educational, political and social institutions that have little, if any, relevance to their problems, needs and life-styles. To the inner-city resident, the library has been just one more institution whose purpose and rationale is both meaningless and unknown, and whose services as a consequence have been directed to an articulate, well-educated, book-oriented elite. The "information imbalance" which exists in the ghetto is perhaps more evident than the one which exists in the larger culture for black people, but both are, nevertheless, jarring examples of "professional negligence" and white indifference.

The situation persists largely because we, as black intellectuals, have either been unaware of or unable to articulate and define the information needs of the black com-

Black Communities and Informational Needs

munity. Nor, until recently, have we had the political power to influence needed change. As a consequence, the information which we require is not organized so as to be readily available to us or our leadership through conventional institutional channels.

To be "informationally deprived" is not to be either intellectually or culturally inferior to the more "advantaged" sectors of the society; it results from the existence of a racist information system at work in this country, which requires for its perpetuation the continued withholding of politically powerful information from black people. Information deprivation can be consciously or unconsciously initiated, and is often the result of the inability of the information agency to be sensitive to the information needs of the community. The consequences of black information deprivation can be serious for the larger white world, as well. Information deprivation provides the "intellectual void" in which rumor, gossip, and deliberate misuse of information abound. When people are deprived of critical information, or their rightful access to it, they become suspicious of, and tend to react negatively to those they know or believe to be responsible for their exploited condition.

Lack of information cannot help but contribute to feelings of powerlessness and certainly does nothing to prevent the growing use of violence as a logical and ready response. Cultural self-determination, basically a positive social movement, has little, if any, hope of success unless groups have available to them the necessary means and intelligence needed to make the critical choices that prognosis mandates. The deliberate withholding of information as a way to maintain white control over black efforts towards self-determination is not only a dangerous practice, but one certain to bring about the forceful seizure by blacks of their information rights. There is no way that information, its use, and interpretation can be separated from the conditions of survival in the black ghetto, nor from the conditions for success in the black liberation struggle.

Information Potential in the Urban Environment

Information in the ghetto must be viewed in dynamic rather than static terms. Information, like the informal network which supports it--the ghetto grapevine--is only as effective as the use to which it is put. Information after the fact is a luxury the ghetto hustler cannot afford; what he needs to know has to be in a hurry, in a context, and inexpensive. Every ghetto resident is a hustler in one context or another. His situation is defined for him: he probably will be evicted unless he finds out in time what the slumlord has planned; he probably will be arrested unless he finds out what rights he's supposed to have; he'll probably miss that job opportunity because he knows absolutely nothing about it; and he'll probably die before morning of an over-dose, if somebody else doesn't know what to do or where to take him. The ghetto is one big twenty-four hour hustle, and the name of the game is survival.

The major problem is that the information potential in the ghetto has never been allowed to develop past the survival or "maintenance" stage. The black inner-city resident will probably learn just enough information, in just enough time, to allow him to move his things the night before the slumlord comes to evict him; but he will never learn how to take the slumlord to court, on what grounds to sue him, or how to make him legally and financially responsible for his inconvenience. The racist apparatus which keeps the ghetto a profitable enterprise for organized crime and consumer exploitation has no intention of changing the picture in the inner-city for the better or for the worse. The survival instincts of ghetto residents which help them to compensate for intolerable conditions maintain, de facto, the white man's investment in black misery.

One can not fault the black community for being survival-oriented, since it is the one thing which has preserved a people and a culture long overdue for extermination. But information utilization could make a difference here. As a social dynamic in the black community, information is one of the most effective tools for organizing. Information can be used effectively to teach and educate people about the conditions around them which can be changed. It is the basis for building black unity, since clarification of ideological and cultural differences among black leadership is facilitated, and the design and deployment of community-based programs of action are made possible. Information about health and welfare rights, about drug traffic and the political basis for its revenue, about organized crime and police complicity, about food co-ops, subsidized housing and other alternatives to the daily exploitation ghetto residents experience, could turn ghetto apathy into organized aggressiveness for control of basic community institutions and the right of self-determination.

Black Communities and Informational Needs

Information Exploitation and Indoctrination

The present information system operating in this country (and that includes the national media, publishing houses, and the institutions of higher education), is designed to keep people ignorant of their exploited conditions while indoctrinating them to accept the continued loss of personal and public freedoms as facism follows racism to the seat of the national capital. Information surveillance and data-bank controls allow a society hell-bent for "law and order" to monitor communities, wire-tap "suspected leaders," and create "instant dossiers" on potential enemies of the State.

The information industry has gone to work to make the black community appear in the eyes of the rest of the nation to be on a collision course toward self-destruction. The federal government finds the money to finance the studies. The universities find the properly credentialed flunky to conduct them, and he finds the time and the social excuse to do it. And the media report and generalize about the new findings. The reports are curiously all the same: in one way or another, the black community is insane, innately inferior, culturally handicapped, psychologically fragmented, politically naive, economically dependent, or else rapidly dying of some unique "black" disease that is communicable. The recommendations always call for some form of black genocide: sterilization of welfare mothers; prevention of marriage between sickle-cell (trait-carrying) blacks; or the administering of passivity serums to "calm down" over-active black youths.

The national media and the white-dominated information studies attempt to prove the social breakdown in the family life of black people, the poverty and sickness which dogs the footsteps of black people, and the crime and political corruption which make up their social environment, until the picture is so painted that, for all intents and purposes, we must be inferior to "appear" so degraded; we must be socially deviant to commit so many acts of violence; and we must be morally bankrupt to want to continue to reproduce a species such as ours.

The exploitation of black people by the white information industry is reflected in the millions of dollars appropriated "for the disadvantaged," but ear-marked for the coffers of white institutions and the bloated salaries of the administrators who keep them open. The white universities have managed successfully to exploit black people through the racist research done on them; through the strict entrance controls kept on those degree programs to which blacks might aspire; by glutting the employment market with white incompetent Ph.D.'s whose degree titles earn them academic welfare benefits; and ultimately by profiting on black bodies, recruited to their white racist institutions to qualify for federal dollars in "overhead and institutional support" to educate "the little niggers." One could ask how many white men have gained their Ph.D.'s from their study of black people; how many of them have achieved tenure and promotion from the publication of those impersonal studies; or how many of them now enjoy leadership positions in government and industry as recognized "niggerologists," at salaries higher than they could ever command in open competition with blacks for such jobs?

The psychological effects upon whites who are thus rewarded to research, discover, and report their findings on the inferiority of blacks are staggering. The mountains of data compiled by white racist-trained and indoctrinated intellectuals not only support the myth of black inferiority and white superiority, but confirm the suspicion that whites are capable of doing in-depth analysis, even in areas in which they know they have no prior experience or competency (e.g., "The Black Experience"). This then becomes the necessary data upon which later decisions will be made to contain (and perhaps exterminate) the black race--<u>in the best interest of the black race.</u>

<u>Information Re-education Programs</u>

There is a vital need to compensate intellectually for the loss incurred by black people who have been the victims of white racist-controlled educational institutions. These institutions have been instrumental in depriving black people of the opportunity to learn about their African heritage. The consequences of such educational information deprivation has been to create a class of black leadership which is dependent upon white scholars and white standards for the design, initiation and evaluation of social action programs for the innercity. The current educational information system is designed to conduct studies and clinically to disseminate information about how black and poor people struggle to survive. It is also prepared to predict for the established authorities how ghetto people are likely to respond to continual degradation and abuse, and to prepare a cost analysis in time and dollars for the white society to maintain their urban slum centers.

White interpretation of educational information for black people invariably leads to discrimination and to the disadvantagement of black people. White people who make decisions for and about black people, involving on their part a determination of whether the black person is "ready" or "qualified" to know about certain information, rely upon a culturally ingrained set of racial values and stereotypes, which are not only inaccurate but are detrimental to the career decision the otherwise informed black person might have made, without their input. Black people who make use of white approved standards are doing an equal disservice to the black community, while they perpetuate the myth of white superiority and maintain a racist status quo in America.

As a people we have a major information problem: to disseminate black culture from a black rather than a white cultural perspective. In doing so we must emphasize to the white, as well as to the black community, the historical precedents in African culture for the design and conduct of cultural and social systems which do not reflect the values or mores of white western culture. We also desperately need an interpretation of issues and problems in the black community from the vantage point of what is essential to our welfare, in order to offset what the white controlled-media and educational institution tell us is in our best interest.

It is obvious that any plan to halt the continued destruction of black minds must involve control by the black community of the educational and cultural institutions in the community: the libraries, museums, churches and schools. Educational and cultural programs must be designed to enable black people to rise and prosper in the midst of a hostile, white environment, while remaining ready and capable of fighting racism and oppression whenever and wherever it threatens the black community. The public library and urban-based cultural centers have a significant role to play in the re-educational process of the black community.

Black Information Programs

Clearly, there are two quite distinct areas to which black liberation efforts must focus more attention--the educational and the informational services. The institutions most central to these two areas are the schools and public libraries. By developing a model for an effective informationtion service for the black community through the public library, we can begin to get some idea of how a comprehensive plan involving the control of all major ghetto institutions could be used to shift power in the community and re-define the terms of existence in the inner-city.

Planning an information service for the black community would involve a three-pronged attack: one aimed at the broad base of the community, another focusing upon the recognized leadership in the community, and a third addressing itself to the survival needs of the community's basic institutions. In every case the information program being designed has as its goal the informing and equipping of the black community with skills and insights to effectively resist and discredit propaganda originating within the dominant white information system.

Community-wide Services:

One of the greatest needs in the black communities is the awareness of their historical and cultural roots. Major educational programs around the black experience, incorporating authentic material about the black man's history in this country and in Africa, and his cultural contributions to the world in the arts, religion, philosophy, as well as socio-political forms of government, should be conducted in every black urban school and college library. The information specialist working in these areas should be in contact with black scholars and educational corporations who are currently producing and disseminating this type of material for use in the black community. The urban school and college library will have to be the prime mover for the larger institution to begin shifting its educational terms and philosophies toward "blackness." The first informational program designed by the academic information specialist should be for the faculty and administration of the school system, to "de-brainwash and re-educate" them about the effective use of their institution in the liberation struggles of black people.

Leadership Training & Support Services:

This is probably the most important aspect of a comprehensive information service program. Black leadership desperately needs an information support system to help it keep abreast of the changing dynamics in the political and social arena. They need to know pertinent information about legislative matters before they arise, so that they can caucus their constituents and fashion alternatives to bills and programs which are not in the best interest of the community. Black leadership locally must be in direct contact with black leadership nationally in order to achieve unity of action and purpose. Black community leadership requires an efficient, well-organized information dissemination apparatus in order to keep its constituency in the black community informed of its actions and decisions, and also to be able to tap instantly the necessary feedback upon which to base its own next strategies.

Community Institutions and Social Action Services:

In many ways this is merely another aspect of the "community-wide service" previously mentioned. This, of course, focuses upon the internal information needs of the agencies and services set up in the community to meet their needs. Information programs to help plan their services, and to disseminate critical information about their services to the community, could be aided significantly by a black information specialist.

Poor organization of files often causes social action agencies to spend precious time which they should be giving the inner-city client, searching through files to locate needed information concerning past services or medical histories. Many health and welfare services turn off community participation by the complicated "red-tape" the recipient has to go through for the services. In most cases this information about the client is already available somewhere else, and only the cumbersomeness of the agency's information systems requires that the client be made to fill out form after form.

Information sharing and client referral are services which grow out of cooperative information program planning among social service agencies; the results would be a lowering of the cost to maintain needed files on community residents, and more time to spend in a professional capacity with the black client.

Other kinds of information services required by social agencies are professional education programs for their own staff members. Health and legal professionals need desperately to keep abreast of professional expertise, even while out in the "field" working with the community. Also, most community action programs have built-in in-service programs for training para-professionals. Educational information materials in the health, legal, or welfare services will aid such "para-professionals" to seek advanced education and possible professional employment in these same areas. Without such information, para-professionalism can easily become a one-way dead-end career for black people.

Agency information planning should not ignore the important realm of locating and tapping sources of funding for the agencies' activities. Most community social action agencies are funded through federal grants, with no guarantee of contract renewal once funds expire; therefore, finding a basis of support within the community, or from foundations and business corporations, could easily occupy most of the time of the social services' personnel.

Black Information Professionals

In talking about information services to the black community we have failed to address ourselves to the critical issues of who would be the professionals responsible for providing such services, where they would be educated, and what they would need to know to be effective. One obvious assumption I am making is that existing personnel, either in the urban school system or the public library, are not the people capable of designing and mounting a sustained information program supporting the liberation struggles of black people, nor are they likely to be willing to become such people. The kinds of information programs envisioned here require a combination and a range of technical skills and "people" expertise which do not follow the traditional status and educational lines of the profession, and which will require entirely new concepts of work roles and the background and education for them. Occupying a black skin is no substitute for life experience in ghetto communities, nor will its tincture enable the black professional to better "understand" what the brother on the street is asking for in the way of a "down" information center designed to meet his particular needs.

In order to create black institutions which are active, purposeful and relevant, these "new" expertises coupled with specialized information preparation are a must. A range of information skills and abilities are involved, as this proposed program reveals. In addition to reference or information problem-solving skills, skills in information program planning, information investigation, media utilization, and information service design must be mastered. Black information professionals will need to adopt a problem-solving orientation which they will bring to every information activity in which they engage. Information is their business; the way it is stored, retrieved, disseminated; the psychological effects it has on the minds of those who come in contact with it; the political and social impact of certain kinds of information analysis upon white leadership in the larger society--these are the daily dynamics these information agents will be dealing with in the streets and in the courts. They must know, and qualify for, membership in the evasive ghetto communication network--"the vine." They must be legitimate enough in the eyes of the black community to receive as many information "tips" as they pass out--in short, they must be ghetto communication hustlers. Their educational preparation will occur wherever committed individuals gather to work, plan and study long enough to exchange valued skills and develop new abilities, until the freedom goals of the Black Liberation Struggle have been realized.

RAT RACE

by Binnie L. Tate

RIGHT ON!	Rat-on rat-on rat-on, RATS on my table, in my closet, SHOOT ME A RAT!!
RIOT'S ON!	Ri-ri-ri-ri-ri-ri Oh-oh-oh-oh-oh-oh-oh-oh-OHN Running, burning, running, REBELLION! POLICE! PEOPLE DEAD!!
RAP ON!	Talk, talk, talk, talk, talk--everybody talk, nobody DOING nothing but TALK, and poverty programs FOR THE RICH!
WRITE ON!	Write about right, RIGHT?--Ain't right to write about me YOU DON'T KNOW ME! Write my own story MAKE THAT MONey!!
FIGHT ON!	Fight's on, everywhere, inside, outside, FIGHT'S ON, wherever you're at--IN YOUR MIND--fight for FREEDOM

or

we will go

RIGHT ON!	rat-on rat-on rat-on, RATS ON YOUR BACK TOO!

The hopes and aspirations of black people have erupted repeatedly in fire and bombs on the streets of American cities. The nineteen sixties and early seventies saw hundreds of ghetto residents storming their neighborhoods with pent-up anger and rebellion. Attention was called to rat-infested slum dwellings, unemployment, poor transportation, and other atrocities heaped on the poor. The slow stolid movement of the King years had awakened the nation's consciousness to the black problems in the South, but had not focused on the blight of our cities' racial

Black Communities and Informational Needs

ghettos. The enactment of civil rights laws did not expose the greater law of racism which penetrated the American mentality and affected institutions and systems everywhere. De facto segregation became equated with segregation in the South. Discrimination in housing and hiring was declared rampant in the North, as was the sharecropper mentality in the South. Consumer fraud, police brutality, pollution and corruption were seen sharply manifested at their worst in minority and poor communities.

The Kerner report of 1968 declared this a nation moving toward two societies, separate and unequal. The report stated that "this deepening racial division is not inevitable. The movement apart can be reversed. Choice is possible. Our principal task is to define the choice and to press for a national solution." The report continued by saying that the healing of wounds would require a commitment toward national action--"compassionate, massive, and sustained, backed by resources of the most powerful and richest nation on this earth."

Power breeding desire for power and repression as the tool of that power were subjects that were not dealt with effectively in the report. Thus the "war on poverty," initiated to correct the problems of the poor, was begun and sorely failed. Those in institutional administration held tightly to the reins of their authority while sometimes unsuspecting white liberals and token blacks were placed in new positions of power over the poor. Monies expended in the name of the destitute were ruthlessly coopted by "haves." The only "massive and sustained" action evident was that of repression and backlash. Within institutions, change was expected to occur without correction. Problems were expected to be solved without recognizing mistakes. Systems which rendered the poor powerless refused to be challenged.

Recognizing these factors, militant blacks and confused whites moved toward a new nationalism, having decided that change would come only through demonstration and confrontation.

> IN THE LATE NINETEEN FIFTIES AND EARLY
> SIXTIES BLACK AMERICANS RESPONDED TO
> THEIR PLIGHT AS SECOND CLASS CITIZENS
> WITH MASSIVE PROTESTS AND APPEALS.
> FACED WITH THE SOCIETY'S INTRANSIGENCE
> THE LATE SIXTIES SAW MORE MILITANT AND

> VIOLENT REACTIONS AND ALSO, THE RE-
> AWAKENING AND WIDESPREAD ACCEPTANCE
> OF BLACK POLITICAL NATIONALISM. [1]

> Since the white power structure, through its black spokesmen, has lost its ability to control the black masses and keep them peaceful, it has now recognized a necessity to do something quick. 'Good housing, schools, and jobs--these are the concrete essentials which the Negro needs.' Hence a host of shotgun crash programs. [2]

> 'Screens' may be found among the countless black Anglo-Saxons who have introjected the values of the white society, including acceptance of their own debasement, to the point that they dream of assimilation on the terms of that society and work feverishly to that end. [3]

Revolts were seen in black and white communities, on college campuses, in high schools, and among other groups which recognized that they were affected by the quagmire of discriminatory practices. A new cry arose, "POWER TO THE PEOPLE!", epitomized in action for decentralization of schools, ethnic studies, and grass roots representation.

Answers were not easy, because issues were not clear. Blacks were constantly called upon to present solutions to what was basically a "white problem." Even the most liberal white groups tired in their pursuit of the problem of racism, for in its solution lay the tearing down of mechanisms upon which they depended. No matter how false these props, many whites could not face survival without them. The call for "accountability" to them meant destruction.

> HISTORY IS REPEATING ITSELF, AND IN DOING SO IS UNDERLINING THE FACT THAT THE INABILITY OF WHITES TO UNDERSTAND THE NATURE OF THE FRUSTRATIONS OF BLACK PEOPLE IS NO EXCUSE FOR THE FAILURE TO PERCEIVE THE ABSOLUTE NECESSITY OF DEVELOPING RESISTANCE TO ALL FORMS OF HUMAN BRUTALITY. [4]

> What is necessary is for whites who really feel
> the need to effectuate law and order to develop
> an appreciation of how that goal can be reached.
> Whites can determine the conditions under which
> black liberation will become a reality. In doing
> so, whites may discover that they too are more
> liberated from a slavery that they have been
> conned into believing is freedom. [5]

Within the institution of libraries, a microscopic view of these cosmic realities has been seen. Few sustained efforts have been made to correct the institutional ills as they affect blacks and other minorities. Much has been said but little has been done to change the structure of libraries to meet the needs of the disenfranchised.

Black librarians have in some cases joined the outer forces for economic and social change. Indictments have been served upon the profession in regard to its systematic racist orientation, job discrimination, and ineffective services. While the institutions are slowly responding to this new awakening, blacks are hopefully breaking free from the shackles of obscurity and secondary citizenship.

> With a few perceptive and original thinkers, the
> Negro movement conceivably could long ago have
> aided in reversing the backsliding of the United
> States toward the moral negation of its great
> promise as a new nation of nations. [6]

Notes

1. Black Review, No. I, edited by Mel Watkins. New York: Morrow, c1971. "Introduction," p. 5.

2. Peter Labrie, "The New Breed," in Black Fire, edited by LeRoi Jones and Larry Neal. New York: Morrow, c1968. p. 75.

3. C. E. Wilson, "The Screens," in Black Fire. op. cit., p. 140.

4. Reginald Major, "Who Shall Civilize the Jungle?" in Black Review, No. I, p. 87.

5. Ibid, p. 95.

6. Harold Cruse, <u>The Crisis of the Negro Intellectual, from Its Origins to the Present.</u> New York: Morrow, c1967. p. 565.

VIGNETTES AND DESIGNS:
SCHOOLS AND SCHOOL LIBRARIES

by Ann Stewart Watt

If we are to believe that the library is the heart of the school, as expressed by school library pioneers, then it will come as no shock to find that as a school librarian one is in a unique position to know something of the general health of the school "organism." At some time during the educational experience every pupil, teacher, and many auxiliary staff members, school board members, administrators, visiting educators and parents come to or through the library. Further, the library is brought before the public in its outreach functions--the materials loaned for outside use, the book fairs held to encourage ownership of books (and sometimes to raise funds for the library).

It is the scene for classes, story hours, research, study halls, pupils waiting for office appointments or examinations, checking books out or in, faculty meetings, student groups (most notably the student government, yearbook, literary club), picture taking, school board meetings and PTA meetings. It is a favorite spot on every school tour and/or "open house" occasion.

Since 1965, the beginning of the Elementary and Secondary Education Act, Title II, for the acquisition of school library resources, textbooks, and other printed and published materials, school libraries have had access to Federal funding totaling over $550,000,000 to date. In this way, many schools have been able to establish and improve school libraries so that they function as learning resources centers (LRC's) or as instructional materials centers (IMC's). These are school libraries in the fullest sense, with access to broadened resources and information in a variety of formats arranged for usefulness and adequately staffed to execute a meaningful program.

The black librarian from this vantage point becomes familiar with educational curriculum, indeed, exerts his or

her best efforts to build a collection of resources to support
the school's curriculum. Too frequently, however, the
librarian does not work with the curriculum committee to
evaluate, study, develop, or revise its courses of study.
The emphases of the various departments and teachers are
conveyed to the librarian by the use and/or lack of use of
the library collection. A sense of the pupil's regard for the
educational tasks assigned is transmitted when the librarian
hears complacent students admit with a sense of urgency,
"I can't go in Mr. McCain's room without that assignment."
The librarian often knows what school projects have generated most enthusiasm among student clientele, is familiar
with their current non-curricular interests, and is aware of
their attitudes toward school. On the professional side of
the coin, the librarian is likely to know which teachers are
taking graduate courses and something about the teachers'
recreational pursuits as well. It is not because he is black
but because he is a librarian that this information reaches
him. This essay will first examine the reactions this
panoply of affairs has evoked in one black librarian, and
then explore some courses of action that are within the role
of the school librarian.

The responsibility for integration in the public
schools is deplorably misplaced. Although it has been 18
years since the Supreme Court decision, we have left the
burden on the pupils. Why haven't we insisted instead
that Boards of Education, administrative positions and
teaching staffs be integrated? In what other situation is
the consumer held so terribly responsible for the quality of
the product? If school integration is to teach pupils tolerance and valid intercultural relations, where are the models
among the administrative and teaching staffs? How does
the white teacher who has never been in a minority position
learn to understand the sensitivities of a child who daily is
the only black pupil on his bus or in his class?

On what basis does the principal assign one black
pupil to each of six sections of the second grade? What
gives him the right to be offended when this placement is
questioned? Why is the only black girl in the class seated
with the boys? Why must tenured, qualified teachers be
given the choice of where they will teach in a district when
they are paid by taxpayers? Why again must the consumer
be made responsible, as in the relegating of "slower" and
"disruptive" pupils to the teacher's aide or paraprofessional
who can "relate" to the children better? Why didn't that

college-trained professional (often a graduate of a state-supported teachers college) get some training in relating to these students? How sound is the rationale for the school librarian denying a second grader a Spanish book ("Because you don't know any Spanish")? Is he to wait until he knows history before he reads about the American Revolution?

I fail to be convinced that American educators seriously believe that segregated patterns of education are educationally unsound. If this were true white Boards of Education would insist on integrated schools. They most assuredly want the best for their pupils. No, the assumption is that black schools are inferior. But where are these black schools? Not buildings--but schools. Examine, if there is one available, a black State Legislature and State Department of Education, a black school board, black superintendent and administrative staff, black faculty and staff, seeking to meet the needs of black pupils and seeking to aid in the realization of black parents' goals. This is what would make up black schools. Since what we have lacks blackness in one or more of these components, no matter how overwhelming a majority of the pupils may be black, there is little basis upon which to conclude that black schools are inferior. Yet, this is the conclusion that has inspired even the most liberal white educators and civil rights workers to say efforts must be made to achieve integrated enrollment. Blacks, on the other hand, are aware that large numbers of blacks have not infiltrated the policy-making levels, know that what passes as black schools is an instrument the power structure uses to maintain the status quo--white supremacy.

This is not to say that there is a need for a total separation on all levels affecting education but that when "black" schools are inferior it may be because blacks have too little responsibility and authority. The whites who have the responsibility and authority lack insight, involvement and commitment in most cases.

School administrators, all too often, have so many preoccupations that they cannot address themselves adequately to the matter of achieving wholesome interracial experiences for students. This is understandable. Administrators cannot manage school lunch programs, athletic programs, foreign language departments or art departments adequately either. The responsibility is met through delegation of authority, usually on some rational basis, to another professional. Yet, the area of interhuman relationships is left to chance or put in the hands of a white or non-minority group teacher whose familiarity with minorities is limited to having played basketball in high school with some good black player or having seen Pearl Bailey, Sammy Davis or Flip Wilson perform. When, by sheer providence, a minority teacher is assigned the task, he finds that progress beyond the study-discussion stage is rare.

The incidents that defeat the success of wholesome interracial relationships too often are not reported, or are disbelieved and/or ignored if they are reported.

The child who complains of being taunted with "Nigger! Nigger!", who in her innocence asks her mother "Why do they call me that?" is told by the principal, "You mustn't make up things like that. I asked all the other (white) children and nobody on the bus heard anyong call you that." The mother is told these children don't know what the word means, and that the principal has taught his son to say "Sticks and stones may break my bones, but names will never hurt me."

The teacher's aide sees black children playing on the playground. One boy is banging another's head against the brick wall. The child's head is bleeding. When questioned as to why she didn't break up this altercation or send for help, the aide replies "I thought they were just playing."

Fifth graders whose study of American history included some discussion and filmstrips on the ignominy of slavery were given projects for homework. Complaining parents came to say, "This is all behind us. It's not the children's fault. You shouldn't bring this up to them. It's too upsetting." Surely one would conclude these children are not to be taught about ancient civilization, the rape of the American Indian, or the American Revolution. Probably our youngsters should not watch television until they are at least 18, because the Vietnam War is too upsetting.

I always marvel at the fact that for three days the carpenter's son remained in the temple talking with doctors and scholars, "both hearing them and asking them questions. They were astonished at his understanding and answers." The reader may explain that "He was gifted." One cannot minimize that. One may respond, so were those doctors

Black Communities and Informational Needs

and scholars who took time to talk to the young Nazarene. I shudder when I think of the remote chance the carpenter's sons of today have to come face to face with scholarship and erudition. There is a disastrous dearth of capable, qualified elementary teachers. By the age of 12 today's carpenter's son is most likely without the skill he needs to find scholastic achievement and, worse, without the desire for knowledge to make the struggle for an education bearable or worthwhile.

When the carpenter's son is black or poor, his parents are generally considered to be at fault and the learning inhibitors are catalogued:

There is no father in the home.
The parents are unlearned.
They live in the ghetto.
There are few books and magazines in the home.
The mother works.
There are five children in the family.
They are on welfare.
His work attack skills are poor.
They moved here from the South.
The parents never come to PTA.
There's nobody home when he gets home from school.
He didn't have breakfast before he came to school.
He doesn't have his own room.

The "inhibitors" become the determinant of the student's destiny and failure, and dropping out becomes a fait accompli. While all of these and more may be accurately identified as inhibitors, a more serious inhibitor is the teacher's attitude. This was brought home clearly in the findings of the Coleman Report.

Many years ago a very wise principal in South Baltimore spoke to her teaching staff about creating and maintaining an atmosphere conducive to learning. She said, among other things, "Wherever the child's eyes rest in your room, he should learn something." She encourages interest in pets, horticulture, art, music, dramatics, jewelry, crafts, literature, sports, needlework, grooming, and a free discussion of these. As she made her frequent rounds to classes she never stopped teaching. The child who said, "that's a pretty pin" was told, "It's an amethyst. I inherited it from my mother. Do you know where amethyst comes from?" This led the child to look up the answer in an ever-open library. Sophisticated language for elementary youngsters? Maybe. Out of place in an inner city school in a poverty area? No! Don't these children need black English? If anybody needs it, the white teacher needs black English so that she can understand her pupils. When the white teacher knows black English she is able to accept "biscuit" as the answer to:

> I am brown and white. You put butter
> and jam on me and eat me for breakfast.
> I begin with the letter B.

Although the teacher's manual says <u>Bread.</u> The experience chart does not make a teaching point of "hog moss" or "hog jaws." More accurate black English translates these as hog maws and hog jowls. The inaccuracies are to be expected, since the teacher doesn't really care enough about the vocabulary to learn it before teaching it. When the teacher knows black English, the child who shows approval of another with "Cool, baby, cool" or "Hang in there" or "Right on!" or "Yeah, Yeah, yeah!" is understood to be using valid idiomatic expression and is not corrected unless the teacher is one who questions the appropriateness of "Bravo"! at a concert, "Amen"! at church, or "Hurray!" at a ball game.

    The proponents of "black English" would have us view as an alternative language system a combination of dialect and colloquialism that is said to be peculiar to blacks. Using this then as a language experiential base, "standard" English would be taught as a second language, in the upper grades. While linguists have been made sufficiently aware of the fallacy of this argument to discourage wide adoption of the idea, there is the informal teaching of black English via a double standard that does not make corrections of poor English usage by black or economically poor white students. The inhibitor is strategically placed. In our society, to gain power one must be able to communicate. To be mute or incapable of clarity of expression is to be powerless in a democracy.

    Teachers decry the lack of respect shown them by students and parents. Pupils have witnessed a mambo-stick decorum (how low can you go?) on the part of teachers. This is evident <u>in the language:</u> "You are nothing but a bunch of animals," and much worse. <u>In the clothing</u> that attracts more attention to the teacher's body build than the youngster could ever devote to modern math. In the preparation for classes where the pupils are asked to list the principle exports of South America; or where teachers declare that a two-year-old revision of a State curriculum (which they haven't seen) is 40 years old, or state blandly that there are no good books in the library. In the performance required of pupils: "What time does the clock show?" asked a teacher of her group of low fifth grade math students. The clock shows 10:43. The pupil answers 10:40. Teacher replies, "Yes." Another pupil says, "That's wrong. It's 10:43." Teacher replies, "It doesn't have to be specific." In the standards of classroom management where some teachers accept participation from some black pupils only when hands are raised, and accept oral outbursts from other pupils as classroom recitation proceeds. In evaluation of tasks assigned that show reams of ditto papers and workbook pages in wastebaskets, unmarked, ungraded and unrecorded. In communication with parents that has degenerated to the level of pre- and/or post-suspension conferences and teacher strikes. In utilization of instructional resources: A teacher returns a filmstrip. The librarian asks if she found it useful. The teacher replies, "Yes." "Did you use the entire filmstrip?" asks the librarian. "Oh, yes we had plenty of time," answers the teacher--as if that were the only consideration.

Not only have parents been given cause to ponder the competence, authority, and concern of the teacher, but the teacher too often fails to exemplify the respect for pupils or parents that he feels he deserves from them. Parents stand in offices and classrooms and wait without recognition. When someone finally gets to them, the most frequent greeting is, "Did you want something?" Children are requested to remain after school to work on a special project without their parents' permission. When parents call school to inquire about a child not arriving on the proper bus, the teacher asserts, "I thought you'd know he would be on the late bus." The decision is reached to show a 20-minute segment of a new daily T.V. program although the school has not decided on its utilization, to parents attending a P.T.A. meeting designed to have parents "go through our child's day." The same PTA program allowed no time for parents of primary children to become familiar with their children's reading program. A pupil who say "that's a staff" to a music teacher who asks "What is this ═══ ?" is told, "You could say that. We just say it's five lines."

A parent who comes in for a conference about a challenged book gathers her belongings and has a book taken from her, because the white librarian assumes she is taking the challenged book.

While the above descriptions have been witnessed by a black librarian, they have by no means been observed only in situations where the majority of the enrollment is black. In formulating designs, then, there is no attempt to discuss the librarian's role only in relation to minority groups. Rather, this is an attempt to discuss courses of action the involved librarian may pursue to direct the library toward fulfillment of its position as the "heart of the school." I am convinced that there is nothing to be done to meet the needs of minority group students, if it is educationally sound, that would diminish the effectiveness of good educational programs for all children.

Librarians cannot afford to be passive. Involvement in world, community and school affairs is mandatory. Much of what the library has to offer never gets into the hands of pupils who need it, because the librarian is not involved in the curriculum or with teachers and pupils to an extent that relates the available materials to their needs. Instead of waiting for clients to come to the library or to ask for material, it is incumbent upon the librarian to reach out to clients with an informed anticipation of their needs and adequate means for meeting them. To hear students talk about basketball, watch them collect baseball cards, observe girls trying new hairstyles or dances, or trying out for the school play, and not to provide relevant materials in these areas is questionable. One librarian who is deeply involved in students interests keeps one bulletin board free for them to post notices of their activities. As often as not, a new title or book jacket is appended to the notice. Newspaper headlines are given depth and meaning by pointing up resources for contrasts, comparisons and backgrounds. New and old titles of interest, periodicals and clippings are sent to teachers with an invitation to come or send to the library for more.

The librarian volunteers to serve on non-library-related committees in the school and professional organizations. It means work, but it pays off in relationships established and insights into needs and interests of the clientele.

A community resource file is established that gives

information on community agencies, organizations and residents who may contribute to students' educational experience. Such a file would include people of all ethnic groups even if the school itself enrolls few minority group pupils.

Professional materials on good educational practices should be abundantly available, and materials for teachers on the life styles and contributions of minorities should be widely distributed to professional and para-professional staff. Professional materials should be made available to school board members and parents. To give options to an uninformed decision-making body on open classrooms in a non-graded primary, British infant school, or on team teaching, etc., is to make their choice invalid.

The school librarian should not hesitate to send announcements of staff openings to minority colleges and meetings of minority professional groups in an effort to balance recruitment procedures.

The school librarian must be a teacher and promote learning. This means convincing administrative and instructional personnel that time in the library is not necessarily time away from social studies, language arts, science or humanities.

The capacity to blend commercially prepared materials with those produced locally and/or with other available materials is essential for effective utilization of the wide variety of media available today. Gifted pupils are frequently capable of assisting in this type of production. The librarian can direct pupils having difficulties in the preparation of materials. Filmstrips especially can be made more useful when a simpler narrative is put on a cassette.

With its wealth of resources, the library is a first port of call for creative writing--poetry, plays, puppet shows, short stories. Here the pupil finds handbooks, dictionaries and factual material to give authenticity to imagination, as well as a tape recorder to enable him to listen critically to his work.

When the library is open to students to come in, other than in class groups, many opportunities for pupil interaction arise. There is an ever-present need for techniques to lead pupils of different backgrounds to encounters with each other as an educational experience, to the end that they will learn skills of citizenship commensurate with the era of which they are a part. The librarian and his or her staff are fair and sensible. The first child requesting the book gets it first. Group activities such as role playing, dramatization, play reading, book discussions, debates, choral reading, and peer teaching help mix pupils from varied backgrounds for meaningful interaction. The library club encourages participation from all types of students. Athletic, intellectual and artistic types can participate in book reviewing and book chats. Standards of conduct and library citizenship are reasonable and are enforced fairly for all pupils. This necessitates provision of some area for normal chatting without distracting other library users. The interaction is a vehicle for increased opportunities to develop leadership and initiative among young people, and to establish wholesome intercultural peer group relationships that may carry over into social and after school pursuits.

Standards of achievement are not diluted. Differentiated educational tasks are set or assigned, but the student is led to execute them thoroughly and accurately and is challenged to go beyond the assignment. The library provides incentives such as display areas for outstanding work; opportunities to tape a story, poem, report, song, to be shared with other pupils; and facilities for simple production of photographs, slides, transparencies and tapes to give an added dimension to assignments.

Using language arts experiences to open doors to the human condition, the librarian will introduce materials on all ethnic groups in displays to promote interest in books and reading. There is just as much justification in pupils reaching outside their own experiences for House of Dies Drear, Egypt Game, Jennifer, Hecate, Macbeth, William McKinley and Me, Elizabeth as there is reaching out for Little Women, Hans Brinker or Johnny Tremain. Librarians should lead teachers to an awareness of this when they ask for suggestions of titles to read to a class or to assign.

Teachers who approach the teaching of black history as though it were a calendar of events or chronology pure and simple should be led to read and absorb the Black Experience so that a more realistic human approach to anger, joy, struggle, hope, disappointment and curriculum soundness is appreciated.

Tutorial stations can be set up using tapes or programmed instruction prescribed by the teacher in a library setting that is not stigmatized. Some reference books, flash cards or other drill devices, including cassettes and players, are available for home use. If security is a problem, parents may be required to pay a deposit, just as they do for musical instruments. Teachers may send messages home to parents by cassette to show how the parents or older brothers and sisters can assist the student. After school hours will give a place for study and enrichment activities. A pupil on the primary level requesting a book that seems too difficult, is allowed to take it with a note to his parents: "Dear Mommy, I may need a little help with this book," or "I'll get by with a little help from my friends," or "This one's tough." Beyond the primary level, the student is led to exercise his own options.

A pupil requesting material for a parent should not be denied it. If pages must be reproduced or a limited loan period set, this should be explained in a brief note to the parent. To deny the loan arbitrarily is to miss an opportunity to reinforce the importance of library resources and services to people on every level of life. Some paperback, pamphlet and cassette material on child development and parental guidance should be acquired (perhaps by the PTA) and made available through the library.

The library should be staffed by adequate professional and para-professional personnel to carry out the program. Duties should be relegated to para-professional staff so that the professional librarian works directly with students and teachers.

Intellectual curiosity, understanding of and respect for young people, a broad liberal arts background, sound judgment, awareness of current affairs, familiarity with resources, creativity, knowledge of the curriculum and educational tasks are essential professional attributes.

In selecting materials for the collection, the librarian should enlist the aid of students, teachers, other school personnel and parents. While the librarian assumes ultimate responsibility, interaction with clientele in this area makes for increased utilization of materials acquired. The library's collection should have both balance and depth, i.e., balance in presenting all sides of controversial issues and depth in the curriculum emphasis.

Book selection is an on-going process that extends beyond acquisition to the matter of replacement, weeding, and utilization. The Standard Catalogs can at best be used as subject guides. They point up subject areas in which materials should be acquired, but the librarian's knowledge of the clientele and school program will determine whether a given title should remain in the collection, be duplicated, be replaced or discarded. As long as The Story of Little Black Sambo remains double-starred in the Children's Catalog, one has reservations about the social consciousness of those experts who serve as advisors to the Wilson Company.

Since it is impossible for a librarian to read every title before it is purchased, cooperative reviewing and cross-checking of criticism is essential. But more importantly, it is necessary to establish a procedure for constant weeding of the collection. Again pupils and teachers may be involved profitably, with the final decision resting with the librarian. The black librarian must become more active in reviewing children's materials from the current reviewing media.

In working with the guidance counselor and pupil personnel staff, the librarian may heighten his awareness of personal problems faced by individual students or groups of students. A bibliotherapeutic approach affords young people the opportunity to view alternative courses of action from the safe stance of vicarious experiences in fiction and biography, role playing and open-ended discussion, films, and filmstrips. "A child will always see even a minor detail in a book if it relates to himself, a detail most adults would fail to notice," writes Clara Kircher, author of Behavior Patterns in Children's Books.

My credo for libraries that serve young people follows. The above designs have grown out of this credo and ultimately are its affirmation.

Libraries for Children Exist in Affirmation of the Right of Each Child

To explore today's universe and man's place in it.

To ask about the solutions of the past and the problems of the future.

Black Communities and Informational Needs

To appreciate beauty and goodness in nature, the arts and his fellow man.

To recognize greatness.

To grow in faith in his own ability to face the future.

To understand the need for critical evaluation and comparison of sources of information.

To help someone.

To pretend.

To believe that life is worth living.

To create the images and sounds that inhabit his inner being.

To feel.

To enjoy life and learning.

To love.

To dream.

To read.

To know.

To sit and stare.

To expect a chance to achieve increasing mastery of basic skills.

To discover with all his senses.

To be challenged to go beyond mediocrity.

To be stimulated to adventure.

To be entertained through a variety of creative expression.

To be amused by the humorous and the ridiculous.

To be free from prejudice of the unknown.

To be accepted at his present stage, in his present mood, with his present problems.

To be encouraged to meet failure and disappointment in a positive way.

To be commended for his efforts and congratulated on his achievements.

To be a part of the solution of the problems that affect him directly.

To be heard.

To be protected from those institutions, persons or laws that deny him freedom to enjoy childhood.

To be secure in the knowledge that someone cares about him.

BLACK PRIDE GROWS IN BROOKLYN

by Edward C. Mapp

About a quarter of a century ago, Betty Smith wrote a novel entitled A Tree Grows in Brooklyn. In chapter two of her best-seller, Mrs. Smith describes Francie's [the heroine] love for the library. She is reading her way through all its books in alphabetical order. Francie loves everything about the place, its books, its ambience, its trappings, even its librarian. This lady, however, does not respond to Francie's adulation:

> A name on a card meant nothing to her and since she never looked up into a child's face, she never did get to know the little girl who took a book out every day and two on Saturday. A smile would have meant a lot to Francie and a friendly comment would have made her so happy.[1]

Francie's Brooklyn is a thing of the past. In recent years, the borough's black and Puerto Rican population has increased to approximately 20-30 per cent of the total, the latest migration coming from Haiti. Brooklyn's ethnic change will be reflected in a future musical production of "A Tree Grows in Brooklyn" which will have an all-black cast headed by Sammy Davis, Jr. Even beyond the realm of theatrical make-believe, there are indications that the challenge of change is reaching out to society's many institutions in the borough.

Since Brooklyn is the largest borough of the largest city in the western hemisphere, observation of its institutions may well carry implications for like institutions in other urban areas.

Colleges

Colleges throughout the borough are responding to the needs of a changing population.

In the early sixties, various community groups urged the Board of Higher Education to establish a new public college that would serve the central Brooklyn area. For the first time in the history of the Board of Higher Education local community representatives participated meaningfully in the planning of a new college and the selection of its first president. The mission of the college was clear from its inception. It would be experimental and innovative in its approach to instruction. It would respond to the occupational needs of the community, offering programs of professional study to its heavy minority enrollments. Medgar Evers College came into being in 1970 and opened its doors to students in September, 1971. Mrs. Medgar Evers, widow of the slain civil rights leader, participated in the formal opening ceremonies. A community council was established to advise and assist the college in following its mandate. An integral component of the college is its Community Service Center, which conducts surveys to ascertain the educational needs and interests of the population, presents workshops and seminars for community residents, and provides consultation to community groups as needed.

Brooklyn College, an older and more traditional institution, sponsors the Martin Luther King, Jr. memorial lecture series on a continuing basis. Individual lectures are organized around relevant themes such as "Black Drama" (Ossie Davis, William Marshall) or "Literature of the Black Diaspora."

The College has acquired the classical music compositions of four black nineteenth century musicians (Joseph White, Lucien Lambert, Sydney Lambert and Edmond Dede). Although the four represent a high level of musicianship, they are not mentioned in the standard histories of music. All four had to go abroad to gain reputations. This rare collection of scores will become a permanent part of the music collection of the Brooklyn College Institute for Studies in American Music.

Brooklyn College students volunteer their time to tutor children in a storefront center in the Red Hook section of Brooklyn. Others have participated in effective projects such as the Boys High School Youth Development Project.

The College's Television Center is a focus of community activity. The Haitian Artist Association Abroad staged an art exhibit which the Center documented on video-

Black Communities and Informational Needs

tape. The Center shared its equipment with a Central Brooklyn Model Cities Television Project, an effort to provide that geographical area with a community-controlled television station and trained personnel. The project is recognition of the fact that the regular media are derelict in their coverage of community news within ghetto neighborhoods. Residents from the community were to be trained in the preparation of television productions (such as a series on black culture) for ultimate viewing over closed-circuit channels in community centers.

At Pratt Institute, community participation is part of the curriculum. Students work with local communities on such goals as improvement of health services, development of block associations and the organization of cultural programs in the Fort Greene, Williamsburg-Bushwick and South Brooklyn areas.

Cultural Agencies

If the colleges in Brooklyn are assuming new roles, the many cultural institutions within the borough are in keen competition. Certainly not the least of these is the public library. It is as though this particular agency were heeding the words of Geraldine Clark:

> We will find that if we are willing to be accountable and responsible to all in our communities, including those who are powerless--the parents of the black and Spanish-speaking and the poor--if we are willing to work with them even when they have the leadership role, then we can make some changes in our libraries. [2]

The Library

Brooklyn Public Library recently established the position of Coordinator of Services to the Disadvantaged and appointed to it, Bessie L. Bullock, former Senior Community Coordinator.

A community news service covering day to day happenings in the black and Puerto Rican communities has been instituted in several branches of the Brooklyn Public Library system. The entire project including subscriptions to the service was undertaken on an experimental basis. The aim is to afford patrons a closer and more accurate view of urban minority problems.

The Brower Park branch has initiated a bilingual program for school children whose first language is not English. French speaking Haitian and Spanish speaking Puerto Rican youngsters make weekly visits to the library for story-telling, films and other presentations just for them. The Brower Park program promotes cultural pride in the young.

As part of the Voice of Brooklyn Festival financed by the National Endowment for the Humanities, Brooklyn Public Library is preparing an anthology of writings by unknown Brooklyn authors. The best of over 300 contributions submitted is being selected and edited by Sol Yurick. Among the wide range of subjects exploring the ethnic roots of Brooklyn's diverse communities are pieces dealing with the black experience, the desperation of the ghetto and racism. The project attempts to identify and encourage literary talents and abilities hidden away in Brooklyn. As a permanent record of the contemporary voices of Brooklyn, publication of the anthology marks an appropriate conclusion to the entire project. "Voices of Brooklyn" consisted of two parts, the anthology phase and the public presentation phase. The latter included a series of programs investigative of African, Spanish-American, and Afro-American cultures. The festivities were celebrated in music (jazz, gospel, spirituals, calypso), poetry, films and folklore. People of various cultures became involved in a common cultural undertaking with reciprocal respect between groups.[3]

Museums

Museums, traditional havens for the artifacts of the past, are becoming more involved with the reality of the present.

Brooklyn Children's Museum, the first children's museum in the world, was founded in 1899. Its buildings were vacated in 1967 as a result of extreme deterioration. Today its programs continue through a neighborhood facility known as MUSE: The Bedford Lincoln Neighborhood Museum. Located in what is essentially a black neighborhood, MUSE puts on exhibits, workshops, and concerts. Once a week, free jazz-jam sessions are offered. Many undiscovered musical talents have emerged from these events. A recent exhibit entitled "A House of Dolls" was another of its successes. The cultures of Africa and the West Indies were represented. Wooden Akua'ba dolls from Ghana and dolls of leather and cloth from Morocco, Kenya and South Africa were displayed. MUSE also presents free educational workshops which are supported by the New York State Council on the Arts.

The Brooklyn Museum, a sister institution, holds an annual "open house" to acquaint the public with its programs and services. The 1971 event took the form of an ethnic dance program. On each floor of the Museum, Brooklyn-based dance groups performed their specialities. On hand were the Sunlanders, the Kelvin Jordan Caribbean Theatre and the West Indian Steel Drum Band among others.

A truly significant cultural milestone, operating in the long corridors behind the African and primitive art section of the Brooklyn Museum, is the Community Gallery. Launched in 1968, the Gallery is reputedly the first facility created within the walls of a major American museum for the purpose of encouraging and fostering community creativity. The Community Gallery has featured the public debuts of local Haitian, Puerto Rican and Afro-American artisans from the surrounding geographic area. Late in 1971, a special fund-raising exhibit to bail the Gallery out of financial difficulty was arranged by its black director, Henri Ghent. More than fifty artists donated their works to the show. It is important that this unprecedented showcase be maintained for those who may not be able to exhibit and sell their artistic wares elsewhere. The Community Gallery should not have to struggle for survival from season to season as it offers important services to every segment of the heterogeneous Brooklyn community.

Yet another vehicle for the exhibition of new talent is the Bedford Stuyvesant Restoration Corporation building where art exhibits, such as Ted Jumola Adetutu's recently exhibited "Black Velvet," are shown.

The renaissance of cultural activity in the borough has been nurtured by the Brooklyn Arts and Culture Association, a volunteer group that organizes neighborhood programs. Concerts, films, art exhibits, dramatic productions and workshops sponsored by the Association afford entertainment and education. Prominently featured in the Association's programs are black groups such as the Afro-Caribbean Folkloric Dance Troupe, the Islanders, the Haitian Theatre Choucoune and the Children of God Gospel Singers.

Community Projects

Numerous community projects and neighborhood activities mark the degree of commitment of the people of Brooklyn.

Borough President Sebastian Leone proclaimed September 10. 1971 as Major R. Owens Day throughout Brooklyn in honor of the Commissioner of the Community Development Agency, a body involved with anti-poverty programs in New York City. Owens was formerly a librarian with the public library system of Brooklyn. The dynamic black leader is an outspoken advocate of community control. The community turned out en masse.

During the same month, the West-Indian American Day Association successfully launched its first carnival. Held in Brooklyn, the festivities included a parade with many picturesque floats, a Miss West-Indian American contest, limbo and steel band musical presentations, as well as a wide range of Caribbean cuisine. The three-day celebration was honored by the appearance and participation of black Congresswoman Shirley Chisholm, who is of Barbadian ancestry.

Plans for a Tompkins Park Community Cultural Center convey something of the unrealized potential of community-based efforts. When completed, the new facility (now under construction) will provide a theatre, a teenage canteen and a Golden Age center for the residents of the predominantly black neighborhood in which it is located.

Black pride grows in Brooklyn and, just like the tree in Betty Smith's classic, "It grows in boarded-up lots and out of neglected rubbish heaps. It grows up out of cellar gratings. It is the only tree that grows out of cement."[4]

In the Crown Heights section of the borough, black youngsters cleared a plot of land which had been used as a dumping ground for refuse. They planted seeds and soon

Black Communities and Informational Needs

transformed the land into a thriving vegetable garden. The youthful volunteers received special service trophies for their civic spirit from local black and community associations.

Local History

Brooklyn has seen a recent surge of interest in local history.

Widow's Son Lodge F. and A. M., the oldest of the Prince Hall Lodges in Brooklyn, came out with its history last year. The Lodge was apparently founded in Brooklyn in 1849. The first place of meeting was at 178 Prince Street, which jibes with the known incidence of blacks in the downtown Brooklyn area. Members were freemen, mostly literate, employed as barkers, carpenters, porters, teachers, machinists, messengers, oysterman, white-washers, farmers and engravers. Over the years, the Lodge has honored such outstanding black Americans as Roy Wilkins, John Hope Franklin, Thurgood Marshall, William H. Booth and Hardy R. Franklin, former community coordinator for the Brooklyn Public Library.

In recognition of the significance of local history, the Landmarks Preservation Commission has designated certain areas of Brooklyn as historic landmarks. Any changes to the exteriors of buildings in areas so designated must secure prior approval from the Landmarks Commission. The Stuyvesant Heights neighborhood, part of the predominantly black Bedford Stuyvesant section, was named the city's 17th historic landmark district. Stuyvesant Heights projects a multiplicity of church images ranging from the spires and cupolas of Mt. Lebanon Baptist to the Gothic traditionalism of St. Paul's Episcopal. Many of its residents are West Indian immigrants engaged in occupations characteristic of middle-class communities anywhere.

Future generations will undoubtedly have reasonable access to study of the Stuyvesant Heights community as a result of preservation of its dwellings.

Discovery and study of Weeksville, an earlier black community in Brooklyn, was not so easy. "Project Weeksville," as the archeological inquiry came to be known, started in 1968 when Model Cities began to demolish the block bounded by Dean, Pacific, Troy and Schenectady Streets. Equipped with shovels and picks, community volunteers began to dig in search of clues about the residents of Weeksville, keeping all the time just a few steps ahead of the bulldozers.

The materials and relics retrieved from archaelogical explorations such as this one tell us a great deal about the occupants of the community, their cultural interests, taste in ceramics, glassware, etc., and their general standard of living. The Weeksville digs yielded a tintype of a fashionably dressed black woman, a bust of a Grecian goddess, handcrafted materials such as shoes, boots, etc., earthenware, stoneware, bowls, urns and items of jewelry. Among the significant documents uncovered was the Constitution and By-Laws of the Abyssinian Benevolent Daughters of Esther Association, a mutual self-help group of black women. Black students viewing the Weeksville artifacts on display in the New York City Community College Library in Brooklyn were fascinated by this opportunity to glimpse their own past, a past that has been denied them too long. The Project's findings tend to contradict the image of Weeksville promulgated by records emanating from whites, which suggest that Weeksville was a slum, occupied by indolent, primitive people. The Weeksville excavation provides documentation for a reconstruction of history to recognize and credit the educated, socially-responsible industrious, tasteful members of the Weeksville community.

Weeksville, to the best knowledge available, was the first settlement of black freemen in the central Brooklyn area. The community appears to have formed before the ending of slavery in New York (circa 1827) and continued until sometime after the Civil War. It figured prominently in the Draft Riots of 1862, when many terrorized black families in Manhattan sought refuge in Weeksville. Project Weeksville has opened a door into what a black community in Brooklyn was like over a century ago.

At Brooklyn's P.S. 243 a curriculum unit has been developed around the history and way of life of the 19th century Weeksville community. The unit has been disseminated throughout the district. "Black Journal," a popular TV network series, devoted one of its weekly programs to Weeksville, thereby publicizing the project. Concerned and interested members of the community formed The Society for the Preservation of Weeksville and Bedford-

Stuyvesant History. The Society's representatives journeyed to Washington, D.C. in May, 1971 to receive from Mrs. Richard M. Nixon a citation and award from the National Trust for Historic Preservation. The award was made to the Weeksville project for identifying and preserving the surviving buildings of the early 19th century free black community. Yet all is not well. For even on a matter of local black history such as this, a growing internecine conflict between blacks and whites over control of the project has emerged. The implications of Weeksville are yet to be fully fathomed.

Introspective examination of the past, coupled with constructive activity in the present, seems to be the course Brooklyn has charted for itself. The deeds and events described here should be a source of pride to the residents of Brooklyn as well as a challenge to concerned community-oriented people everywhere. Is it any wonder that so many outstanding librarians have found professional fulfillment in Brooklyn?

Notes

1. Smith, Betty. A Tree Grows in Brooklyn, a Novel. Harper, 1947, p. 20.

2. Clark, Geraldine. "Bureaucracy or Commitment?" Library Journal, January 15, 1970, p. 210.

3. Nyren, Dorothy. "Voices of Brooklyn: Report on a Project Funded by the National Endowment for the Humanities," Wilson Library Bulletin, January 1972, pp. 443-445.

4. Smith, op. cit., p. ii.

PART III

On Academic Libraries

DEMOCRATIZATION OF THE
URBAN UNIVERSITY LIBRARY

by Etta Stanton Bullock

The university library has traditionally been a symbol of the intellectual glories of the past. It has been in a sense a repository of the accumulated wisdom of the culture. Scholarship was its stock in trade and the intelligentsia its patrons. Contemporary university librarians have gracefully inherited this tradition. As a result, university libraries are ready victims of the strong winds of rapid cultural change which are blowing in this country and throughout the world. This is especially true of urban university libraries which find themselves in the midst of a complex and often bewildering variety of urban problems.

The kernel of contemporary cultural change is, in my opinion, the drive for individual self determination. Although this nation was founded on "democratic" principles and the United States Constitution has long been regarded as the bulwark of the protection of individual rights, it has for the most part been an authoritarian nation. Social regulation, like the regulation of the armed forces, has been effectuated through a chain of commands in which policy was determined at the top and handed down through various echelons. This has been the essential structure of governmental, industrial, religious (in many instances) and educational institutions. In the last two decades groups of black people, students, and women have seriously challenged this nation's constitutional structures. Other ethnic minorities, including Puerto Ricans, American Indians and Mexican Americans, have joined the fray. What might be called cultural life-style minorities--hippies, communal-livers and homosexuals--have made their impact. Most currently, inmates of penal institutions, whose complaints of inhuman treatment have long been ignored, have broadened their protests to embrace a revolutionary political stance. The protest activities of these groups have been sparked by anger and frustration if not always by ideology. Their activities, nonetheless, have been accompanied by a burgeoning intellectual substructure based on psychological and psychiatric literature, political leftist writing and a kind of fundamentalist democracy in which current protest is likened to the protest of the American colonists against Great Britain.

Traditional institutions were unprepared for the unexpected assaults upon them. Although some personnel of the institutions often recognized the injustices which lay behind the protests and conscientiously desired to adjust themselves to them, they failed to recognize that the protestors, sometimes consciously and sometimes unconsciously, were objective not always so much to what the institutions did as to what they were. They were often objecting not primarily to particular decisions but to the decision-making process from which they were excluded. Many a conscientious administrator has asked, "What can I do?" whereas the person with whom he was dealing essentially objected to his having the power to determine what should be done.

We are all aware of some of the major changes which have occurred in universities in recent years as a result of the pressures of various groups: increased enrollment of black students, special programs for so-called disadvantaged students, usually the institution of a Black Studies Program, the opening up of formerly all-male schools to females and vice versa, and the increased participation of students in the management of university affairs. Urban universities, however, are being pressed by another group with which they have not yet come to terms to any appreciable degree--the community, in many cases a black, "disadvantaged" community. In the latter cases the pressures of the community and of the black students are not clearly distinguishable.

Although specific pressures may be treated on an ad hoc basis, universities--and from this point I shall focus on university libraries--cannot avoid some basic general questions. What groups have a legitimate right to participate in the determination of library policy? Is merely advisory participation feasible? What is the best structural form for the participation of various appropriate groups? How should the request for participation by any "inappropriate" groups be handled?

Let's take some examples of library "problem" situations which we have known to exist: (1) Several black school teachers from the community desire to borrow books from the library but balk at the administrative procedure and its delays; (2) Black clerical workers feel trapped in the lowest-paid non-maintenance positions and charge that they have been discriminated against with respect to promotions; (3) A group of Puerto-Rican students complain that Spanish music and literature are inadequately represented in the collection; (4) Neighborhood youths tend to monopolize the music-listening facilities and "frighten" students away; (5) Members of the Black Studies faculty charge that the library devotes insufficient money and attention to materials about black people; (6) The staff is being pressed by union representatives to join a union in order to have more voice; (7) Many women staff members complain that top library staff positions always go to men and that no non-whites are in high administrative posts; (8) A politically or racially "radical" group from the community desires to use the library auditorium for a meeting.

Confrontations such as these are certainly departures and distractions from "traditional library functions." Each of these problems, however, involves a group which feels that the library is insufficiently responsive to its needs and concerns. Each of these groups, in addition to having what it sees as a specific, practical problem, feels that it is a victim of a large, unwieldy and impersonal system. Since being resentful of a system without being resentful of the people who run the system is a state of mind of which most people are incapable, the library administration finds itself the object of hostility and often of vilification. In the midst of recrimination and response, the original practical issue gets lost in the shuffle. Even if the original demand is granted, the recrimination may continue. Often the library administrator is powerless to grant what is requested by reason of budgetary limitation or of what he interprets to be university policy. Under such circumstances, whether a library administrator is "liberal" or "conservative," friendly or unfriendly, is not likely to make much difference. He is at the same time a victim of his power and his lack of power. Although he may wish to be responsive to groups within and without the library, he may not legally abdicate his own role of decision-maker. At the same time his decision-making power may be sharply limited by factors beyond his control.

It seems to me, therefore, that what must be searched for is a different format for library governance, a format which could vary according to the needs of a specific library but one which could receive the input of the various groups

On Academic Libraries

that have a library concern in any way and digest it as part of the decision-making process. We are here facing on a small scale the challenges of making a democracy work. The first step in this process is commitment to the principle that determination of library policy is a cooperative process in which all who are affected by it should be privileged to participate. Inherent in this concept is the proposition that whether or not a person or group is affected by library policy should be determined by the particular person or group, not by somebody else. At present, at least the following groups claim such an interest: students, faculty, library administrators, library professional and non-professional staff and community residents. Some of these groups have obvious sub-groups. I am not going to attempt to draw a blue-print for a decision-making functional process based on the principle suggested. Such a process would have to evolve from the people concerned within the context of the principle, for institutional processes and the people who participate in them are interdependent. That is to say, it is at the very least a two-way street. Particular institutions tend to foster a certain type of people and particular types of people tend to foster certain types of institutions. It is unrealistic, therefore, to talk about changes in institutions without also talking about changes in people.

Libraries have historically, I believe, tended to attract a certain type of people--people who looked for a kind of refuge in hallowed halls, who felt more comfortable in a world of books than of people and events. It is not without some justification that the stereotyped library scene involves a middle-aged spinster librarian shushing ebullient intruders. I think it noteworthy that as one reads the news media, it is rare that one reads of a librarian speaking out on public questions or deeply involved in political issues and activities. There is little in the atmosphere of most university libraries that would encourage librarians into activity in keeping with social change. Moreover, in the problem-laden context of today, librarians, like other people in bureaucracies, are always fearful of being caught taking a position which might be disapproved of by their superiors. Tenure, which might protect the freedom of tenured faculty to speak out, is most often denied librarians, despite the educational qualifications for their positions.

Librarians, like other personnel in academe, are presently going through a painful process of "survival of the fittest." Given the variety of groups lodging protests against urban university libraries, librarians with the ability to get along cooperatively with such groups are a necessity. The librarian who is afraid of his shadow will be by-passed by such groups, with a negative report to his superior. Similarly, librarians showing conscious or unconscious prejudice against any of the groups they deal with are in for considerable criticism. This creates special personnel problems for the top library administrator since the most manageable, cautious and conservative librarians with spotless work records are often most likely to be the ones who become foci of outside criticism. Similarly, more maverick type staff members who are less inclined to be scrupulously responsive to authority are often the ones who can best deal with the protesting forces.

The various contemporary currents of change in academe are emphasizing what kind of a person one is and deemphasizing the assigned role. Essentially, personality, rather than status, is the principal concern. Such an approach is very frightening to an insecure person who hides behind his degrees and his university status. Young people today have justifiably charged many of their elders with hypocrisy. In an academic setting it seems particularly appropriate that teachers, librarians and other persons who are part of the educational process should impress students, not with degrees, roles and other academic indicia of status, but with themselves as human beings who have learned something about what it means to be human. After all, if universities are not primarily concerned with the kinds of human beings they employ and the kinds of human beings they help to produce, they become little more than glorified trade schools. I do not mean to suggest that universities should attempt to produce individuals from a standard mold, but rather that the focus in all their activities should be on the humanity of human beings however its unfolding is facilitated in each particular case.

This essay has been written from the point of view of a black librarian and a citizen of this country who is skeptical about its future unless certain realities are grasped and acted upon positively. University libraries, like other American institutions, are inheritors of racism. But racism, virus within the society that it is, is only one manifestation of man's inability to accept his full humanity. An understanding of racism, however, may lead to an understanding of the basic problem of reaching human openness to other human beings. What I am trying to say is that it is important for university library administrators, as well as for those above and below them in the hierarchy, to understand the cultural trends of which they are willing or unwilling parts. This means understanding the frustrations of the people who are causing them "problems," and recognition that the resolution of these problems lies ultimately in the direction of formulating institutional processes which must incorporate into the decision-making process the concerns of all affected. Wherever one is on the totem pole of authority, he must think of the other people with whom he is dealing as human beings and treat them as such. Perhaps it should not be, but this is a big order. In every generation there seem to be people who in one way or another have learned to do this. So far, however, most of humanity throughout history has not been able to rise above its own egocentricity. In any event, at this point in history, logic, if not feeling, must prompt us not to hold rigidly to past practices but to experiment with new ways of doing things which emphasize co-operative rather than authoritarian decision-making.

Urban university libraries can no longer be ivory towers passively preserving the cultural heritage of the mainstream and thereby reinforcing the status quo. The students will not permit it. The surrounding communities will not permit it. Soon the women's liberation groups will not permit it. Attempts to maintain the status quo do nothing but permit pressures to build to the exploding point. There has been enough experience in recent years for library administrators to understand what is happening. To wait for crises instead of acting to prevent them is now an obsolete, band-aid approach. The library schools should already be teaching understanding of the problems of urban university libraries. Library administrators should be creating offices whose principal responsibility would be to diagnose and anticipate problems, but from within and without, which are part of the waves of change. Nor can trouble be avoided by window dressing. There must be commitment to an ever-increasing understanding and desire to meet the real needs of people.

Librarianship is a service profession, but the concept of service must be expanded to include others in the decision as to what library service should be. We must question the sacred assumptions about libraries and about our roles as librarians. In so doing we may find that we become broader people, more able both personally and professionally to contribute to the solution of current cultural crosscurrents from which libraries cannot escape.

A BLACK LIBRARY IN A WHITE UNIVERSITY

by Mary D. Walters

When Dr. Lerone Bennett, Senior Editor of Ebony magazine, addressed an audience of black students and faculty on the challenge of Black Studies, he stressed the importance of Black Studies in determining the direction of the black liberation struggle.

> Black Studies should be a preparation for and an initiation into a life of service in the black community.
>
> Black Studies should be adapted to black people's needs and make scholars responsible for solving social problems. It should also allow us to see and handle our own reality. It should help us abandon the frame of reference to our oppressors whose education taught generations of black people to believe they were inferiors who contributed nothing to America's civilization.

He concluded by saying that Black Studies must challenge the authors of books who present information that blame blacks rather than whites for poverty and slum conditions:

> we must challenge the oppressive institution they would create as a result of their works.
>
> Most important, Black Studies is a challenge to black people to internalize black teachings, give up poverty, and play and get our hearts, souls, and minds together.

Early in the development of the Black Studies Division at Ohio State University, I was appointed Chairman of the Library Committee, specifically charged with the responsibility of writing a proposal for the establishment of a Black Studies Library. At OSU the Library Council, upon the

On Academic Libraries

advice of the Director of Libraries, is responsible for the approval of all libraries within the University library system. Knowing the history of denials of requests for new department libraries, I submitted the following proposal, substantiated with pretty strong language, to the Director of Libraries. The proposal had the full support of the staff of the unapproved Black Studies Division.

Establishing A Black Studies Department Library to Support a Black Studies Curriculum at the Ohio State University

The concept of a Black Studies Program at the Ohio State University grew out of the growing urgency of educators and administrators to satisfy the demand of its younger generation of students to provide them with an education which is relevant to their daily needs. The Black Studies Division has developed the following objectives:

To provide a means for the systematic and scholarly examination of the past, present, and future of Afro-American people in particular, and African people in general;

To develop a comprehensive curriculum in Afro-American and African studies;

To make available the full resources of the University community for the liberation and advancement of Afro-American and African peoples;

To provide specialized programs and services to Afro-American and African communities;

To conduct essential and vital research in areas deemed important by Afro-American and African peoples;

To develop institutions for the survival, creation and perpetuation of Afro-American and African life;

To assist Afro-American and African peoples in the development of ideological concepts and strategies necessary to overcome European and other colonial domination;

To assure that all institutions and universities like Ohio State provide equal opportunity for all Afro-American and

African peoples throughout the world;

To work with all people interested in building a humane and equitable society for all.

The recent trend in establishing library collections representative of ethnic groups in America, such as the East Asian, Hebrew, and Slavic, is a significant step in the perpetuation of understanding among races and groups which make up the United States of America.

Because America has been guilty of neglecting the contributions of black Americans to the development of this country, students have had to rely on either very limited library resources found in many of the black university libraries or on word-of-mouth experiences. Publishers, because of the demands of students for more meaningful education, have tried to bridge the "fact gap" by reprinting whole library collections held by black university libraries. Consequently, some universities have been faced with a financial dilemma in attempting to keep pace with the output of materials from publishers and reprinters. Fortunately, many programs for blacks in universities throughout the country have found very fertile grounds from financial support given them by private foundations as well as the federal government.

Because Ohio State University Libraries have been insensitive to the needs of the black students, last spring several demands were made by the students relative to library needs, among which were (1) a Black Studies Library, and (2) an Oral History Library. These demands grew out of the needs for personnel services sensitive to the problems and needs, as well as the aspirations of black students. They had found that, historically, Ohio State University Libraries had never hired a black professional librarian to head a department library; that only one black professional librarian serves in the public service area of the entire university library system; and that there has never been a black male professional librarian on the staff of the Ohio State University Libraries.

Keeping in mind the above inequities, the Black Studies Division adopted the following objectives as supportive of the Black Studies Library for the Ohio State University:

On Academic Libraries

--To provide an atmosphere and conditions under which black students at Ohio State University can study effectively.

--To hire adequate personnel who are trained to be sensitive to the needs of black students.

--To develop programs and collections to support the curriculum of the Black Studies Division.

--To acquire on a systematic, continuing basis, all relevant materials necessary to acquaint the black student with the contributions his race has made to the development of American civilization.

--To acquire any oral testimony from contemporary personalities which would not be available from any other source.

--To work cooperatively with other library units on campus to give maximum service to all students.

It is generally agreed by experts in the field of libraries that university libraries are the most difficult to evaluate quantitatively, because their value cannot be measured in quantitative terms. This is to say that the worth of the library program, to the student and faculty served, cannot be measured by looking at the number of volumes in the collection or the number of staff who service it.

The proposals presented below stem from experience as well as contact with library users, and are aimed at the maximum objectives derived from the use of these library materials. We realize these proposals will result in changes in the organizational structure of the University Libraries, thereby requiring additional funds for staffing as well as for purchasing of library materials, but they only reflect the increased pressures exerted on virtually every aspect of university activities throughout this country.

1. We are proposing that a separate department library be established to be called "The African-American Library" and that an "Afro-American Oral History Library" be established as a part of the African-American Library.

2. That this Library be staffed with black persons of American and African origin who would represent different cultural backgrounds.

3. That the size of the Library be determined by the annual rate of increased enrollment which would be determined by its allocations. Ideally, the annual rate of increase would be approximately three thousand volumes and an equal number of videotapes, films, etc., and a staff of three carefully chosen professional librarians with ample clerical assistants. As the services increase and the number of students enrolled in the Black Studies Division increases, we would hope that the library budget would increase equally.

4. That this Library be ample for seating one-fourth of the students enrolled in the Black Studies Division.

5. That the personnel be responsible for the book selection, circulation, and reference services, and the administration of the collection.

6. That this Library be set up in the Main Library -- first choice; or as a second choice, in the Dieter Dunz Language Hall. That the second floor area of the Main Library which now houses the Undergraduate Library be given first choice. While the Black Studies Committee realizes it would not be economically feasible to attempt to shelve every book which may be relevant to the Black Studies Program in any one room, the Main Library would offer many advantages such as: (a) accessibility to expensive reference tools which are necessary for the continued acquisition of library materials; (b) accessibility to expensive book forms in the Microform Room and the necessary equipment for use; (c) accessibility to newspapers and periodicals already in the library's collection and which would pose special shelving problems if removed from their present location; and (d) having the advantage of being contained in a building which is secure at night with ample janitorial services; (e) the desk for circulating materials is already there and this expense would not be incurred; (f) accessible stacks are there for the growth of library materials; and (g) ample seating, proper lighting, chairs, tables, desks, etc., are already there.

Nevertheless, the detailed summary of the cost of operations is based on standards developed by the American Library Association for determining minimum library needs.

SUMMARY

Regular Library[1] (First Year)

Number of students (undergraduate)
    Majors in Black Studies, Undergraduate Degree ... 350
    Students taking one or more courses in Division .. 3,500

Number of faculty
    Full-time in Division 15
    Teaching one or more courses in Division 30

Size of collection
    Books or monographs 10,000
    Journals (current subscriptions) 50
    Back volumes of journals 500

Staff
  Professional
    Head of Black Studies Library
    Reference Librarian
  At least two clerical

Hours of service (The same as all other department libraries)

Space needs
    Shelving .... 1,300 linear ft.
    Seats .... 80 seats
    Floor space for seats .... 2,000 sq. ft.
    Floor space for staff .... 300 sq. ft.

The Black Studies Division will be responsible for the following:

1. Obtaining space for Black Studies Library;

2. Personnel salaries--Obtaining personnel salaries;

3. Approval of personnel in cooperation with the libraries;

4. Selection of materials on a day to day basis;

5. Providing office space for Head of Black Studies Library, in the Black Studies Division until floor space is made available for library.

Section I - Detailed Schedule of Personnel Services

5 students to aid in curricular development	8,000
Guard for Afro Center	7,000

Section II - Detailed Schedule of Learning Resources

Oral Library:
Curator (includes travel budget)		15,000
2 clerks		10,000
Materials		2,000
Equipment		6,000
	Total	33,000

Regular Library:
2,000 volumes at $20,000
Retrospective buying at $1,500
Current Books, Continuing Budget at $1,500   23,000

Periodicals - 30 to 50		
Current Subscriptions at 13¢ each		650
Back runs - 500 volumes at $20 per volume		10,000
	Total	10,650

Personnel
Cataloguer at $10,000/yr.
Acquisitioner at $5,000/yr.
Library Assistant at $5,000/yr   20,000

                                          Grand Total   86,650

Section III - Detailed Schedule of Space Required - Second Choice

Summary of Proposed Use of Space

Dean Babcock's intention is to allocate rooms 236 and 236A of Dieter Cunz Hall as the administrative offices of the division. Room 235 is 20 ft. x 8 ft. and could serve as the reception area, with room for two secretaries. Room 236A is 12 ft. x 16 ft. and would be used as the Chairman's office. In addition, Dean Babcock is reserving three faculty offices in Dieter Cunz Hall should they be needed. Conversion of Room 232 of Dieter Cunz Hall to provide space for advising, counselling, etc, will be requested by Dean Babcock.

From the spring of 1969 to the summer of 1971, the Director of the Black Studies Division, with the help of the Associate Director and of the Black Studies Committee, labored with the following proposal and submitted it to the Council on Academic Affairs:

PROPOSED MAJOR PROGRAM IN BLACK STUDIES

August 12, 1971

Introduction

The Black Studies Division is a new academic and administrative unit of the College of Humanities. Its purposes are to establish a program which speaks directly to the needs, aspirations, and history of the black man in America and to establish learning programs which focus upon the actual lives and problems of urban and rural black Americans. In accordance with these objectives, the Division encourages students to take courses with a solid academic content and to participate in community projects that will aid in the liberation of the black man.

The Division's program also emphasizes the establishment of close ties with African people around the world who are engaged in the quest for liberation. Consequently, students in the Division are encouraged to spend time studying and working on the African continent and in other significant places where black people are engaged in the common pursuit of freedom.

With these goals in mind, the Black Studies major seeks to acquaint students with a wide body of knowledge bearing on the liberation experiences of black people across the world. Accumulated knowledge in the area of Black Studies is so vast that it could not possibly be codified in one academic discipline. The Black Studies major program anticipates that students will take a wide range of courses across a broad span of academic areas serving to enhance their knowledge of the Black Experience while simultaneously preparing them to cope with the practical realities endemic in the quest for rewarding post-college vocational careers. Thus, the Black Studies major is interdisciplinary in nature, drawing on a wide array of academic resources of the University to provide a unique combination of intellectual and inspirational stimulation and vocational training for students interested in centering their educational pursuits around a total understanding of and involvement in the ongoing struggle for black freedom.

The proposed baccalaureate program in Black Studies is based on the B.A. and B.S. curricula of the Colleges of Arts and Sciences. The major program contains two parts. The first part (central theme) consists of at least forty (40) hours selected from the attached list of available courses offered by the Black Studies Division or by other Departments. As a part of this forty (40)-hour requirement a student must take at least three (3) courses above the level of 200 designated as core courses by the Black Studies Division, at least one of which must be from the student's area of interest. These courses, which should be scheduled early in the major program, will provide a foundation for later courses. For example, a student with an historical interest must take as one of his three (3) core courses, a history course designated as a core course by the Black Studies Division. The other two (2) core courses might be from political science and philosophy. Similarly, if a student were interested in education, his two (2) other core courses might be from literature and sociology. This provision for core courses assures that all student majors in Black Studies will receive training in areas which the Division deems essential to a rounded educational experience. Further it provides a central point around which students can build comprehensive, cohesive and productive programs of study within the realm of Black Studies. As a result, themes or tracks ... can be built to allow students to bring order and reason out of the many course options available to them through Black Studies.

The second part of the Black Studies major (Coordinate Theme) consists of at least twenty (20) hours taken wholly in one Department or divided between two Departments. This requirement provides the student with a healthy variety of course options, thus making the major program immensely flexible and infusing it with considerable academic strength. While the Central Theme will provide the principal paradigmatic thrust of the major, the Coordinate Theme may be vocationally directed to strengthen the student's preparation for his later career. It is hoped that courses of the Coordinate Theme will sharply intersect at various points with the Central Theme of the major, thus facilitating a broadening of tracks and themes to encompass broad sweeps of rationally connected knowledge across traditional academic boundaries.

At least 25 of the 60 hours of the major must be at the 300 level or above. No more than 15 hours of the total major may be in individual (-93) or group studies (-94) courses.

When the announcement came that an academic major program in Black Studies leading to a baccalaureate degree had been approved on the Council on Academic Affairs, and that the Library Council had agreed to establish a Black Studies Library, we had lived to see the results of our efforts materialize into the actual implementation of some of the demands made by students throughout this land--an education which would be more relevant to the young people of this age.

I suppose Lerone Bennett summarized it adequately when he spoke briefly at the dedication of the Black Studies Library:

> There is need for understanding the black experience, because it relates the struggles as well as the scholarship of the black people ... and though on opposite ends of the spectrum, they are both great, and people remember greatness. The importance of a Black Studies Library is in compiling and researching information about the history, psychology, sociology, and culture of black people.
>
> Until recently the enemy knew more about black people than we knew about ourselves; and he distorted this information to use against us. An example of this distortion is The Unheavenly City by Dr. Edward C. Banfield,[1] who heads President Nixon's task force on model cities. Like Moynihan before him, Banfield blames blacks rather than whites for the conditions of our society.

Among his solutions to Negro problems are: Black children should be taken from their parents at an early age and raised in a cultural atmosphere that is normal; lower-class (black) children should be sold to highest bidders and prices should be as high as possible as an incentive for lower class parents to sell their children. Enclaves of lower-class people should be semi-institutionalized. They would be forced to give up their privileges of marrying, owning property, and having children.

Let us make this a repository of good examples of black men and women who taught us how to live and how to die....

History is entombed here because it was made and was recorded. In the name of all the long black lines from Slavery to Columbus, Ohio, we dedicate this Library to the truth which shall be our liberator.

According to Mrs. Eleanor Daniel, the Black Studies Librarian, the Ohio State University Libraries contributed most generously (although funds were limited) from a budget already taxed and weighted with priorities. In fact, there is every indication that the financial support received surpasses that of institutions of comparable size and rank. In order to supplement and support the curriculum adequately, it is felt that a separate collection will best serve the special needs of the students and faculty. To keep abreast of the increasing demands for materials by or about blacks, it is necessary to build the collection rapidly. The goal of the Black Studies Library at Ohio State University is to become a major source of research and study. The total black heritage will continue to be explored and revealed; the most significant and best contributions will be explored from all available sources for inclusion in the collection.

With continued awareness and support, the Ohio State University Libraries hope to become an unparalleled repository of the black man's experience.

Note

1. Edward C. Banfield, The Unheavenly City: the Nature of Our Urban Crisis. Boston: Little Brown, 1970.

BLACK RAGE AND BLACK ACADEMIC LIBRARIES

by Casper LeRoy Jordan

The Sixties have ended. Although filled with a host of dramatic and significant events domestic and foreign, the decade will be vividly remembered in the United States by swift and lasting advances toward racial equality. The Federal Government pushed through legislation guaranteeing certain basic rights and took steps to establish political equality for all people. The conscience of the country generally was aroused to the evils of discrimination and its consequent violations of the moral principles basic to a truly democratic society. These activities assailed abuses along the whole spectrum of rights--from voting privileges and equal access to education, to housing conditions, employment practices, and consumer services.

In the past, major progress toward the goal of free and open access to education has had to await legal action in the courts, but now educational opportunities are expanding as the result of wider and more telling use of political power and social pressure. These opportunities are themselves necessary before comparable advances can be made in employment opportunities, for today, education and technological training are the keys which unlock the doors to the preferred occupational fields. Without open access to education at all levels, to the untutored and unskilled the right to employment without regard to race will largely remain an empty dream.

Education also gives renewed strength to the entire movement for equal opportunities. Black college students dramatized this role of education in the early 1960's when they began to demonstrate for equal opportunities, beginning in North Carolina and then in Alabama and Georgia. These demonstrations, together with the enrollment of the first black students in previously all-white state universities in Georgia and Mississippi, focused the eyes of the nation on the colleges that these students attended and sparked an interest among many in the character of the education they provided. Questions come to mind. What were these colleges really like? What role did they have to play in the whole fabric of American higher education? What were their basic needs? What were their standards?

At least five times in the past fifty years students of American higher education undertook to answer these questions.[1] In 1917, 1928, 1942, 1960 and 1962, and 1965 studies appeared with many facts about higher education for Negroes. Smaller studies were also undertaken from time-to-time (the infamous Jencks-Riesman study comes readily to mind).[2] The 1965 study, the published version of which is known as the "McGrath study,"[3] was undertaken by the Institute of Higher Education and financed by a grant from the Carnegie Corporation of New York in 1963; it has had a profound affect on black higher education and particularly on the libraries. Recently the Carnegie Corporation published a further study of black colleges.[4]

The McGrath study discovered that although black colleges included less than six percent of American institutions, and their enrollments comprised less than three percent of all college students, these colleges enrolled over half of the black students attending institutions of higher learning in the United States. It also established the fact that black institutions run the entire gamut of quality within American higher education, except at the topmost level of excellence represented by a few celebrated institutions. It further stated that these schools should be strengthened and preserved, rather than dissolved as some suggested. The closing of these institutions would deprive thousands of blacks of any opportunity for higher education.

The study looked closely at the libraries in these black institutions. There was a report on four major features of the library: material resources of facilities and collections; human resources of trained staff members; use of these resources by student and faculty members; and administration and financial support of the library. The findings showed the following needs: new quarters; increases in the rate of support for collections; increases in staff size and training; regional workshops for continuing education of in-service library personnel; cooperative ventures among these libraries, especially in the area of technical services; the establishment of strong library orientation program for beginning black college students. The study summed up the condition of library services in most black college libraries:

That the physical facilities are in general more adequate than the books, journals, films, and records they contain, or the number and training of the library staff. Their collections and staff need extensive strengthening to rectify a history of insufficient support and to help lift teaching and learning out of ritual and routine.[5]

Trained librarians are at a premium everywhere, but the shortage is especially acute in black colleges. There is grave need for more trained librarians than in the ordinary school. Only the best librarians are capable of meeting the demanding challenges in these schools. In the mid-1960's, through a large grant by the Rockefeller Foundation to the Atlanta University School of Library Service, a program was inaugurated to increase the number of trained librarians. Atlanta University had long produced the majority of the black librarians in America, and this was an effort (and a successful one) to increase the pool of black librarians. In addition, institutes were sponsored to improve the lot of the in-service black librarians.

In 1968, with a grant from the Ford Foundation, the School of Library Service was able to enlarge its program with a three-year project aimed directly at improving the black academic libraries. The fellowship program would educate sixty people over a three-year period, and they were obligated by accepting the grants to work for at least two years in a black academic library. In a sense, these schools were being provided with 120 man-years of library service--or longer, if the individuals chose to remain.

The in-service librarian was not forgotten. A series of three workshop-intern programs were planned. These workshops would cover the areas of improving technical services (1968-1969), reader services (1969-1970), and building collections (1970-1971). The participants were brought to Atlanta for a two-week workshop with the assistance of noted consultants; they then spent a two- to four-week internship at a "model" library where they were able to observe and participate in excellent library service. These workshops have been very successful, and rewarding to both the participants and the host libraries. Opportunities for professional exchanges have been meaningful and relevant. There has also been a corresponding improvement in library services at "home" libraries.

The year 1968 also saw the formation of a cooperative plan for six black colleges in Alabama and Mississippi.[6] The United Board for College Development in Atlanta underwrote a feasibility study for centralized library purchasing and technical processing for six black colleges in Alabama and Mississippi. UBCD was established with the primary objectives of engaging in research and overt action to improve the quality of a group of black, church-related and independent colleges. The study recommended the establishment of single processing center for the selection, ordering, cataloging and processing of materials for the institutions. Other institutions would be invited to join the group after the pilot study was underway. The cooperative College Library Center was opened in the fall of 1969 through a grant from the Carnegie Corporation of New York. It is perhaps the first academic cooperative serving libraries in more than one state.

The first project of the Cooperative College Library Center was to sponsor a workshop on classification conversion--one of the requirements for membership in the Center is to convert to the Library of Congress Classification. Over twenty black college libraries--all prospective members for the Center were invited to attend the two-week institute. Many areas of further cooperation were explored during this Atlanta-based meeting. The response was very encouraging, and many libraries were eager to join the group immediately.

Other projects have "snowballed" since 1968. The 3M Company, in cooperation with the Hill Family Foundation, Atlanta University, and the United Negro College Fund, sponsored two workshops in the fall of 1969 centering on the use of microprint in black libraries. Thirty-eight libraries who were under the UNCF umbrella and two other libraries were given microprint resource centers and selected materials on microfilm from the Schomburg Collection of the New York Public Library. This is a three-year project and other materials will be added to the collection in subsequent years.

The School of Library Service also sponsored a workshop on the utilization of personnel under the direction of a noted consultant in the field of library management during the month of October 1969.

Fisk University has sponsored two institutes focussing

on black studies librarianship. Several score librarians, black and white, have availed themselves of these enriching experiences to broaden college library services in a long-neglected field. Fisk is also undertaking a black oral history project, and combined with it will be workshops to provide expertise in this field to other librarians beyond the limits of Nashville.

In 1969, COSATI (Committee on Scientific and Technological Information) became concerned with black research libraries. A task force on black academic libraries has been working with COSATI, Federal libraries, the Association of Research Libraries, and the Black Caucus of ALA to identify needs in this area.

The School of Library Science of North Carolina Central University in Durham, with a federal grant, has sponsored a pilot program to identify black collections in six Southeastern states.

The United Negro College Fund has constituted a steering committee on library planning and development for the forty college libraries of its members. This group will be concerned with UNCF college libraries, but its findings will have great interest for non-UNCF libraries in the private and public sectors.

So there is evidence that the long-neglected black academic libraries are receiving some long needed attention. Elaborate statistics on future college enrollments need not be displayed again to demonstrate that the demands on all the constituent units of the enterprise of American higher education will increase intensively and irresistibly in the years ahead. The nation will need every existing institution, and many more, to accommodate the youth who seek and deserve the advantages of higher education. All the existing black colleges and many more institutions will be required to accommodate these oncoming legions. It is imperative that the "hearts" of these institutions be in good shape to serve these legions.

Notes

1. Thomas J. Jones, Negro Education. <u>A study of the private and higher schools for colored people in the U.S.</u> (Washington: Bureau of Higher Education,

1917). Arthur J. Klein, Survey of Negro Colleges and Universities, prepared in the Division of Higher Education, U.S. Office of Education Bulletin, 1928, no. 7 (Washington: U.S. Government Printing Office, 1929). National Survey of the Higher Education of Negroes: Ina C. Brown, Socio-Economic Approach to educational problems (Misc. no. vol. 1); General studies of colleges for Negroes (Misc. no. 6, vol. 2); Lloyd E. Blauch and Martin D. Jenkins, Intensive study of selected colleges for Negroes (Misc. no. 6, vol. 3); Ambrose Caliver, A Summary (Misc. no. 6, vol. 4) (Washington: U.S. Government Printing Office, 1942 and 1943). "The Negro private and church-related college," Journal of Negro Education, vol. 29 no. 3 (Summer 1960); "The Negro public college," Journal of Negro Education," vol. 31, no. 3 (Summer 1962). Earl J. McGrath, The Predominantly Negro Colleges and Universities in Transition. (New York: Bureau of publications, Teachers College, Columbia University, 1965.

2. Christopher Jencks and David Riesman, "The American Negro College," Harvard University Educational Review. vol. 37, (Winter, 1967), 43-60.

3. E. J. McGrath, op. cit.

4. Carnegie Commission on Higher Education. From Isolation to Mainstream: Problems of the Colleges Founded for Negroes. McGraw-Hill, 1971.

5. E. J. McGrath, op. cit. p. 136.

6. Annette H. Phinazee and Casper L. Jordan, "Centralized Library purchasing and technical processing for six colleges in Alabama and Mississippi; a report," College and Research Libraries, vol. 30, no. 4 (July 1969), 369-370.

PINHEAD LIBRARIES AND LIBRARIANS, IN PRAISE OF

by Margaret Perry

> Every library should try to be complete on something, if it were only the history of pinheads.
> --O. W. Holmes

The departmental library at some colleges or universities is looked upon as a pariah or, in less derogatory terms, as a confusing nuisance in a world (the library) which is already full of arcane language and rituals and mythic-like rules and regulations. In the orderly manner characteristic of the taxonomic librarian, some definition of a departmental library and an investigation into its genesis and history should be presented before advancing in an organized manner towards the heart of this essay-- the delineation of the nature and role of a subject-oriented departmental librarian.

In 1898, George H. Baker, Librarian of Columbia University Library, presented the following definition of a departmental library:

> Departmental libraries are collections of books, usually looked upon as a part of the general book stock of the institution, selected for the special use of a department and usually kept in a convenient place in the building or section of a building devoted to that department.[1]

The simplicity of this definition lends itself to such flexible interpretation that one is hard put to deny its applicability. Later definitions that refine or qualify Mr. Baker's retain the basis notion of a generic separation of books (and other materials, of course) into a pattern of library decentralization.

The history and development of departmental libraries is remarkably clear, straightforward, and plausible. In an article that explored the early development of departmental libraries, it was stated that

> Departmental libraries started as a protest.
> Nothing much was said, but now we can see that,
> at a certain juncture in American education, books
> were imperatively needed--and the university library, so called, was asleep. On the whole, it
> had never been awake, and it was very slow in
> waking.[2]

A combination of an unavailable and/or inadequate collection in the main body of the library, and an imitation of the seminar libraries in Germany, allowed for the development of departmental libraries before a name was given to the phenomenon. Often these libraries were nothing more than donations from a professor's own collection; other collections simply formed from an outgrowth of an overcrowded main library. As scholarship improved and post-graduate study transformed institutions into true universities, and as the administration of libraries evolved into a more exacting and recognizable discipline, departmental libraries were given closer scrutiny to estimate if, indeed, they served a valid purpose. The questions of who was to care for them and who exerted the power to direct them had to be answered. In 1901, two problems that would plague departmental libraries for some time to come were pointed out: the cost of running a separate collection (especially when expensive duplication of material could be demonstrated), and the problem of control and management of the adjunctive library. As was stated at the beginning of this century:

> ...the librarian ... will note before all other matters one against which his professional pride and business convictions cause him to rebel instinctively. The sense of possession, of ownership, of control, so strongly manifested by these several 'groups' [i.e., academic departments] will strike him at once as a new factor in his problem.... No librarian, probably, would consent to responsibility minus power....[3]

It was during the 1920's that a general shift away from departmental libraries evolved: for one thing, many of the original buildings--sadly overcrowded and, therefore, a reason for the establishment of many departmental libraries--were replaced, and reassessments concerning the concepts behind departmental libraries were made. One

On Academic Libraries 115

reason, given as valid, was:

> The care of a department spurs on the lazy librarian. Heaven deliver an ambitious librarian from an assistant who regards his position as a literary lounging ground or as a background to display his talents as an author; ... let him be given a task where, working alone, results can be accurately measured, and where responsibility and pride will spur him on. [4]

The general consensus at this time was that the library's strength within the framework of academia would be enhanced through reorganizing into or establishing a centralized system. Louis T. Ibbotson pointed this out in his 1925 article, and he indicated some of the reasons for this shift of emphasis in library administration. Departmental libraries, however, did not disappear; indeed, they multiplied despite some real animosity toward them. Selection, upkeep, and service were always three of the more serious problems because the usefulness of such a collection (especially for the student) was greatly affected by these considerations. Inasmuch as there seems to be little abatement in the construction of buildings, or the provision of room(s) for departmental libraries (this is most often true for the fields of Science, Medicine, and Law), such libraries, like the old cliché about the poor, will be with us ad infinitum; and, rather than debate the rise and fall of what appears indestructible, it seems more useful and rewarding to probe the more illusive matter of the role of the departmental librarian.

The nature of the librarian who is a specialist in a subject area is a bit like the line from Archibald MacLeish's poem, "Einstein":

> So he knows
> Less than a world and must communicate
> Beyond his knowledge.

The breadth of a subject area has that limitless quality one senses upon watching and following the earth's horizon, and the librarian who grasps this reality, either dialectically or intuitively, possesses one key to a healthy perception of his profession. Armed with this humbling notion which is, after all, the beginning of wisdom, the librarian sees to it that he secures solid knowledge about the basic and more specialized literature (selectively chosen, according to personal inclination) of a specific discipline. The practical matter of giving reference service demands no less than this. The most direct, perhaps the simplest step, is to acquire a master's degree in his subject area; but a degree is not the sine qua non for the possession of specific academic knowledge. The acquiring of basic, remote and then more complex facts, truths, information within a body of knowledge is a personal matter; the desire for this knowledge must possess the librarian. This demon, or saint--for this phenomenon of desire is not totally unrelated to the sentiments expressed by some mystics--is also what keeps the librarian's mind active in the drive towards new and/or expansive insight into his subject. Whitehead and others have remarked that the mind is always active, but the world is full of delusive stimuli which deflect even the true thinker from his specific goals in life. A subject-specialist librarian needs a probing as well as an open mind; a belief in searching for the truth of matters; intellectual restlessness; a respect for scholarship; and an unsurfeited curiosity about areas of knowledge related to his special discipline. There are other needed qualities, to be sure, but an enlightened mind and a respect for intellectual pursuits are paramount.

One final quality necessary in a departmental librarian is a combination of dedication and loyalty to the department he serves. Dedication and loyalty cannot, however, be exacted by fiat; they must be deserved. If there is not mutual regard between the librarian and the faculty within a department, there can be no fulfillment of the task to which both parties are dedicated: the acquisition and expansion of knowledge.

The librarian will be, first of all, a professional colleague of the teaching staff; will be--in the words of Whitehead--part of "a band of scholars." The possession or lack of academic status does not enter into this notion; for, in this role the librarian must be a scholar in his own right. The librarian has chosen specialization as opposed to general reference or technical work, and he must live up to his professional choice. As in the iterative stylistic form of St. Francis's verse-prayer, the librarian who feels his scholarship is faulty or faltering must say to himself: where there is lack, let me sow erudition; where there is weakness, strength; where there is doubt, resolution. In other words, search for the problems hindering success, face them, and work in a positive manner to obliterate them.

On Academic Libraries   117

Accepting, then, that the librarian, endowed with intelligence and a zeal for knowledge, is a master in some area of a subject and a colleague who occupies a singular role within a department, let us bring closer scrutiny to bear upon some of the specific roles he performs. If the table of organization does not allow for an assistant librarian, or if technical work is not centralized, there will be very practical tasks to perform. But since the performance of work tasks and the assumption of a role are exclusive, in part, the latter will be examined because it is more important. It is how one presents oneself as a colleague and fellow-scholar that defines the distinctive nature as well as the unique strength of a subject-specialist librarian.

There are three definable roles one might single out for the departmental librarian. One depends on the possession of academic status--i.e., the general adviser to students, not all of whom would be in the librarian's department. Depending on the particular college or university, of course, the librarian might perform this function without the advantage of academic status. The two other roles, however, are possible without benefit of any particular status except as a departmental librarian who is a member of that "band of scholars" in a specific school. It is in the role of bibliographic adviser to both the faculty and the students that the departmental librarian assumes one of his most important functions. It is in the nature of his position that the solid bibliographical knowledge possessed by the librarian be illuminated and shared with colleagues. No matter how deeply a librarian may investigate one aspect of his subject, he will be compelled to keep himself well-informed in a general manner in order to fulfill this role as bibliographic adviser. The role confers upon the librarian the necessity of reinvestigating the old, searching for the new, and then sharing his knowledge and insight at various points of the quest.

The last role (at least, the last chosen for the purposes of this essay) is closely related to the idea expressed earlier, concerning dedication and loyalty, posited as being a part of the nature of the departmental librarian. The role can be described--hopefully, not too loftily--as a priestly-like dedication to the students of the librarian's particular department. This may be difficult to explain; and the notion may be unacceptable, if not too idealistic or plain silly, to some. But this is the unique role the departmental librarian can assume, for the relationship with one group of students on a continuous basis in a variety of activities is an opportunity afforded almost exclusively to the departmental librarian. The extent to which the librarian can be a mélange of teacher, explicator, clarifier, energizer, friend, colleague, and seer is unlimited. And this role can be as complex as the theory of relativity or as simple as the pure enjoyment of beauty unexplained. In this way, the librarian aids the student in his heuristic as well as scientific approaches to knowledge and, at the same time, forms a nexus to the department and the faculty in a manner that is complementary rather than usurpative.

There can be no simple summation, in one or two words, of the nature and role of the departmental librarian unless "humanistic-scholar-librarian" evokes the image of a person who possesses some of the aforementioned qualities. Does this mean that those who do not serve as departmental librarians need not have these traits or need not function in such a role? Of course not; there is nothing exclusive about the nature and role of the departmental librarian. On the other hand, this type of librarian must focus on a specific field and a particular clientele in such a manner that his role is, in a sense, unique. In a way it is akin to the remark that all cognac is brandy but all brandy is not cognac. Satis verborum!

Notes

1. George H. Baker, "Relation of seminary and departmental libraries to the general university library." Library Journal 23:103 (1898).

2. Louis T. Ibbotson, "Departmental libraries." Library Journal 50:853 (1925).

3. William Warner Bishop, "The problem of the departmental system in university libraries." Library Journal 26:17 (1901).

4. Edith E. Clarke, "Departmental libraries." Library Journal 16:267 (1891).

5. Ibbotson, pp. 853-858.

Background Bibliography

Baker, George H. "Relation of seminary and departmental libraries to the general university library." Library Journal 23:103-106 ([July?] 1898).

Bishop, William Warner. "The problem of the departmental system in university libraries." Library Journal 26: 14-18 (January 1901).

Bruno, J. Michael. "Decentralization in academic libraries." Library Trends 19:311-317 (January 1971)

Centralization and decentralization in academic libraries: a symposium." College and Research Libraries 22:327-340+ (July 1961).

Clarke, Edith. "Departmental libraries." Library Journal 16:264-268 (September 1891).

Dixson, Zella Allen. "The departmental libraries of the University of Chicago." Library Journal 20:375-377 (November 1895).

Ibbotson, Louis T. "Departmental libraries." Library Journal 50:853-858 (15 October 1925).

Legg, Jean. "The death of the departmental library." Library Resources & Technical Services 9:351-355 (Summer 1965).

McAnally, Arthur M. "Departments in university libraries." Library Trends 7:448-464 (January 1959).

Maizell, Robert E. "The subject-departmentalized public library." College and Research Libraries 12:255-260 (July 1951).

Newhall, Suzanne K. "Departmental libraries and the problem of autonomy." ALA Bulletin 60:721-722 (July-August 1966).

Thompson, Lawrence. "The historical background of departmental and collegiate libraries." Library Quarterly 12:49-74 (January 1942).

Venn, Mary C. "Departmental libraries." Libraries 34: 193-196 (May 1929).

Wildes, Karl L. "What the college or institution expects of its departmental libraries." Special Libraries 27: 53-55 (February 1936).

BLACK MATERIALS:
TIME FOR A NATIONAL PLAN

by William D. Cunningham

> If a race has no history, if it has no worth-while tradition, it stands in danger of being exterminated
> --Carter Woodson, "Negro History Week," 1926.

Carter Woodson inaugurated Negro History Week because "the Negro knew practically nothing of his history and his 'friends' were not permitting him to learn it."[1] He and others toiled the vineyards to unearth and bring to light the supposedly nonexistent records of the Black Experience. The long years of lonely labor appear to be approaching some degree of fulfillment in the black awareness of the 70's. Books In Print overfloweth with the trade publishers' wares of black materials, offered with pangs of guilt mixed with dollar incentives. The reprint houses continue to reach back in time to pull out more of what, a few years ago, wasn't there. Foreign bookmen offer German, Italian, French and Dutch versions of the black experience; a testament to the blackman's universal presence and his traveling ability. Schomburg and the Moorland Collections emerge as national treasures of Afro-Americana. Indeed, it has been proved that blacks, regardless of geography, have a rich and storied history and tradition. The emerging written record is our link to the past and our direction for the future. However, before the librarian begins patting himself on the back for the pivotal role of overcoming the lost, strayed or stolen syndrome (as it relates to black materials), there is a need to pause and do a bit of serious reflection.

Despite the fact that we are obviously riding a tidal wave of interest in and need for black materials, the good ship Afro-Americana could go the way of the Titanic without major and continuous effort on the part of librarians--especially black academic librarians.

> ... so far as the American world of science and letters was concerned, we never 'belonged'; we remained unrecognized in learned societies and academic groups ... after all, what had Negroes to do with America or science?
> --W. E. B. DuBois, Autobiography, 1968.

For some time, it has been recognized that there was a need for a union catalogue of black materials. Some efforts in this direction were initiated during the Depression via WPA. In Chicago, at the Good Shepherd Community Center, A Union Catalog of Printed Materials on the Negro was organized to include titles on all phases of Negro life and achievements in the Chicago Public Library, the John Crerar Library, the Newberry Library, and the University of Chicago Library. About 40,000 main entry cards were gathered and about 100,000 additional cards were filed in the title and subject files.[2] In 1938, Howard University initiated a Union Catalogue of Titles By and About Negroes. The catalog contained titles on the Afro-American, as well as on the African, West Indian, and Afro-Brazilian. These and similar projects were discontinued with the end of WPA assistance. In the absence of a union catalog, we have utilized book catalogs of major collections such as those for the Schomburg and Moorland-Spingarn. We have also substituted available bibliographies. These latter items are exemplified in the extensive ones of Dorothy Porter; the special-materials type (children's material) by Augusta Baker; or the handy brochure type ably done by Edythe Cawthorne. None of these substitute formats, however, perform the basics of a union catalog; i.e. record print and non-print items published anywhere in any language, or provide geographical locations. Even the Library of Congress' National Union Catalog is not a satisfactory alternative to a union catalog of black materials.

Related to the absence of a union catalog is the lack of an adequate retrieval tool. Standard indexes and abstracts do not include the nitty-gritty of black information sources. It is doubtful that any of the established indexing services would touch Muhammad Speaks or the Kansas City Call. Yet, in their respective fashion, these publications are core types of black information sources. Like the early union catalog projects, there have been sporadic attempts at developing a retrieval device for black information and materials. While the attempts are all praiseworthy, the results have not produced a "Chem. Abstracts" of black materials. Many such indexes were no more than a synthesis of Wilson indexes; the citations were culled from a data base of publications already covered by Reader's Guide and other Wilson tools. Those few indexes that have used a data base of black publications have limited effectiveness, due to the absence of locator information.

Location information is an essential feature for any retrieval device of non-general, obscure publications. The reason for this added feature is the lack of availability (to the user) of the materials indexed. The question of availability brings to the surface an additional problem facing black materials. This is the matter of access to library holdings. Planning and development of a union catalog, plus the indexing and abstracting devices, need to include a means of getting user and material together beyond identification and location. Granted the presence of interlibrary loan as the primary avenue of accomplishing this; however, in this day of teletype, telex, telefacsimile, etc., interlibrary loan in its traditional reliance on mails does not appear to be apropos. Aside from the cooperative program between the Alabama Colleges (Tuskegee, Alabama A&M, Alabama State, etc.) there has been no real networking between sources of black materials. It seems somewhat incongruous, considering the thrust of network development beyond the general interfacing of public-school-academic library resources into specialized areas such as medicine, that there has been no move in this direction among black libraries. Yet this, undoubtedly, is the level and kind of access that must be developed for black materials.

> I am invisible, understand, simply because people refuse to see me. Like the bodiless heads you sometimes see in Circus sideshows, it is as though I have been surrounded by mirrors of hard, distorting glass.
> --Ralph Ellison, Invisible Man, 1952.

Black academic libraries, by tradition, have a special interrelationship with the black community. In many cases, this tradition stems from the fact that the academic library was the only information source available to the black community. The libraries of Tuskegee and Texas Southern, among others, practiced community involvement long before the concept became an acceptable part of library theory and practice. Fisk's BLACAP (Black Libraries-Community Action Project) is based on the presence and continuance of this tradition. Binnie Tate, in BLACAP planning, hammers home the fact that this relationship means an active commitment (on the part of black libraries) in collection and dissemination of black materials. Mrs. Tate sees the realization of this activism in terms of libraries assuming the leadership role in production as well as in utilization of materials. Production, in this sense, means unilateral and/or joint efforts, by libraries and black publishers, in the development and issuance of materials. The scheme, in implementation, would assure that a percentage of new materials would be more closely related to the black community, the primary consumer. Mrs. Tate's premise, coupled with such projects as Annette Phinazee's pioneer effort in search, identification and analysis of regional black materials, adds new dimensions to the total concept of acquisitions of black materials. It is a concept that adds a regional and national level to our present localized collection and development programs; and also requires some division of labor ("Farmington Plan") among black academic libraries. Acquisitions, within this new framework, includes the continuous ferreting out of original source material, such as diaries, letters, organizational records, scrapbooks, that are still in their overlooked yet to-be-discovered state. It is a concept that includes the establishment of direct lines to non-US sources of black materials (Africa, South America, Carribean areas); and bypassing the programs of white institutions which acquire African and related materials without a commitment to make such acquisitions available to the black community.

A final problem area is the matter of personnel. Too many public and school librarians have been forced to become instant "Black Experts" without benefit of orientation or training that would give credence to the lie. Too often, "expertise" is derived from indiscriminate use of whatever is readily available in the form of guides, lists, articles. At the other end of the scale, there is no regular, formal educational program that will produce the specialists needed to develop standards, bibliographic tools, technical applications, etc., for black materials. Recognition of this lack in professional library and information science education has forced a program of internal education on the part of individual libraries. Unfortunately, such programs are limited to the staff of the particular library. The enormity of the training gap has not forced any interchange between these kinds of programs.

Because of the present and projected needs of students, scholars, researchers and, above all, the black community for black materials; and because of the non-directed development (either in kinds and types of materials, or in assemblage of such resources) to respond more effectively to these needs, a concerted program, national in scope, for the organization, collection and dissemination of black materials is long overdue.

The basic elements of such a program should include:

1. Development of a central referral system for access to resources of major subject collections.

2. Development of a central repository, through copy of one-of-a-kind items, acquisition of special and fugitive materials, and development of an identification retrieval system of such material in the holdings of other libraries.

3. Development of an educational program for library and information science specialists, to improve the organization, selection, and servicing of materials.

4. Development of research and evaluation, and stimulating experimentation in materials development, packaging, handling, etc.

The operable components of these basic elements could be organized as follows:

Information Storage and Service

Accomplishment of the information, access, and repository purposes necessitates an information storage and service system. The basic components of such a system would consist of:

1. Data base;
2. Information gathering and storage mechanism;
3. Collection development;
4. Service mechanism;
5. Exchange (Network) mechanism.

Data Base: The catalogue of a major black resource library (i.e., Fisk, Howard, Atlanta, Schomburg) would be the core of the data base. To this would be added machine-readable records of the non-duplicated holdings as identified in the printed catalogs of the other major black resource libraries.

Information gathering and storage: A computerized catalog of holdings will be developed from the data base and:

    1. record of on-going acquisition program of the data core library.
    2. record of special acquisitions of the data core library.
    3. record, through a depository system, of unique acquisitions of other major black resource libraries.
    4. record, through a depository system, of acquisitions from selected resource development projects that emphasize identification of local and regional materials (such as the North Carolina Central Project, or Southern University's Oral History Project).

Preparation of data:

    I. Analysis of source materials; for documents acquired, the following:
        a. Bibliographic description and subject analysis of separately-published items;
        b. Subject analysis of items within certain classes of documents, i.e., periodical articles.

    II. Coding:
        a. Fugitive items--involves transcribing results of bibliographic/subject analysis to coding sheets;
        b. Bibliographic references--involves transcribing relevant data from bibliographic references.

    III. Editing:
        a. coding sheets;
        b. punched cards.

Control of subject heading terminology:
    I. Development and maintenance of subject heading authority;
    II. Examination of bibliographic references received from outside the system to reconcile differences in assignment of headings.

Data conversion of transcription:
Data on coding sheets will be punched on 80-column punched cards and later on magnetic tape via the MTST.

Computer processing:
Storage of bibliographic records;
Maintenance of data base;
Searching of data base;
Printout of search results, statistics, etc.

Forms of output:
I. indexes;
II. lists of records (i.e., accessions);
III. bibliographies.

Collection Development: This component is a necessary assurance of continued acquisition of "difficult" material. This material has been previously characterized as that which falls and/or is not traceable through standard tools outside of trade publications. At the present time, it probably represents the bulk, and most significant, of black materials. This material specifically consists of:

1. Black periodicals and newspapers--current and retrospective; local, regional and national.
2. Monographs, and occasional papers (including broadsides, pamphlets, bulletins, etc.), current and retrospective, of black organizations, local and national.
3. Manuscripts (including diaries, scrapbooks, etc.).

Service Mechanism: The service part of this program element would be developed to provide an on-call information retrieval response, as well as a directed, scheduled information retrieval response. The former situation refers to response to such user inquiries as: (1) physical location of items recorded in the storage system; (2) bibliographical information; (3) requests, loan and/or copy, for material; (4) literature and subject searches; and (5) special indexing. The scheduled information response refers to informational tools generated. Such tools might include a monthly index to black serial publications, monthly acquisition list, abstracts.

Exchange (Network) Mechanism: This segment of the operation is an extension of a function briefly mentioned under Collection Development. Part of the acquisitions program involves off-site photoduplication (for hard copy) of materials located in other collections. It is a prime necessity that the core library's collection eventually include an actual copy of at least 90% of all that is reflected in the data base. It is an equal necessity that such duplicates, from copies, are available to other libraries for their collection development and informational needs. The network is designed to facilitate such information transfer.

Initially, the operational part of the network would consist of a media processing unit into which copies of off-site material are fed, and from which processed material is added to the core collection and/or supplied to users or other libraries on request. A field staff and a communications system should be added as a second phase of the operation. The field staff would serve the collection development function as well as direct and refine the objectives and exchange process. The communication system, either teletype or telex, would be the principal medium of tying together the efforts between staff, processing unit, source locations and requesting locations into a kind of Black Information Network. Moreover, the network operation should be expanded to allow direct access to the core by the individual user. This is possible through the establishment and development of access points on a geographical basis, among black academic libraries.

Educational Program

This component is predicated on the obvious fact that collecting, organizing and dissemination of materials requires trained personnel. The increase in demand and interest in black materials has not produced a related effort in upgrading skills in dealing with these materials. Education and training in this area has largely been substained through infrequent institutes and workshops sponsored by such agencies as the National Endowment for the Humanities and, more recently, the U.S. Office of Education (under Title IIB of the Higher Education Act). The educational experiences and models produced from these institutes or workshops have not filtered into the curriculum of the accredited schools of library and information science. The objective of this part of the project is to alleviate this lack of a regular, on-going program of continuing education and training related to black resources.

The Fisk Institute on Black Studies Librarianship offers an ideal building block on which to develop educational and training priorities. The contents and structure of such a program should be geared to deal with the problems of identification, analysis, bibliographic control, retrieval, and machine applications. The contents and structure of the program should be flexible so as to allow presentation via the workshop format as well as the possibility of packaging. By the latter we mean the development of self-help or self-instructional materials such as guides, handbooks, programmed instructions or training kits.

In addition, provision for on-the-job training must be made as an essential complement to other training approaches. The OJT (on-the-job-training) may be conceived as a feature within a workshop/seminar format. It could also be developed as a separate training experience. In any event, the content should provide exposure to the technical aspects related to subject materials, through a sequential work experience in areas of the resource libraries.

Research and Evaluation

The remaining component relates to the need for standards, evaluation of materials, a source for "state-of-the-art" information, and a stimulus for continued production of materials. The major functions of this part of operation would be concerned with:

1. Development, through test and survey method, and publishing of standards of bibliographic control of materials. Such standards should relate not only to forms of entry, but also include such problem areas as preservation of materials, and forms of media.
2. Development and publication of guides to aid in selection and evaluation of materials.
3. Monitoring inception and progress of research, studies, demonstrations, etc., dealing with all aspects of Afro-American materials. Acquiring and analyzing all final or complete reports of projects for dissemination.

The implementation of the foregoing program will provide a workable and viable national plan not only for the systematic acquisition of black materials and resources for information and research, but more importantly, it will also ensure access to these materials for informational purposes, study, and research.

PART IV

An Intellectual Freedom Question

WHAT PRICE FREEDOM, ANGELA DAVIS?

by Jeanne English

Gus Hall, General Secretary of the Communist Party of the U.S.A., calls the struggle to free Angela Davis, "the central and major ideological question facing America today."[1] I agree, perhaps for reasons other than Mr. Hall's. Striving not to choke on the deep, deep sand at hand for burying educators' heads, I have opted to present a more open approach to Angela Davis than the heavily antagonistic, closed views projected by the mass media and other spokesmen for the Establishment. This option I have had to defend at Evanston Township High School; thereby hangs my tale of intellectual freedom. But first, let me develop the relationships of the issues raised by Angela Davis to intellectual freedom, to black people, to young people, and to the problems of Evanston Township High School.

One night during the week of October 13, 1971, which marked a year Angela Davis had been held in punitive detention without bond, a friend and I posed to ourselves this question: "Will black people, to whom Angela has avowedly (will the press ever speak of her without using that word?) dedicated her life, let her burn; the way they let W.E.B. DuBois burn; the way they led Paul Robeson burn?" My friend, with pessimism, concluded: "I'm afraid they will. They show little sign as a group of grappling with the issues, or, if they do, they are agonizingly quiet about it." We considered how those who do publicly express support, smitten in conscience at the ill-treatment she has received but fearful of the association with communism and revolution which might becloud their names, anxiously preface their statements with: "...Although I do not agree with Miss Davis' political views..." As if a mere difference of views were the issue at stake!

The night after the attack on Attica by state police forces, when 43 persons lay dead, I listened to Walter Cronkite consign the entire responsibility for the prison disaster on "revolutionaries," in particular, George Jackson

An Intellectual Freedom Question

and Angela Davis. He went on to say, in a strained voice, that "we" do well to put such individuals behind bars to shield society from their monstrously evil influence. His sweeping condemnation, representing that kind of "thinking" which conceivably precedes a lynching, reflected the hysteria rolling in from all over the country as many Americans sought to place the blame for Attica on some cause outside our own society. When Angela Davis' lawyers claim that it will be next to impossible to assure her a fair trial in the United States, may not their doubts have basis in reality? In a poll taken to support a motion of the defense for a change of venue, it was found that 72% (of the 46% of those questioned who expressed an opinion) thought she was guilty as accused.[2]

In considering the relation of the Angela Davis case to intellectual freedom, the question is not only that of freedom to read and to think, but of the freedom of what to read, and how possible it is to think freely while imprisoned in the web of what we have read. Is intellectual freedom even possible, in this case? I think not. Intellectual freedom cannot exist until somebody (why not those guardians of public information, librarians?) coaxes the tiny spark beneath those dead coals of Red baiting, race baiting, sexism et. al., into a brisk and biting flame of judicious inquiry. How serious are we in our search for Truth?

The media have released many "facts" about Angela Davis which are simply expressions of opinion, bias, and worse. "... A great many people, mostly blacks, believe Angela Davis should be freed even if she was involved in the San Rafael matter--that whatever was the crime, it is society that is to blame...."[3] This airy fiction from the Chicago Daily News series on her life, "The Riddle of Angela Davis," implies that black people do not recognize crime as crime, do not distinguish the issues in the Angela Davis case, and that there is no reason for them to be distrustful of "white" law.[4] The writer relies on their total ignorance of black history to permit most white readers to swallow the ultimate in race baiting.

"... Her other activities were not, however, of the nature to endear her to white parents of the middle class sending their children off to freshman year...."[5] From the same series, this statement blithely baits white middle class parents, schools, and teachers, all in one blow. In yet another installment, we observe the implication that emotional instability goes hand in hand with her dissidence: "... Although she did a job above reproach in her classes, Miss Davis' outside activities had become frenetic...."[6] My kids at school, however, think Angela Davis is really "together." They recognize the superb personal qualities of intellectual and moral integrity which she has consistently manifested while imprisoned.

From the Dallas Times Herald, here is the word on the $10,000 gift to the Angela Davis Defense Fund by the United Presbyterian Church in the United States: "... The 'no-fair-trial' bit is strictly a propaganda play. Is an accused conspiratrix, an avowed Communist ... just as deserving of aid as ... a struggling businessman? ... Who can blame so many Presbyterians for being so upset? In the name of racial justice, they have been had."[7] I suppose one good propaganda deserves another.

The very male National Review sounds the alarm: "... And she is a woman! She will electrify Femalelibs. And some men--apparently including all reporters--find her attractive! Sex! ... when she is extradited to California, and her trial commences in Reaganland, it will be time to batten down the hatches and ready the lifeboats on every American campus."[8]

Time leads another chorus: "... Disciple Davis once spoke approvingly of the Che-Lumumba Club's concept that 'revolution must be tied to dealing with specific problems now, not a lot of rhetoric about revolution, but real fundamental problems'.... Was the armed invasion of a California courtroom designed to force release of the Soledad Three, a way of 'dealing with specific problems now?'..."[9] Conviction without benefit of trial?

The New York Times slaps the labels on: "... Whatever the eventual outcome, the tragedy is that one who might have made a significant contribution to the nation's normal political debate and to its needed processes of peaceful change became so alienated that she finally went over to revolutionary words and perhaps worse."[10]

Compound these examples by thousands more and it can be easily seen, as one of my students says, that Angela Davis has been made into a "media myth" and duly convicted. I submit, therefore, that the prevailing view that she is guilty is based on public disapproval of her dissidence, her

An Intellectual Freedom Question 135

dissonance with our society, and that she is herself a victim of conspiracy. In America today, is not dissidence equated with criminality, even as communism was in the McCarthy era? Is it difficult to demonstrate that our highest law enforcement agencies, indeed our highest administrative officers, treat dissidents as if they are criminals, vilifying them through a generally cooperative media, locking them up on occasion without due process, slapping on them dubious charges of "conspiracy," categorized by the late Clarence Darrow as "this worn-out piece of tyranny?"[11]

Is a Supreme Court appointee, who, in a statement of position to the people, touts our "democratic forms" while failing to mention their inbred racism,[12] prepared to discuss a fair trial for Angela Davis or any other black person? When Lewis Powell seems to use "persons accused of crime" interchangeably with "criminals," is it because these terms are synonymous in his mind? He insists that: "... Foreign powers, notably the Communist ones, conduct massive espionage and subversive operations against America...."[13] Sorry if we can't get too worked up over that, Mr. Powell, when we see America conducting "massive subversive operations" against herself--crime-infested slums, degrading welfare programs, unequal access to housing, paternalistic educational programs, dual application of criminal justice, vicious abuse of black personnel in the armed forces, and lack of national moral leadership. It is a system programmed to self-destruct, with or without the help of revolutionaries like George Jackson and Angela Davis.

HR 11120, introduced in Congress by Representative Richard Ichord, and designed to create an inquisitorial agency called the Federal Employee Security and Appeals Commission (FESAC), subjects those who do not present the silhouette of a WASP to the possibility of rejection for government employment and/or criminal prosecution. President Nixon, by means of executive orders and revival of the SACB, Subversive Activities Control Board, apparently seeks to perpetuate America as one vast, suburban, sleep-in community. The far-reaching effects of these moves will affect so many Americans that it is incredible that the outcry against them has not drowned out even the advent of Red China into the United Nations. Why have not the Establishment media aroused us to these dangers, sensational as they truly are?

If a person today does not range ever more widely

for information, testing avenues he might not have felt a
need to seek even two years ago, now that escape from the
omnipresent media is impossible, his mind will be made up
for him by powerful agencies and persons who <u>are</u> ranging
widely for information, who have at their disposal all manner of electronic tools and techniques, and hirelings, and
who are demonstrating not only serious moral and intellectual
befuddlement as to the proper course for this democracy and
the just implementation of the law, but above all an inclination to settle for less than the Truth if it supports the bases
of power.   Consider this ominous romance with might and
expediency and know that we the people have been carefully
prepared to label Angela Davis, as well as any other dissident, "criminal."   Pavlov strikes again!

    In order, therefore, for the people to exercise intellectual freedom, realize the political and physical freedom
which accrue from it, and as a consequence, emerge both
as individuals and as a nation from the present impasse of
outmoded forms and rituals, it is necessary to increase infinitely the range of sources from which we seek information.   We need to delve into political and social viewpoints
of a far wider range than is provided by the customary conservative, liberal, moderately left and right vehicles of information resting on our library racks.

    Angela Davis is on trial for her life.   A prime necessity, from her point of view, at least, is that the American public, without delay, apply the exercise of their intellectual freedom to her case.   It is true that the Communist Party mounts a massive worldwide defense movement
in her behalf, greater than that for the Scottsboro boys, or
perhaps that for Sacco and Vanzetti.   In both these cases
there is evidence that the courts acted from political motives.
In the Scottsboro case, the decision of the court in the end
was completely reversed.   Many persons avoid real thought
about the Davis case because Angela Davis is a Communist,
a "revolutionary," and a "radical."   But the questions which
arise out of the situation are thought questions, for anyone
who thinks to tackle them: Do the Marxists have a monopoly
on principle?   Do the Communists have the most advanced
position on racism in the U.S. today?   Are laws made to
meet the needs of government more important than those
made to meet the needs of people?   Do America's decisions
to protect her institutions preclude decisions to protect her
people?   Can it be proved impossible for black people to
receive equal justice in our courts?   Why are there so

An Intellectual Freedom Question   137

many black people in jail; is it simply because they are
criminally inclined? Is that revolutionary spirit, characteristic of early Americans, entirely out of place in a complacent, contemporary America, surfeited with the good
life? Is a genuine moral position on any issue an impossible
stance for America today? Do the needs of today demand
the jettisoning of past theories and ways? These, to my
mind, are some of the key issues which make the struggle
to free Angela Davis, who leads a broad front against institutionalized racism, especially as it is exemplified in our
criminal justice system, "the central and major ideological
question facing America today."[14]

To imagine that schools and educators can somehow
sidestep the issues which confront the larger society is to
bury one's head in the educational sandbox. To imagine that
Evanston Township High School can somehow avoid contact
with the larger society is an illusion. The question of
Angela Davis and the defense of the black community has
visited itself upon our school in a natural enough way, as I
will relate.

When I arrived almost four years ago at E. T. H. S.,
any casual observer could have told that the school was in
trouble. One had only to walk through the halls to see
many black youngsters out of their classrooms. Not evident
to the casual observer was that the situation was very much
on teachers' minds. In their council meetings, the talk was
all about "these" students, and about "discipline" as the
answer to all problems. Earnest study was devoted to de-
vising adequate "disciplinary" procedures, culminating in
suspension and expulsion, which would result, happily, in
alleviating the "problem." Not apparent to enough teachers
was the reality that no matter how fervently one goes about
it, black children cannot be "disciplined" into becoming
white; hostility and frustration resulting from economic disadvantage and racist rejection cannot be "disciplined" into
nonexistence. Not apparent to enough teachers was the
reality that the important words are not "discipline," "suspension," and "expulsion," but "empathy," "insight," "social
change." As signs of change strive to emerge, and black
faculty struggle to be heard through centuries of inattention,
"discipline" as a solution to black student disaffection per-
versely continues to waft through the atmosphere--an old,
cold, familiar refrain.

At present E. T. H. S. has a population of about 5,200

students, of whom approximately 17% are black. The campus encompasses four administratively separate but physically united schools. The high school itself comprises the school district, which includes Evanston and part of nearby Skokie. E. T. H. S. has long been known for the high percentage of its graduates who attend college, its rich and diverse course offerings, the excellence of its faculty and its innovative approaches to education. However, in spite of its reputation as a great American high school, E. T. H. S. has yet to make history for black youngsters. It is doubtful that two black students have won National Merit Scholarships in the past ten years. The community takes it for granted that scores of black students will not graduate!

Evanston has a population of 79,800, and a median income of $14,000, 61% above the national norm. Ninety percent of the population is native born, of Scandinavian, German, English, and Polish extraction. The black community, small, vulnerable, fragmented, and proud, makes up 16% of the total. There is also a sizeable Jewish population, which the brochure distributed by the Chamber of Commerce fails to mention.[15] With 66 churches and four synagogues, Evanston has held tenaciously to the past, until recently has been "dry," and is still loathe to welcome social change. When my father was a medical student at Northwestern University in 1916, natives told him that black people "didn't even go up to Evanston," except as servants to rich, white, North Shore residents. Although the "North Shore" has steadily inched farther north and new people now live by the lake, the hostility manifest in school conflicts was first planted in the class-conscious soil of old Evanston, which now has its share of both white and black poor, and in spite of itself, a good share of "urban problems."

The black community, like many another black community in the nation, began to awaken to certain racial realities in 1968, with the assassination of Martin Luther King. A protest was organized by a small group of black students with the help of some interested adults, and demands were made of the administration to hire more black faculty (there had been a few black teachers) and to implement courses in black history and literature. As a result, the Board of Education set a quota for the accelerated hiring of black faculty, and initiated courses in Black Studies. Efforts were made as well as to integrate black experience into all social studies and literature courses. At the present time, cutting across all departments and most levels of

An Intellectual Freedom Question

operation, there are 35 black members of the faculty, four of them administrators.

The Human Relations Department was created and a black counselor appointed to head it. From this department, admittedly a mechanism for defusing racial animosities, many programs have come to improve the status of black students and faculty at E. T. H. S. The Human Relations Department was, in fact, the administrative apparatus by means of which the question of Angela Davis has remained an open question in the school, although attempts were made to suppress it.

My advent to E. T. H. S. as an "instant" black faculty member took place in 1968 at the time of the escalation of racial crises. The absence of communication between the school and the black community, the disorientation of black students at E. T. H. S., were, in my estimation, of grave proportions. Most distressing to the few black teachers (eleven in a faculty of about 400) was the observable personality disorganization of many black students, the high percentage of their academic failure, the use of a tracking system which automatically eliminated black students from many advanced courses and even average courses, the almost exclusive dependence on "discipline" by faculty in dealing with the problems of black students, and the shifting of the responsibility of the racial problems to the few black teachers who had recently been added to the staff. It was as if everyone said to us, "Now, you're here, black folks. It's for you to put Humpty Dumpty together again." I will cite instances which provide a representative view.

Early in the school year in 1968, as a Human Relations activity, the 700 or more black students were divided into groups, and one black teacher assigned to meet with each group. We were given released time to try to communicate with them about their grievances, a list of which had been presented to the administration the previous year; obviously a "clean up" job for us. At this meeting, communication was hardly achieved, but I made some observations: "A peculiar inversion seems to have occurred with many black students here (not all, by any means), whereby what has been traditionally promulgated by white racism, i.e., that black people are inferior, incompetent, criminal and inadequate, is being absorbed by many black students as their 'style of life.' By some tragic irony, they have been successfully brainwashed into accepting an inferior role as essential life philosophy." The bitter, black children of Evanston. These notes of mine become relevant now as I consider comments by Angela Davis: "... Disengaged from normal social life, its revelations and influences, they must finally be robbed of their humanity...."[16] Is the depth of psychological isolation of these black youngsters any less than that of prisoners Angela Davis speaks of behind stone and iron walls? Perhaps their condition might be termed worse, since they suffer the illusion of physical freedom.

Not only I, but other black teachers became aware that some black students are fighting to the death to stay on the bottom rung of the achievement ladder, their hostility turned inward against themselves. We realized how deep the mark of slavery is upon some of us still, and therefore, still upon us all. Could these thwarted young black people-- victims of racist indoctrination, destined to defeat, too late aware--be the youthful counterparts of the "political prisoners," who have indeed met their intended fate?--"... anonymous ghetto inhabitants, who, if [President Richard M.] Nixon had his way, would all be buried away in dungeons ...."[17] As our attention now focuses on a penal system defined by the disproportionate number of black people comprising its population, I am led to conclude that many black youngsters are being "educated" into the prisons of this country, or to put it another way, education seems not to be saving them from this unhappy destiny.

This conclusion, in turn, leads to others concerning the effects of "integrated" education. The truth is that integration of black children into a white educational system, when there exists no compensatory support in community institutions, brings about the psychological destruction of many, many black children. Only when revolutionary changes in the structure of the program are deliberately made to promote the psychological well-being, as differentiated from the academic progress of black children, are their developmental needs met. I am not aware that the necessary change have taken place generally in the schools of the United States. The entire educational system seems designed to support the points of view and the egos of the white community, and by white consensus suppress everything which does not conform to these norms. The problems of personality disintegration of black children in mixed schools, arising from the devaluation of blackness and consequent behavior and penalties, resulting in academic defeat for scores of black students, must be laid at the feet of programs engineered to defeat all authentic black aspirations. That so many black people survive and succeed is due not to their achieving true fulfillment but to their complicity with this white system. Those who in their pain rebel, are "disciplined" out of the system --therefore, Angela Davis. From my observations, many, if not all black people sustain a deep and abiding anger as a result of this "education." They manage to bury it deep in their consciousness, where it throttles their energy and destroys their spirit. "Black rage"[18] is not an idle phrase; it is the natural product of racism and the psychological burden of all black people. The high rate of crime among black people may very well indicate a high degree of rebelliousness and resistance.

Another racial crisis occurred at E.T.H.S. as Martin Luther King's birthday came around in 1969. In previous years there had been walkouts and rebellious disturbances of various descriptions, rising and falling like the seasons. This time, students came to us, wanting to make a demonstration of "black solidarity." They asked us to join them in a walkout, in effect to dare to defy the white establishment. I had just arrived; this demand placed me in a quandary, which was, however, soon resolved. That night, at home, I received a call from my principal, giving me "permission" to stay away from school on the crucial day, and suggesting that I might want to join the black students in their commemoration of King. I made an instant decision; I would participate in no segregated activity which I knew to be the result of the historical institutionalized isolation of black students. And so I came to school the next day, to work, and to wait for the time when the entire school community would decide to plan a commemoration worthy of Martin Luther King. This year, for the second time, the school as a whole commemorates Martin Luther King on his birthday. Martin Luther King lives!

As we black teachers consulted together about the development surrounding that day in 1969, we reached a consensus that the free day had been offered all of us in the hope that we would "supervise" the black students and keep things "under control." We were, as usual, the "clean-up crew." We did not think the story at E.T.H.S. unusual; it must have been and still is being repeated a hundred thousand times in schools all over where there are black youngsters in a mixed racial setting. My first two years at E.T.H.S. were extremely significant in apprising me of the full extent of America's racial sickness. It is often said that E. T. H. S. is America in microcosm; the meaning of that paradigm is manifold, and the racial aspect is clear. When will this institution, and others like it, ask why the periodical expectoration of racist bile in its hallowed halls is as predictable as the seasons?

During the transition to a more democratic society, we the "black faculty," even as the "black nation" in the United States, carry the load of history. During my first year at Evanston, a strangely antagonistic black community, angry with the white establishment for years of rebuffs, angry with the black teachers whom they perceived as collaborators with the white establishment, castigated all indiscriminately. On one occasion, a local political organization demanded that we black teachers attend a public meeting and offer solutions about the "problems at the school." As individuals, with individual opinions, we apparently did not exist. To compound this obliteration of our individuality, this dehumanization, administrators took up the habit of writing to us, addressing their messages to the "Black Teachers." This practice was also adopted by the teachers' organization. In true racist style, it was assumed by community, administration, and faculty that, because we were black, we should be lumped together, with the additional responsibility (not appearing as a requirement on the personnel forms) of solving the "problem." Our bitter question: "Is it for this we were hired?"

Rather than be completely cornered, like rats in a trap, or black panthers up a tree, we actually did begin to form politically, and to hold regular meetings, just to compose ourselves sufficiently to answer the "charges," assumptions, allegations, and fantasies which forced us to take positions on racial issues with which the school, like the nation, was and is obsessed. Needless to say, our meetings were regarded with suspicion, and occasioned many rumors. We came to the conclusion that if such incidents were happening to us teachers, how much more must be happening to black youngsters, whose fragile defenses and entrapment in the oppression syndrome could hardly hold up under the constant buffeting of subtle antagonisms. We began to understand some of their poignant reasons for taking to the halls.

"Think black" was the word as Martin Luther King's birthday rolled around again in 1970. The national scene was blistered with a spate of cases against the Black Panthers, and with protesting dissenters of many varieties. On

An Intellectual Freedom Question 143

January 5, the week before our commemoration of King, Angela Davis was arraigned at San Rafael, after a vengeful FBI chase which pushed all other headlines from the front pages. Although all black people were not sympathizers of the Black Panthers or of Angela Davis, few missed their symbolism or lost the message of the intensification of the repression of black people. Fred Hampton, shot dead in his bed in Chicago in 1969, was remembered in the black community with mass action to indict the perpetrators of that travesty. Various shootings of black children by police in the ghettoes too frequently and too routinely noted by the media. Evanston, sequestered away on the North Shore, no doubt considered itself "safe" from the effects of these events. But with us black faculty, E.T.H.S. had also unawares imported a consciousness of the all-pervasiveness of the racist society and the deep need to combat it.

As black students came to us teachers again, we realized it was a time to answer back, a time to resist or go under. The sense of oppression reached all of us to the point of physical suffocation. Black students, thinking that only by going "underground" could they express their aspirations, had to be convinced that the struggle for freedom is not a subversive activity, and that the fear of exercising their freedom is as much to be overcome as the oppressive society. The tragedy would have been to remain quiescent. We therefore became a visible legal organization and students named it "Black." We found the superintendent willing to help us carry out our plans.

Black Liberation Week, 1970, culminating with the birthday commemoration of Martin Luther King, will be remembered for the poetry, the songs, the speeches, the dance, the insistent beat of African drums. It will be remembered by us, who, for too short a time, became a visible black nation in the midst of racially tense Evanston Township High School. The student committee had asked me to talk about Angela Davis, for contrary to the wails of woe emitted by the media, her message to young people was one of inspiration, a call to all freedom fighters, a voice crying in their wilderness.

As the week began, we threw up five displays at strategic points throughout the sprawling complex of buildings, carrying out the theme of Black Liberation: "The Prince," on Martin Luther King; "Take up the Search," on Malcolm X, Frantz Fanon and their vision of freedom;

"Africa," on the beauties of that continent; and "What Price Freedom, Angela Davis?"--an exhibit of clippings, pictures and related books. No one, old or young, wandering the halls, could have missed the message.

Intellectual freedom and the absence of censorship are truisms at E. T. H. S.; Evanston is one community where the parents do not try to make judgments which teachers and librarians are expected to make, although it is a community with a sizable number of vocal watchdogs of school policies. It came, therefore, as an unexpected development when, one morning, my principal asked me, summarily, to remove my Angela Davis exhibit. He stated that "some people" looked upon the Davis case as merely a criminal case, very much like the Manson case, which was also in the news at that time. I did not argue. I left his office and straightaway sought out the Human Relations chairman of my particular school. Before the day was over, a letter voicing my objections to his interference with my intellectual freedom was in the principal's hands, and also those of my school's Human Relations chairman and of the Coordinator of the total school Human Relations operation. At last, a use for the bureaucracy!

As the word of the incident spread, like fire, black teachers became incensed at the traditional white negation of the black point of view. Several options presented themselves to me at this juncture, including a perverse notion to air the situation in the press. Suppressing this impulse, I placed the matter in the skillful hands of the Coordinator of Human Relations. She took the issue to the superintendent, who in turn called me in. Aware of the two societies in which black people must live, I took with me to the superintendent's office "counsel," the black teacher who was chairman of human relations in my school. Our meeting, which waxed warm over the fears of the administration of "white backlash," Angela Davis, and "white liberation," resulted in a letter of apology from the superintendent for the arbitrary directive. He cautioned me, however, to present always a "balanced" point of view. I thought to myself that an obscure display in an isolated high school could hardly "balance" the super job of character assassination the media was busily carrying out on Angela Davis. I continued the discussion with the superintendent by writing what eventually emerged as <u>Thirty-Three Points Which Show Why the Angela Davis Trial is a Political Trial.</u>[19]

An Intellectual Freedom Question   145

It is clear that, had not a protest been raised, both principal and superintendent were willing to arbitrarily cancel my intellectual freedom, although they would have expected to defend a student's right to it.[20] The exhibit on Angela Davis was only one of several, all featuring rebels and revolutionaries from Martin Luther King to Bobby Seale, and revolutionary literature from Eldridge Cleaver's Soul on Ice to De Anne Sobul's discussion of the Bill of Rights. None of these other exhibits was questioned; only that on Angela Davis. What, then, is the special power of Angela Davis to evoke such awakening? Will Before and After Angela Davis mark the turning point in the history of institutionalized racism?

The suburbs have taught me what the inner city never could. Black people are not free and are not likely to be free for an indefinite period of time. Our captivity is marked by economic, social, educational, judicial, and civil repression. We are bent, in spite of ourselves, to the uses of the captor, helpless in our impotence. Our massive personal frustration comes from continuing to believe that we are free, and acting from this basis of unreality, which the media, among other influences, brainwash us into absorbing. Being an oppressed people, we must learn to understand the syndrome of our oppression.[21] We must take the only moral stand possible. That moral stand is a commitment, not to accommodation, not to pacification, not to integration, not to separatism, not to nationalism, not to survival, and above all, not to identification with the oppressor--our commitment must be to Liberation. We must develop collectively an ethic of Liberation, a day-to-day defense of the black community, and a long range total offensive against oppression. Academic excellence, pursued heretofore so obsessively by educators, is discovered to be not the goal but merely the means. Recent heavy emphasis on career orientation is years too late. Liberation is the only course which will provide spiritual resources powerful enough to sustain our humanity in the midst of dehumanization, motivate our children to struggle, and eventually, by many avenues, lead to a transformation of society. The hard lesson, from Jesus to Malcolm X and Martin Luther King, is that true liberation can be achieved only with a large measure of suffering and sacrifice. Perhaps those who are so antagonistic to Angela Davis do not recognize in what she says the same hard truth.

As I read (not in the commercial press) of the misfortunes of supporters of Angela Davis--some being humiliated, fired, injured, arrested, and even indicted--I think I came off better. However, I am somewhat more aware of the kind of country I live in: I perceive ever more clearly the dual nature of our society. We, no less than Angela Davis, are security prisoners. Begone the days when the sacrifice of black children is the price of living with the white establishment!

DECLARATION OF COMMITMENT TO BLACK LIBERATION[22]

We find it necessary as black people to recognize and affirm our unity in the value black, realizing that this value is neither appreciated nor adequately implemented in the mores of our society and with ever-increasing frequency is violated. We declare that this recognition and affirmation by ourselves to ourselves, as well as before the whole of society is an essential beginning to our full development. This recognition causes us to commit ourselves actively and intensively to BLACK LIBERATION, pursuing these specific objectives:

1. We set ourselves to the task of identifying in all the institutions and practices of this country, and subsequently ridding ourselves of, every fantasy and abuse which ignores, represses, or causes neglect of the human, social, educational, and civil needs of black people.

2. We will methodically and relentlessly root out of our own personalities and those of our children, and of our brothers and sisters, all traces of the racist mentality which rejects what is black in us and thereby constitutes a rejection of self, making consistent fruitful action, if not altogether impossible, next to impossible.

3. We will, every moment and by every means possible, protect, nurture, love, develop, and temper as fine steel those special qualities in black people deriving from their African heritage, their black identity, their historical and social experiences in this their second country, which make them a Black nation within a nation.

4. We will vigorously take up anew our search to pierce

An Intellectual Freedom Question 147

the agonizing obscurity of our lost identity. Although forcibly severed from the lifeline of our African heritage and through violence induced to forget it, we will fit the pieces into a dynamic whole, in spite of the pain this may bring to us and to those who continue to resist an idea whose time has come.

5. Welded together in the unity of black, with all black people of Evanston, the State of Illinois, the United States, and all the countries of the World, we will stand and deliver the challenge of the black nation-- which is to understand freedom, to suffer and to struggle for Liberation, and to transform a racist society!

LONG LIVE THE CHALLENGE OF AN ANGELA DAVIS!

Will Evanston Township High School continue to be great by meeting the challenge?

Notes

1. "Gus Hall Discusses Issues as Candidate for President," Daily World, Vol. IV, No. 33, September 21, 1971, p. 2.

2. "Trial Date Set for Angela Davis," New York Times, Vol. CXXI, No. 41546, October 24, 1971, p. 38.

3. "Sheltered Child Became Marxist Rebel," Chicago Daily News, 95th Yr., No. 166, July 12, 1971.

4. Heywood Burns, "Can A Black Man Get a Fair Trial in This Country?" New York Times Magazine, July 2, 1970, p. 5+, September 27, 1970, p. 21+.

5. "Letter Starts Angela's Downfall," Chicago Tribune, 125th Yr., No. 198, July 17, 1971, p. 11.

6. "Student-Agent Exposes Angela," Chicago Daily News, 95th Yr., No. 162, July 16, 1971.

7. "They've Been Had," Dallas Times Herald, 95th Yr., No. 173, June 21, 1971, p. 20A.

8. "The Girl Who Has Everything," National Review, Vol.

XXII, No. 43, November 3, 1970, p. 1144.

9. "Personality," Time, Vol. 96, No. 9, August 31, 1970, p. 14.

10. "The Angela Davis Tragedy," New York Times, Vol. CXX, No. 41,172, October 16, 1970, p. 40.

11. Jon R. Waltz, "This Worn-Out Piece of Tyranny," Nation, Vol. 212, No. 19, May 10, 1971, p. 589-92.

12. See Report of the National Advisory Commission on Civil Disorders, Bantam, 1968.

13. Lewis Powell, "America is Not a Repressive Society," New York Times, Vol. CXXI, No. 41,556, November 3, 1971, p. 47.

14. See footnote, no. 2.

15. Evanston Around's About, Vol. 1, No. 2, November, 1971, Evanston Chamber of Commerce, Evanston, Illinois.

16. Angela Y. Davis, "Lessons: From Attica to Soledad," New York Times, Vol. CXXI, No. 41530, October 8, 1971, p. 41.

17. Angela Davis, "Rhetoric Vs. Reality," Ebony, Vol. XXVI, No. 9, July, 1971, p. 119.

18. William H. Grier and Price M. Cobbs, Black Rage, Bantam, 1968.

19. "Angela Davis Source Paper Available," Wilson Library Bulletin, Vol. 46, No. 3, November, 1971, p. 291.

20. "Policy on Student Expression," Pilot, E. T. H. S. 71-72. Thirty-Third Edition, Evanston Township High School, Evanston, Illinois, pp. 18-21.

21. See Paulo Freire, Pedagogy of the Oppressed, Herder and Herder, 1971.

22. Closing statement of my talk to students during Black Liberation Week, 1970, entitled, "What Price Freedom, Angela Davis?"

PART V

Critical Issues in Library Education

AGAINST ALL ODDS, WE HAVE BEEN BELIEVERS

by Mohammed M. Aman

After a series of summer riots, civil unrest and waves of hate culminated in the assassination of Dr. Martin Luther King, Jr., America was alerted in 1968 to the fact that it was moving towards two separate and unequal societies.[1] The report of the President's Advisory Commission on Civil Disorders warned that unless the nation took drastic and immediate measures to compact racism, the division and polarization of the races would delibitate and weaken American society. The alarm was sounded from a very high place, its message was comprehensible, and the mass media promulgated it throughout the country.

What was the effect of the alert on black and white America? On its people and institutions?

The alarm did not appear to trigger any undue apprehensions or fears within black America. In fact, a majority of black people viewed the report with a matter-of-fact detachment, and with the knowledge that the conclusions were a gross understatement of a condition that had been endured for more than three hundred years. For black Americans, life is not simply separate and unequal, it is unjust, dehumanizing and destructive.

Blacks in America have been denied justice, pride, privileges, dignity, education, employment, adequate health care, decent housing and full stomachs. Black Americans have had to endure hardships and hatred and have had to fight for their rights to be recognized as men and women. The words of the black poet Langston Hughes aptly describe the distressing condition of the black man:

> Life for me ain't been no crystal stair,
> It's had tacks in it,
> And splinters,
> And boards torn up,
> And places with no carpet on the floor--
> Bare.[2]

The report of the commission was not new, neither was the warning. The message had been told before in the poems and songs of black artists, in the actions and deeds of black martyrs, and in the handicapping conditions of the minds and bodies of little black children. The dramatic effects of racism had been aired in the mass media during the marching, rioting, looting and bombing of the mid-sixties. White America did not have to have a scholarly study to document the fact that racism was destroying the country. And yet, for many blacks, the study represented all that America was willing to do to change the character of the society. To some blacks, the report gave the issue of racism a cool detachment; to others it appeared as just another avoidance tactic of white America; to most it was a a clear indication that white America was fully aware of black sufferings and was content to see it continue.

How did white America respond to the report?

Had vast numbers of white Americans accepted the fact that the United States was and is not a white nation? Did white citizens abandon the evils and inherent dangers of racism empathy and understanding? The monitoring of day-to-day events in newspapers and television indicates that white America has responded to the crisis with little self-examination and commitment for change, that its prevailing characteristic remains self-interest.

White America still demonstrates that fear and hate can initiate ugly riots, bombings and other acts of violence to prevent black families from moving into its communities, its schools and social institutions.

The report, therefore, did receive negative criticism and inaction from some quarters, yet its analysis and conclusions received laudatory comments from the people who were invested with the power and responsibility for this nation.

Did the leadership of this country mobilize its strengths and resources to combat racism? What is the evidence?

The government has demonstrated a great reluctance to initiate programs that would move this country towards an equalitarian society. In many instances, it has used its power and influence to impede integration in the schools, the courts, the military and the voting booths. It has failed to provide leadership to the average American citizen who looks to the government for guidelines and directions.[3]

In the examples of their private lives and public actions American leaders have shown that they are not prepared to take seriously the warnings of the advisory commission. Instead of responsible leadership, America has been provided with examples of hypocrisy. Many political leaders choose to support the concept of racial integration as long as it is an abstraction for debate, or a symbol for political expediency. They also choose to reject the concept when it interferes with the location of their homes, or the education of their children.

Business and industrial leaders have continued their old segregated practices, or have changed their employment practices and policies from total racial exclusion to tokenism, which in turn has only heightened the frustration, tension and suspicion between black and white America. Financial leaders have also done little to share their power with the poor and the black; thus access to capital and other material resources continues to be severely limited.

Does racism still permeate the major institutions of our society? A ready answer can be found in social reports and indicators published by learned societies and the federal government.[4] Perhaps, for a better comprehension of the problem, introspection is needed. We should examine our roles and the institutions of which we are a part. Perhaps measuring awareness, questioning motives and actions will help us find solutions to the problem.

How responsive have libraries and the library profession been to the black and other minority groups?

As an American institution, libraries and the library profession cannot claim the distinction of being free from hypocrisy, or from racist policies and practices. Libraries and the library profession have consistently ignored the needs of black people.

The library profession responds to the black community with: insufficient and inadequate library service; attitudinal barriers which have hampered deliverance of services; and failure to incorporate sufficient numbers of minority groups within the profession.

Library services are insufficient in quantity and inadequate in quality. Few library facilities are readily available to blacks and other minority groups living in depressed areas, urban as well as rural. There are instances where large urban public library systems have failed to build new branch facilities to meet the needs of a rapidly growing population in minority neighborhoods. There is little black and minority group participation in community surveys and planning. There is the resulting evidence of oversight and the belief that blacks and other minority groups do not care about books and reading. Oversights and false assumptions have led to the establishment of more libraries in the suburbs and upper-middle class areas and fewer libraries in ghettos and predominantly black neighborhoods.

For most minority groups, the library, if one exists, is like other community institutions in their neighborhood: inadequate and irresponsible to its unique differences and needs. The library should be a vital force in a community, but particularly so in a minority community. The library should be the place where adults can go to start or continue their education; the student of limited means should find the resources of the library an extension of the classroom; and the library should serve as a cultural center where educated blacks and whites help their fellow young men and women improve their skills and overcome cultural and educational barriers. For the school drop-out, the library should serve as a center for the renewal of hope, and for the small child it should be the beginning of hope. Unfortunately, few minority group patrons can realize these dreams in their community libraries.

There has been a paucity of ethnic literature and reference tools available in these libraries. Book collections were developed without considering the community's reading habits, interests or abilities. Many minority group patrons found library catalogs and shelf arrangement confusing and difficult to comprehend, especially without orientation programs, individualized help, or courteous treatment for those who dare to inquire.

The black sociologist Andrew Billingsley wrote that racism is not limited to strategies of action and inaction, but is extended to attitudes, beliefs and values.[5] These attitudes based on "illusions" of value do much to effect racism in our society. The illusion of wisdom and excellence can do much to create professional biases, class distinctions and attitudinal barriers to services which will prevent black people from participating in the benefits of the nation's institutions. The library profession is not without its own notions of worthiness. The profession prefers the image of intellectual selectivity and exclusion. Some librarians even convey the impression that the keepers of the books are as wise as the most brilliant author in the library's collection. Along with the air of intellectual snobbery is the inference of stupidity, failure and rejection, which is most keenly imagined or felt by a group of people who have repeatedly experienced failure with other professionals and institutions.

The library profession, like other professions, has failed actively to recruit, train and employ blacks and other minority groups into the full range of the library profession. Library schools have failed to extend incentives and scholarships to minority groups that would enable them to enter the profession. There is only one library school outside the deep south with a federally funded program designed to attract blacks to "one aspect" of the library profession, i.e. (urban information specialist).[6] Compare this program to the number of library science programs, institutes, etc., developed to attract foreign students. Can library school administrators feel a sense of pride for international understanding or a deep sense of shame for neglecting the darker fellow countryman?

Librarianship suffers from a lack of black talent, not only in numbers but in positions of responsibility. Library schools have resisted the appointment of black professors and black deans. Major public libraries have resisted the appointment of black directors. To date, there are only two major municipal public library systems that have black administrators.

If black visibility in the library profession and in its program can be viewed as an indicator of the institutions' intent to reform, and reflect the existence, needs and contributions of blacks, then the library profession must be charged with the insidious crime of racism. It is unfortunate that the spirit of liberalism and enlightenment which dominated the free library movement in this country was allowed to die as the profession became preoccupied with one ethnic race and one value system. This has resulted in the development of library programs and services which are mainly oriented to the white middle-class people who are able to read.

Buried deeply in the safety of its traditions, the library profession seems to reflect a little of the spirit of liberalism and enlightenment only in its preoccupation with the defense of intellectual freedom.

Very recently, the concern for social responsibility found its way into the structure of the profession. Concerns over budgetary matters, lack of organizational guidelines, planning and leadership have diminished the profession's near support for scholarships, research and programs in the black community.

As we deepen our introspective inquiry we must also question ourselves as black librarians. Have we been so concerned with self-attainment and professionalism that we also proclaim exclusion and erect barriers for our less fortunate black brothers and sisters? Have we mobilized and deployed our resources in a delivery pattern that is meaningful to our black clients? Are we helping to provide the necessary commitments and leadership to the black community?

A review of the personal experiences, concerns and accomplishments of twenty-five black librarians, reveals their commitment to the struggle for the dignity of all men.[7] It provides, too, a history of commitment and leadership to the black community. Black librarians were instrumental in maintaining the visibility of the black man in America; they helped to keep alive the history and culture of black people during the long ignominious years when the black past was unmarketable in America. Black librarians assumed the responsibility for educating and recruiting other blacks into the profession, establishing workshops, seminars, and library science curricula in black colleges. They developed imaginative and creative programs for the black community despite the financial and personal handicaps. Black librarians have encouraged the young to dream, to pursue excellence and to contribute to the history of the black man, and have worked diligently and consistently for the universal recognition of the identity, rights and talents of all men.

The Kerner Commission's alarm over the pervasiveness of racism, its cost to society, and the urgent need for this nation to translate the complete freedom of black people into a meaningful reality does have credence. The truth of those statements is evident in marchings, killings, bread-basket campaigns, and in the chants of "right-on."

> So boy, don't you turn back.
> Don't you sit down on the steps
> 'Cause you find it's kinder hard.
> Don't you fall now--
> For I'se still goin', honey,
> I'se still climbin',
> And life for me ain't been no crystal stair.[8]

All epitomize the black man's efforts to define himself, to force society to redefine itself and to develop strategies of actions that will eventually lead to complete emancipation.

As each person and institution responds to these urgings, it becomes clear that certain courses of action are necessary for a rapid reformation of the society, and that black people must have specific responsibility in developing the black experience into a viable and powerful force. For the purposes of this essay, it means that the black librarian must take cognizance of new attitudes, responses and behavior, and must develop new initiatives, responses, positions, and actions.

Specifically, black librarians must respond to:

1. The need for more effective education and deployment of black manpower in the profession.
2. The movement toward community control of institutions.
3. Availability of federal funding.
4. Inadequacy of research in the field.
5. A sense of black oneness.

The above-mentioned goals cannot be implemented without a black organizational structure, the nucleus of which can be the present ALA Black Caucus. This proposed organization will combine strength in the states with national coordination; it will be genuinely interested in promoting total black involvement in the profession.

Such an organization will seek to promote and recruit black talent to the library profession through organized and coordinated efforts. Although individual efforts of black librarians to recruit other blacks have resulted in a modest increase in the number of blacks in the profession, a national black drive is necessary. Traditional and non-tradi-

Critical Issues In Library Education 157

tional techniques can be adopted in this area, not only to attract young black talent, but also to secure a place for them in library schools, and to provide grants and scholarships for those who are qualified. Follow-up plans can also be implemented. Opportunities for advanced education to the doctoral level should be made available to interested black librarians. Coordination with the scholarship programs of other civil rights organizations, and with black colleges and their alumni associations should be established so that overlap in national and local black efforts may be reduced to a minimum.

It would be naive to assume that library schools will open their arms to these black recruits. Experience has shown that the influx of a handful of blacks in a school of a few hundred white librarians results in an educational crisis.[9] In cases where such crisis become apparent the black library organization should use all its resources to block racist attitudes and to ensure quality education and peace of mind for black students and everyone concerned.

A proposed plan for censuring can be adopted. Thus, as the ALA now accredits and the AAUP censures, so a black national organization must be able to censure library schools indicted of racist attitudes.

A second goal for organized black librarians should be to explore the inadequacy of library programs and services for the black community, and to attempt to strengthen these areas. Black librarianship should be instrumental in strengthening black participation in governing and shaping the policies of the library.

Experience of blacks and whites alike has shown that community control of services and institutions has resulted in better services. Schools, hospitals, and churches are a few examples of institutions that have moved toward community control.

Interested black leaders should be persuaded to serve on public library boards of trustees. This will certainly bring the public library and its services within the focus of community organizations and action groups. It may result in closer scrutiny of hiring practices, better utilization of library volunteers in community programs, provision of more varied and more socially responsive service patterns, e.g. library collections in store fronts, community centers and day-care centers. It can also change the orientation of library operations from passive to active service.

A third goal for black librarians, though it should be the first, aims at exploring and securing federal and local funding to support different library programs. Experience has shown that in the past federal monies and grants have gone to the well established institutions, leaving the black population without financial support and without noticeable change. Effective lobbying by black librarians on behalf of their constituents will make every official and layman aware of the injustices which have been done to blacks, even when money for improving services has supposedly been available. Securing funds is crucial to black programs and services, but even more crucial is the knowledge and awareness of who receives the funds and how they are spent.

Through the present black congressional caucus, librarians can identify, for their elected representatives, areas in need of funding, and in some cases they can point out the specific institutions which need to receive such funds. A coordination between black legislators who do not trust the system and librarians who act as watch-dogs of funding patterns may very well benefit the black community which has been cheated of federal and state funds for a long time.

Black efforts should also be coordinated to assure qualified men and women of their professional rewards and to support them in their fight for equal opportunity. Black librarians are underpaid, overworked and rarely rewarded. Promotions have been denied to many excellent black librarians because of the racist attitudes of some trustees. Many admittedly unqualified candidates have been selected as deans of library schools and directors of major libraries in preference to highly qualified blacks who have applied for the jobs.

Instead of having the positions and salaries of black librarians mentioned indirectly in the profession's annual statistical surveys of salaries and status (cf. Frarey's annual study in Library Journal), let us provide specific surveys of black librarians' earnings and the extent of professional growth. The results may not come as a shock to the library profession, which realizes how underpaid black librarians are, but they will have value in establishing a solid basis for comparison which will enable black librarians to demand equality in jobs and pay.

It is now a valid assumption in the field of social research that the best qualified person to understand black problems is a good black social scientist. It is equally valid to assume that only a good black librarian can study, evaluate, and recommend action for black library problems. Research in the social aspect of library science is far from being depersonalized. Admitting that a black librarian may be biased in favor of his race, as whites are, the black library science researcher may come up with a good model or design for social research in librarianship. The black community has special library needs that should be studied and creative programs should be developed, tested, and evaluated. So far, library scientists have not concerned themselves enough with those who are not library users. As a result, misinterpretations and lay information become accepted as scientific theories. Black library scientists will no doubt take a different approach and attitude to black problems and concerns with reading, knowledge, libraries and neighborhood cultural centers. Black research in librarianship should also attempt to relate to black academic problems, e.g. surveys of library resources for Black Studies, availability of black children's literature, attitudes and reactions to racist books. If the University of Michigan accepts bibliographic compilations such as those on the Suez Canal, Ghandi, or the prophet Muhammad, as part of the Ph.D. program, blacks can be encouraged to make similar contributions on the history of Colonial Africa and slavery in America.

There are needs for a comprehensive guide to African reference books, similar to Winchell's guide and its Japanese and South African counterparts. Through a combined black effort, black librarians can and should launch comprehensive biographical guides to Who's Who in Black America, Who's Who in the Black World, and other similar reference tools. A joint effort led by black librarians can result in accomplishing W.E.B. DuBois' dream that there be available on any library's shelves a complete Encyclopedia Africana.

Black oneness is a reality that no white media can distort. The feeling of brotherhood among blacks should be extended to mutual actions between blacks in the United States and their brothers and sisters in Africa. Blacks on both continents should realize that white Europe and America have used the slogan "united we stand, divided we fall," yet when blacks adopted their motto of black unity, it was met with adverse reactions from whites and with uncertainty by some blacks. Black librarians are in a position to bring black people of the two continents together in order to achieve their mutual dreams and aspirations of freedom and dignity.

Black librarians can be instrumental in holding the first All-African library science conference to be attended by black librarians from every part of the world. Such a conference, besides its educational, cultural and social influence, will enable black librarians to help one another. UNESCO's continuing policy of recruiting library advisors from Anglo-European professional circles for work as experts in the developing countries of Africa and Asia constantly reminds Africans and Asians of the psychological superiority that white Europe and America have exerted internationally.

A cultural exchange program between black Americans and Africans can be conducted under the auspices of the permanent secretariat for the proposed All-African library science conference and the proposed local black library organization. Aside from the clear results of the mutual exchange of information, visits, and cultural understanding, the program can also provide further opportunity for American black library leaders to conduct advanced training programs for African librarians. American black librarians will also learn from their African brothers and sisters the ways and means to involve the library and the cultural center in combating illiteracy and spreading reading and knowledge in poor cultures.

A medium for communication among librarians in both continents can also be developed, using perhaps <u>Nigerian Libraries</u> as the first such vehicle to convey news about black librarians and writings about black library experiences in both continents.

If there is truth in the common belief that blacks will spearhead social reform in this country, the lack of this color in our profession reminds us of the long struggle still ahead. Creativity and imagination are the prerequisites for social reform. If necessity is the mother of invention, then blacks would be the best inventors of non-traditional library services. Black librarians can provide the profession with the best methods to make the library a vital force in the black community in particular, and in America.

We have been believers yielding substance

for the world.
With our hands have we fed a people and out of our strength have they wrung the necessities of a nation.
Our song has filled the twilight and our hope has heralded the dawn. 10

Notes

1. U.S. National Advisory Commission on Civil Disorders, Report. Washington: Gov't. Print. Off., 1968.

2. Langston Hughes. "Mother and Son," in his Selected Poems. New York: Alfred A. Knopf, 1969. p. 187.

3. Willie Morris. Yazoo--Integration in a Deep Southern Town. New York: Harper's Magazine Press, 1971.

4. White House Conference on Children, 1970. Profiles of Children. Washington, 1970.

5. Andrew Billingsley, Black Families in White America. Englewood Cliffs, N.J.: Prentice-Hall, Inc., 1968.

6. James C. Welbourne, Jr. "Black Recruitment: the Issue and an Approach," in: E.J. Josey, ed. The Black Librarian in America. Metuchen, N.J.: Scarecrow Press, 1970. p. 92-97.

7. E.J. Josey, ed. The Black Librarian in America. Metuchen, N.J.: Scarecrow Press, 1970.

8. Langston Hughes. op. cit.

9. Mary Lee Bundy. "A Crisis in Library Education," Library Journal, 96:797-800, March 1, 1971.

10. Walker, Margaret. "We Have Been Believers" from her poem: "My People," in: The Poetry of the Negro, 1746-1949, edited by Langston Hughes and Arna Bontemps, N.Y., Doubleday, 1949. p. 181.

References

Billingsley, Andrew. *Black Families in White America*. Englewood Cliffs, N.J.: Prentice-Hall, Inc., 1968.

Bundy, Mary Lee. "Crisis in Library Education," *Library Journal*, 96:797-800, March 1, 1971.

Hughes, Langston. *Selected Poems*. New York: Alfred A. Knopf, 1969.

Hughes, Langston and Arna Bontemps, eds. *The Poetry of the Negro, 1746-1949*. New York: Doubleday, 1949.

Josey, E.J., ed. *The Black Librarian in America*. Metuchen, N.J.: Scarecrow Press, 1970.

Morris, Willie. *Yazoo--Integration in a Deep Southern Town*. New York: Harpers Magazine Press, 1971.

U.S. National Advisory Commission on Civil Disorders, *Report*. Washington: Gov't Print. Off., 1968.

White House Conference on Children, 1970. *Profiles of Children*. Washington, 1970.

LIBRARY EDUCATION AND NON-PRINT MEDIA:
THE STATE OF THE ART

by Herman L. Totten

In 1972, it seems self-evident that the increased demand for information which we've experienced in the last thirty years is not suddenly going to subside. It is more likely to increase as time goes on. To handle it, new methods of communication have been and will continue to be developed by information scientists around the world. This ever-rising flood of information will be available to all who know how to use the various media which give access to it.

What does all of this mean for library education? It means that if the librarian is going to be near the center of the communications systems of tomorrow, he must learn how to handle this information today. This task belongs to the library schools, for they have traditionally taught students the science of selecting, storing, retrieving, and disseminating information. However, the profession has not always risen to the challenge, so the possibility that librarians' functions may some day be taken over by another organization is a real one.

The purpose of this paper, then, is to investigate how library education has been and can be further altered to prevent this unhappy outcome. Along the way we'll try to show why such changes have been opposed, and what can be done to counter the opposition. Finally, we'll take a look at where it all leads.

To begin with, the library school educator who is worried about tangling with the new media should remember this essential fact: that the objectives for teaching with or about the new media are essentially the same as those used in teaching with or about books.[1] The theoretical as well as the practical aspects of the new media should be pursued.[2] The message, not the medium, should still be of primary concern.[3] However, the importance of communications resources should also be stressed throughout the curriculum, to the extent that every library school graduate student knows how to examine, evaluate, organize, and administer the new media.[4] The fear of non-book materials can be easily overcome.

This, in fact, has been happening every year as more schools have instituted courses about multi-media materials into their curricula. Whereas Lieberman's 1952 survey showed only seven out of sixty-one library schools (11%) teaching anything about media, Hertz's 1965 survey showed that fifteen out of thirty-two schools (50%) were then teaching about media to some degree.[5] Thus, Stone's claim that "it is fair to report that a majority of academic training activities now encourage separate course work or laboratory studies of audio-visual materials, equipment, and other newer media,"[6] is probably correct.

Another area of Hertz's survey showed how the schools examined taught about multi-media materials. The majority (13) of these, such as Columbia and Illinois, offered one course.[7] Because the New York school's "main concern is the development of film literacy,"[8] its students spend most of their time viewing movies in class, at commercial theaters, and at the New York Public Library,[9] and comparatively little time is spent on inexpensive film production and bibliographic control of materials.[10] Likewise, Illinois estimates that it spends 40% of its class time in viewing 16 millimeter films and 20% each on sound reproduction, television, and publicity.[11] Only one school, Kansas State Teachers' College, offers a complete multimedia curriculum,[12] consisting of four courses on materials and three courses in administration of media centers.[13] Finally, those schools, such as Indiana, that don't offer any audiovisual aids courses of their own, do cooperate with other on-campus departments, such as education, to give their students exposure to this information.[14]

Beyond teaching about different types of media, some organizations, such as UNESCO, are also teaching with them. With the aim of establishing a program to teach the fundamental principals of librarianship to prospective South American practitioners,[15] this agency created a curriculum consisting of ten classes on librarianship in general, six on administration, 14 on cataloging, 14 on classification, 16 on reference and bibliography, and six on book lending.[16] All the information was put on 18 magnetic tapes, which were accompanied by 640 slides, two sets of exercises, two sets of class work, one set of bibliographic material and one guidebook.[17] The course, which lasted 2 1/2 months, was conducted by a monitor who was responsible for selecting the students, organizing the class, leading the discussions, and presenting both an oral and a written final examination.[18]

The performance of the program was astonishing: of the 185 students selected to take the course, only 24 (12%) did not complete it.[19] Of the remaining 161, only six (3.7%) failed the final examination.[20] Such success should be impressive to any library science staff considering using these methods.

Even more important may be the reactions of the students. Eighty of them thought that the course exceeded their expectations,[21] and seventy-five felt that there was enough practical work.[22] However, only sixty-eight of the students were satisfied with the manner in which the course was handled,[23] indicating that there might have been something lacking in the way the monitors conducted the class.[24]

UNESCO concluded that the slide-tape-exercise approach was an excellent way to teach the basic skills of librarianship.[25] It not only made up for a lack of adequate faculty,[26] but succeeded in producing truly professional results. Finally, it was also felt that with a minimal amount of money and manpower, this approach could be expanded to include a much wider range of subjects,[27] thereby providing prospective librarians with additional practice on the equipment of the future.

It seems clear that the multi-media approach to teaching library science should have great appeal for professors who have already used it extensively. Unfortunately, this did not seem so in 1966 when I surveyed "the extent to which educational media ... are used in the teaching of library science in accredited American graduate library schools."[28] Although faculty members admitted that some materials in almost every form were available, only transparencies and films were used to any extent, and even these did not play an important part in their programs. Not even the size of an institution influenced the use of more modern forms of media.[29]

Why, then, if these multi-media teaching techniques are so successful, are they so shunned? One reason, as stated earlier, is that library educators are reluctant to tangle with them. Conservative by nature,[30] many faculty members take the view that teaching with or about multi-media materials is an exercise in senseless gadgetry.[31] They fail to see that the principles for teaching with or about non-book materials are really the same as those for teaching with or about books. Were this not so, they would not wonder how these "new" practices could be related to "old" theories,[32] or how such courses could be conveniently added to the core curriculum--whose aim is to train academic and public librarians, not school media specialists.[33] A third reason for their refusal to accept this approach is the fear that their colleagues in other schools, and even their own students, would rebel against the use of media, causing the school to lose its accreditation and its student body--which would also be a financial disaster.[34] Fourth, and finally, some faculty members are simply not interested in changing.[35]

Even faculty members who are willing to change are reluctant to do so--but for other reasons. Since most research on the use of multi-media teaching techniques has been confined to practice at the lower academic levels, and since most library science research is centered on bibliography (an area that has little application to the teaching or development of new multi-media materials), many graduate library school educators are at a loss to know how to use the newer media.[36] Furthermore, once they decide to use them, they need to know where they can get materials suitable for graduate students rather than high school or college students. Frequently, such materials are nonexistent, or, if they exist, they're difficult to find.[37] Finally, progressive faculty members are discouraged from using the newer media by their students' lack of experience with it on the undergraduate level.[38] Unless these students have been sold on it during a pre-registration seminar, for example, the graduate school that wants to teach with or about multi-media materials will have to wait until a new generation of applicants appears, one that's been exposed to "Sesame Street."

Examining very closely the situation I've described, it becomes obvious that some changes in library education are urgently needed if the profession intends to gain a central position in the communications field of the future. Some of the changes are, in fact, long overdue. Following are some suggestions that, if implemented, would dramatically improve the situation.

Faculty attitudes toward the new media rate our attention first, for here is "the most important place to break the circle of apathy and ignorance regarding media."[39] To accomplish this, deans and directors of library science schools and departments will first have to evaluate their teaching methodologies in the light of multi-media techniques.[40] In situations where the staff members are neither competent nor comfortable with all forms of media,[41] "they must be informed concerning the full range of materials which have significant implications for library science."[42] As my survey suggests, the best way to do this is to offer library educators the opportunity to take in-service training courses to acquaint themselves with the new media and with the techniques of teaching about as well as with the new media.[43] We hope, of course, that those who participate in such programs will be inspired to practice what they learn.

With faculty attitudes toward media changing, curriculum changes are bound to follow. The report of the USOE Workshop held at Western Reserve University in 1963 offers many suggestions for using media in all areas of library education. For instance, one group at the conference stressed the need to teach reference and bibliography with field trips, tapes, transparencies, television and teaching machines.[44] Another section decided that cataloging and classification were the courses which were "most amenable to the use of visuals and programmed instruction."[45] (In fact, Stone and Osborne were preparing transparencies for teaching these courses at the time of the conference.)[46] As for teaching the history of books, the members of this group felt that "the best visuals are the books and manuscripts themselves,"[47] when they are available. Finally, regarding selection, they felt that both good and bad materials and equipment should be used to demonstrate the principles and problems of building a good multi-media collection.[48]

Since the workshop, a new area of interest has been added to many library school curricula: data processing. Since we recognize that the librarian of the future "should understand the basic principles of machine operation and have a fairly clear notion of the types of work that can be done,"[49] "a number of schools have either instituted or are planning to institute courses in data processing or information retrieval"[50] and "some introduction to information science is now an accepted fact of the librarian's education."[51] These courses, however, must remain general for the time being, because most of the students have yet to be exposed to such information at the undergraduate level.[52]

When the faculty of the library schools put these new programs into operation, new materials and facilities will be needed. In fact, the analysis, evaluation, selection, and design of printed and audiovisual materials; the utilization of materials by students and professors; and the organization and administration of materials and services are of primary importance in the ALA's Standards for School Media Programs.[53] Somehow these objectives must be met.

As we pointed out earlier, the supply of commercially produced multi-media materials suitable for showing to graduate library science school students is severely limited. Also, the indexing of the materials that do exist makes it difficult to find out what's really available. To correct these shortcomings, library educators should work more closely with the producers of both materials and indexes so that the tools which they want will be available. If this doesn't work, they should produce their own materials and indexes,[54] just as public libraries' in-service training programs[55] and Lieberman have done.[56] Of course, "library school faculties ... will be faced with the ... reorganization of the curriculum"[57] to provide their students with the proper training for carrying out this function in the future, just as Carolyn Whitenack does at Purdue University's Department of Audio-Visual Instruction.[58] Such production of materials by library educators is essential because "without these, 'instructional technology' is likely to be only a collection of gadgets."[59]

To make use of these new materials, however, a certain number of "gadgets" are necessary. Ideally, this equipment will be located conveniently in library school libraries, materials and demonstration laboratories, and computer programming centers, and these should be near the classrooms used for library education. If this arrangement proves impractical, then multi-purpose study desks, each with a television screen, typewriter, record player, and earphones, should be installed for each student in whatever place is available.[60] Some schools, such as Western Michigan University, have already installed systems that use closed circuit television, 16-millimeter films for individual viewing, and other modern equipment.[61] Either way, both the materials and facilities for using them should be available to professors and students for their use in or

Critical Issues In Library Education 169

out of class. Finally, as in the case of materials, faculty members should change their courses to include training in planning for and handling the machinery of the new media.[62]

Computer programmed instruction, too, is adaptable to the teaching of library science. With today's large classes and small faculties, it is impossible for student responses to be reinforced in any other manner than by machine. Mr. Wendt of Southern Illinois University feels that, since "the payoff in learning is the application of knowledge to the real life situation"[63] (or something very close to it), then, "some of the knowledge we need about this transfer ... may well be best found through construction of programmed sequences within various courses."[64] So, since library science is often taught by simulation of activities in selected areas (cataloging, reference, acquisition, etc.), computer programmed instruction could probably be applied to it with good results.[65]

The advantages of such an approach are obvious. The course's content could be varied to meet the needs and abilities of each individual student based upon his answers to questions. It could be adjusted for fast or slow readers or learners, for those who need pictures, and for those from various socio-economic levels.[66] In short, "it is inconceivable that library science should stand idle while other areas of study benefit from use of the computer for instruction."[67]

There has, however, been some criticism leveled at the use of laboratory techniques to teach basic library skills such as classification and cataloging. The critics claim that these procedures are too concerned with practice, detail, and the "nuts and bolts" of the equipment, rather than with the theory which supports their use.[68] This objection has some truth in it but, since library education does stress these mechanical skills so strongly, the worth of these simulated learning centers shouldn't be minimized.

True, making changes in faculty attitudes, curricula, materials, and facilities may be impossible for an out-of-date library school to accomplish overnight. However, with cooperation from other departments, the existing faculties, courses, materials and facilities of the entire campus can be employed to cope with the situation, either temporarily or permanently.[69] Such a system, in fact, works well at San Jose State College where the departments of librarianship, instructional technology, cybernetic systems, speech-communications, journalism, and industrial studies cooperate to provide subject specialization to meet their students' needs.[70] The pitfall to watch for here is that other departments may be even less open to change than the library school.[71] In this case, the only thing to do is to wait patiently until personnel, planning, and financial support permit progress within the department itself.

However training with and about multi-media materials is done, it seems certain that a longer time investment by the student will be needed. Since undergraduate library education is out of favor, the only other choice is to extend the graduate program for a sixth year.[72] Such a program is primarily aimed at those students who are interested in administering media centers and systems and consists of courses in educational supervision, curriculum development, systems analysis, educational communications, data processing, and research methods.[73] This sounds more like an education department's curriculum than a library school's and, in fact, this is the way the University of Missouri School of Library Science treats it.[74] As a part of the University's College of Education, courses in cataloging, organizing and administering of audiovisual materials are not required to complete the program.[75] Obviously, such shortcuts would not be allowed if the sixth year program were administered by the library school, as of course it should be.

All these suggested changes are offered as a means of meeting new user and learning needs brought on by the new media. As other materials create other needs, library education should see them as new challenges, and meeting them should be the final criterion for curricular change.[76] Only in this way will library education be able to prepare professional practitioners for the future.

Some of these changes may not seem radical to those staffs who have already adopted them, or soon will. Praise should go to these people for their progressiveness, however beleated it might be. On the other hand, for those staffs who resist all change outright, we should make a determined effort to show them the benefits of the new media. If not, they and their students will surely not be at the center of the information and communications network of the future.

To avert this latter outcome, several different avenues of influence are open. Firstly, to compensate for the lack of qualified faculty to teach the ever-increasing amount of library science students, library schools may be forced to put their best professors' lectures on video-tape and to program the rest of the course.[77] Secondly, the American Library Association, by the implementation of a more stringent accreditation policy for library schools,[78] as well as a more rigorous enforcement of the Standards for School Media Programs,[79] could emphasize audiovisual instruction to such an extend that the schools would have to teach it and use it in order to obtain the Association's approval. Thirdly, the practitioners in the field who deal daily with the increasing volume of available information and the corresponding requests for it, should demand that their new employees know how to handle the materials and techniques of the new media. This would place the responsibility for teaching these techniques squarely on the shoulders of the library school staff.[80] Fourthly, and finally, library educators will have to adopt multi-media teaching techniques simply because that's the way upcoming generations will have been taught at the lower levels, and "they will tolerate less and less our fumbling with materials strange to us but familiar to them."[81]

If these pressures are not powerful enough to bring about the desired improvements, then the outlook for the librarian is bleak at best. The handling of information has become too complex for an agency which is unwilling or unable to provide general access to all of it in any form.[82] Ultimately, then, "another agency might ... arise to serve a future population in ways we seem to minimize or avoid,"[83] for, "unless the media communicator undertakes a leadership position..., he scarcely merits the high social responsibility delegated to the profession."[84]

With this in mind, it's little wonder that the audiovisual and information specialists are waiting in the wings to steal the stage from the stodgy librarians. As these specialists increase their presence in the libraries, they'll become less receptive to taking the spatial and monetary leftovers from the book-oriented librarians.[85] They are trained to approach their materials as more than mere custodians (unlike many librarians), and they may be better able to meet the information needs of the future than the traditionally trained librarian.[86]

It is possible that while "the book may not be obsolete ... the bookman very soon will be."[87] Hopefully, this will not be the outcome for the librarian of the current information explosion. Librarians in the future should, instead, find themselves working with communications analysts, systems designers, program administrators, television directors, engineers and technicials, computer programmers, instructional programmers, sociologists and psychologists in the operation of an expanded library organization.[88] An agency so oriented should succeed, "because it is an essential extension of the fundamental print-oriented learning services of the library."[89]

Notes

1. A. M. Rees, "What We Should Teach Special Librarians," Special Libraries, LVIII (January, 1967), pp. 33-34.

2. M. I. Rufsvold, "Library Education and the Newer Media," ALA Bulletin, LV (February, 1961), p. 142.

3. Ibid.

4. C. W. Stone, "An A.-V. Report Card for Librarianship," Wilson Library Bulletin, XLIV (November, 1969), p. 291.

5. F. R. Hertz and E. A. Pringle, "Education for Instructional Media Centers," Drexel Library Quarterly, II (April, 1966), p. 172.

6. Stone, p. 291.

7. Hertz and Pringle, p. 172.

8. "Schools in Transition," Library Journal, April 15, 1969, p. 1736.

9. Ibid.

10. Ibid.

11. H. Goldstein, "Audio-Visual Services in Libraries: What One Course at Illinois Attempts to Do," Illinois Libraries, XLV (February, 1963), p. 69.

12. Hertz and Pringle, p. 172.

13. "Schools in Transition," p. 1736.

14. Ibid., p. 1735.

15. C. L. Penna, "Library Training by Audio-Visual Means," Unesco Bulletin for Libraries, XXIV, (September, 1970), p. 235.

16. Ibid., p. 237.

17. Ibid.

18. Ibid., p. 238.

19. Ibid., p. 239.

20. Ibid.

21. Ibid., p. 240.

22. Ibid.

23. Ibid.

24. Ibid.

25. Ibid.

26. Ibid.

27. Ibid.

28. I. Lieberman, "The Use of Non-Print Media in Library School Instruction," Library Education: An International Survey, ed. L. E. Bone, (Urbana: University of Illinois Graduate School of Library Science, 1968), p. 267.

29. Ibid.

30. W. Meierhenry, "Strategies and Plays," Library Journal, XCIV (April 15, 1969), p. 1728.

31. A. M. Rees, "New Dimensions in Library Education: The Training of Library Information Personnel,"

Special Libraries, LVI (October, 1963), p. 500.

32. Ibid.

33. Ibid.

34. R. Warncke and R. Davis, "Is the Traditional Library School Meeting the Needs of the Profession?--Two Viewpoints," *Special Libraries*, LIV (October, 1963), p. 496.

35. H. Goldstein, "The Importance of New Media in Library Training and the Education of Professional Personnel," *Library Trends*, XVI (October, 1967), p. 262.

36. P. Wendt, "New Library Materials and Technology for Instruction and Research," *Library Trends*, XVI (October, 1967), p. 204.

37. Lieberman, pp. 264-265.

38. Goldstein, "Audio-Visual Services in Libraries," p. 68.

39. Goldstein, "The Importance of Newer Media...," p. 264.

40. "The Future of Library Education: The Proceedings of an Institute--Suggestions, Recommendations, and Proposals," *Journal of Education for Librarianship*, III (Summer, 1962), pp. 57-58.

41. H. Goldstein, "Media Standards and Education for Media Specialists," *Illinois Libraries*, LII (September, 1970), p. 662.

42. Lieberman, p. 264.

43. Ibid., p. 268.

44. Ibid., p. 265.

45. Ibid.

46. Ibid.

47. Ibid., p. 266.

48. Ibid., p. 265.

49. R. H. Parker, "Basic Concepts of Data Processing for Libraries," Proceedings of the National Conference on the Implications of the New Media for the Teaching of Library Science, ed. H. Goldstein, (Urbana: University of Illinois Graduate School of Library Science, 1963), p. 109.

50. Ibid., p. 113.

51. D. E. Ryan, "Library Education in the Soaring Seventies," Southeastern Librarian, XX (Winter, 1970), p. 238.

52. Parker, p. 113.

53. Meierhenry, pp. 1728-1729.

54. W. Johnson, "Filmstrips as an Aid in Teaching: Implications," Proceedings of the National Conference on the Implications of the New Media for the Teaching of Library Education, ed. H. Goldstein, (Urbana: University of Illinois Graduate School of Library Science, 1963), p. 62.

55. "Clearing House for Non-Conventional Teaching Materials," Aslib Proceedings, XX, (February, 1968), p. 90.

56. S. S. Reed, "Conference Summary," Proceedings of the National Conference on the Implications of the New Media for the Teaching of Library Science, ed. H. Goldstein, (Urbana: University of Illinois Graduate School of Library Science, 1963), pp. 164-178.

57. Rufsvold, p. 140.

58. C. J. McIntyre, "The Librarian's Role as an Educator in the Production of Non-Print Materials," Library Trends, XVI (October, 1967), p. 267.

59. Ibid.

60. M. E. Monroe, "Graduate Library Education in Space," Journal of Education for Librarianship, V (Summer, 1964), p. 7.

61. M. Miller, "A Graded Curriculum," Library Journal, XCIV (April 15, 1969), p. 1732.

62. C.R. Carpenter, "Strategies of Learning and Learning Resources," Proceedings of the National Conference on the Implications of the New Media for the Teaching of Library Science, ed. H. Goldstein, (Urbana: University of Illinois Graduate School of Library Science, 1963), p. 18.

63. P. Wendt, "Programmed Instruction for Transfer to the Real Life Situation," Proceedings of the National Conference on the Implications of the New Media for the Teaching of Library Science, ed. H. Goldstein, (Urbana: University of Illinois Graduate School of Library Science, 1963), p. 98.

64. Ibid.

65. Wendt, "New Library Materials...," p. 205.

66. Ibid., p. 206.

67. Ibid.

68. P. Dunkin, "Good Teaching Methods in Library Science Instruction," Library Education: An International Survey, ed. L.E. Bone, (Urbana: University of Illinois Graduate School of Library Science, 1968), pp. 282-286.

69. "The Future of Library Education," p. 57.

70. J.W. Brown, "The San Jose Model of Media Personnel Preparation," Illinois Libraries, LII (September, 1970), p. 680.

71. Goldstein, "The Importance of the Newer Media...," p. 263.

72. Miller, p. 1732.

73. Ibid.

74. R.W. Evans, "Specialization in Educational Media at the University of Missouri--Columbia," Illinois Libraries, LII (September, 1970), p. 679.

75. Ibid.

76. Miller., p. 1732.

77. Lieberman, p. 264.

78. Stone, "An A.-V. Report Card...," p. 293.

79. L. Asheim, "Education for Librarianship in the United States: Some Problems and Challenges," Australian Library Journal: XVIII (December, 1969), p. 405.

80. Rees, "What We Should Teach Special Librarians," p. 33.

81. H. Goldstein, "A./V.--Has It Any Future in Libraries?," Readings in Non-Book Librarianship, ed. J.S. Kujoth, (Metuchen: Scarecrow Press, 1968), p. 380.

82. C.W. Stone, "The Library Function Redefined," Library Trends, XVI (October, 1967), p. 181.

83. Goldstein, "A./V.--Has It Any Future in Libraries?," p. 380.

84. P.R. Penland, "Towards the Competencies of the Media Communicator," Illinois Libraries, LII (September, 1970), p. 665.

85. McIntyre, p. 271.

86. Rees, "New Dimension in Library Education," p. 449.

87. Asheim, p. 405.

88. McIntyre, p. 271.

89. Ibid.

Bibliography

Arrizzi, M. "Professional Library Education: Progress and Prospects," Focus on Indiana Libraries, XXIV (September, 1970), pp. 122-123.

Asheim, L. "Education for Librarianship in the United States: Some Problems and Challenges," Australian Library Journal, XVIII (December, 1969), pp. 401-406.

Brown, J.W. "The San Jose Model of Media Personnel Preparation," Illinois Libraries, LII (September, 1970), pp. 680-682.

Carpenter, C.R. "Strategies of Learning and Learning Resources," Proceedings of the National Conference on the Implications of the New Media for the Teaching of Library Science, ed. H. Goldstein, pp. 5-22. Urbana: University of Illinois Press, 1963.

Cheney, F.P. "The Teaching of Reference in American Library Schools," Journal of Education for Librarianship, III (Winter, 1963), pp. 188-198.

"Clearing House for Non-Conventional Teaching Materials," Aslib Proceedings, February, 1968, p. 90.

Clement, Evelyn and Totten, Herman L. "Problems in Organization and Administration of Multi-Media Resources," Oklahoma Librarian, XVIII (October, 1968), pp. 126-127.

Coughlin, V.L. "Improving Library School Teaching," Library Education: An International Survey, ed. L.E. Bone, pp. 289-316. Urbana: University of Illinois Graduate School of Library Science, 1968.

Dunkin, P. "Good Teaching Methods in Library Science Instruction," Library Education: An International Survey, ed. L.E. Bone, pp. 273-288. Urbana: University of Illinois Graduate School of Library Science, 1968.

Evans, R.W. "Specialization in Educational Media at the University of Missouri--Columbia," Illinois Libraries, LII (September, 1970), pp. 678-679.

"The Future of Library Education: Proceedings of an Institute--Suggestions, Recommendations and Proposals," Journal of Education for Librarianship, Summer, 1962, pp. 53-60.

Goldstein, H. "A./V.--Has It Any Future in Libraries?" Readings in Non-book Librarianship, ed. J. S. Kujoth, pp. 373-380. Metuchen: Scarecrow Press, 1968.

──────. "Audio-Visual Services in Libraries: What One Course at Illinois Attempts to Do," Illinois Libraries, XXXXV (February, 1963), pp. 67-71.

──────. "The Importance of Newer Media in Library Training and the Education of Professional Personnel," Library Trends, XVI (October, 1967), pp. 259-265.

──────. "Media Standards and Education for Media Specialists," Illinois Libraries, LII (September, 1970), pp. 661-664.

Hayer, R. "Directions for Library Education," Special Libraries, LIV (October, 1963), pp. 508-510.

Hertz, F. K. and Pringle, E. A. "Education for Instructional Media Centers," Drexel Library Quarterly, II (April, 1966), pp. 168-175.

Johnson, W. "Filmstrips an Aid in Teaching: Implications," Proceedings of the National Conference on the Implications for the Teaching of Library Science, ed. H. Goldstein, pp. 61-62. Urbana: University of Illinois Graduate School of Library Science, 1963.

Lieberman, I. "The Use of Non-Print Media in Library School Instruction," Library Education: An International Survey, ed. L. E. Bone, pp. 247-272. Urbana: University of Illinois Graduate School of Library Science, 1968.

McIntyre, C. J. "The Librarian's Role as an Educator in the Production of Non-Print Materials," Library Trends, XVI (October, 1967), pp. 266-273.

Meierhenry, W. "Strategies and Plays," Library Journal, XCIV (April 15, 1969), pp. 1728-1730.

Miller, M. "A Graded Curriculum," Library Journal, XCIV (April 15, 1969), pp. 1731-1733.

Monroe, M. E. "Graduate Library Education in Space," Journal of Education for Librarianship, V (Summer, 1964), pp. 5-9.

Morton, F. F. "Library Education for the Seventies," Catholic Library World, XLI (January, 1970), pp. 285-292.

Parker, R. H. "Basic Concepts of Data Processing for Libraries," Proceedings of the National Conference on the Implications of the New Media for the Teaching of Library Science, ed. H. Goldstein, pp. 103-115. Urbana: University of Illinois Graduate School of Library Science, 1963.

Penland, P. R. "Toward the Competencies of a Media Communicator," Illinois Libraries, LII (September, 1970), pp. 665-677.

Penna, C. L. "Library Training by Audio-Visual Means: A Conclusive Experiment," Unesco Bulletin for Libraries, XXIV (September, 1970), pp. 234-241.

Reed, R. S. "Conference Summary," Proceedings of the National Conference on the Implications of the New Media for the Teaching of Library Science, ed. H. Goldstein, pp. 116-120. Urbana: University of Illinois Graduate School of Library Science, 1963.

Rees, A. M. "New Dimensions in Library Education: The Training of Science Information Personnel," Special Libraries, LIV (October, 1963), pp. 497-502.

_____. "What We Should Teach Special Librarians?," Special Libraries, LVIII (January, 1967), pp. 33-36.

Rufsvold, M. I. "Library Education and the Newer Media," ALA Bulletin, LV (February, 1961), pp. 140-142.

Ryan, D. E. "Library Education in the Soaring Seventies," Southeastern Librarian, XX (Winter, 1970), pp. 232-240.

"Schools in Transition," Library Journal, XCIV (April 15, 1969), pp. 1735-1737.

Sexton, P. B. "To Kill a Whooping Crane: A Fresh Approach to the Problem of Educating Librarians," Library Journal, XCI (January 1, 1966), pp. 5327-5332.

Shera, J. H. "Toward a New Dimension in Library Education," ALA Bulletin, LVII (March, 1963), pp. 313-317.

Slavens, T. P. "Films for Teaching," Journal of Education for Librarianship, IX (Fall, 1968), pp. 149-151.

Stenstrom, R. "Some Thoughts on the Future of Library Education," Journal of Education for Librarianship, IV (Summer, 1963), pp. 9-14.

Stevens, R. E. Instruction on Microfilms: Its Place in the Library School," Journal for the Education of Librarianship, VI (Fall, 1965), pp. 133-136.

Stolurow, L. M. "Programmed Learning and Teaching Machines," Proceedings of the National Conference on the Implications of the New Media for the Teaching of Library Science, ed. H. Goldstein, pp. 63-76. Urbana: University of Illinois Graduate School of Library Science, 1963.

Stone, C. W. "An A.-V. Report Card for Librarianship," Wilson Library Bulletin, XLIV (November, 1969), pp. 290-293.

──── . "A.-V. Task Force Survey Report," American Libraries, I (January, 1970), pp. 40-44.

──── . "A Design for Tomorrow," Proceedings of the National Conference on the Implications of the New Media for the Teaching of Library Science, ed. H. Goldstein, pp. 25-45. Urbana: University of Illinois Graduate School of Library Science, 1963.

──── . "The Library Function Redefined," Library Trends, XVI (October, 1967), pp. 181-196.

Totten, Herman L. "An Analysis and Evaluation of the Use of Educational Media in the Teaching of Library Science in Accredited American Graduate Library Schools," Dissertation Abstracts International, XXVII (October-December, 1966), p. 1846 A.

──── . "Educational Media in the Teaching of Library Science," Texas Library Journal, XLIII (Spring, 1967), p. 27.

_____. "Self-Evaluation Instrument for Educational Media Utilization in Teaching," East Texas Teachers News, XXIII (September 25, 1966), pp. 24.26.

Warncke, R. and Davis, R. "Is the Traditional Library School Meeting the Needs of the Profession?--Two Viewpoints," Special Libraries, LIV (October, 1963), pp. 493-496.

Wendt, P. "New Library Materials and Technology for Instruction and Research," Library Trends, XVI (October, 1967), pp. 197-210.

_____. "Programmed Instruction for Transfer to the Real Life Situation: Implications," Proceedings of the National Conference on the Implications of the New Media for the Teaching of Library Science, ed. H. Goldstein, pp. 98-99. Urbana: University of Illinois Graduate School of Library Science, 1963.

LIBRARY SCHOOLS AND BLACK PEOPLE

by Robert L. Wright

> I am not you --
> but you will not
> give me a chance,
> will not let me be me.[1]

Education has been characterized interestingly (perhaps prophetically) by its advocates as the "major fallacy" in man's quest for life's panacea. The late Dr. Martin Luther King, in a speech in Washington, D.C., said, "The Negro today is not struggling for some abstract, vague rights but for concrete and prompt improvement in his way of life.... Education and learning have become tools for shaping the future and not devices of privilege for an exclusive few."

The field of librarianship is fast promoting the second major fallacy, namely information power. Information will cure all ills. Let the "Brother" know from whence he's being screwed and he'll solve his own problems. Seeking ways to dispense their cure-all are the community librarian, the "floating librarian," and the "information interpreter"-- or whatever generic title seems appropriate at the time and place. Our librarian type revolutionist might sloganize this concept as: "Give me liberty or give me death? Hell No! Give me information. I'll take the rest!"

In anticipation of my conservative critics, I should allude to the claim of a third major fallacy (in the truest sense of the word). The present national administration enthusiastically continues to prophesy the day (as conditions deteriorate) when all Americans will have a "piece of the action." My colleague, James C. Welbourne, puts down this notion quite aptly in his essay in The Black Librarian in America, edited by E.J. Josey:

> Not only is this type of approach naive, simplistic and patronizing, it is quite irrelevant to the prob-

lem at hand (namely, self-determination). It is precisely the white man's 'action' (which he now wants to give blacks a piece of) that has resulted in the social turmoil of today's society, and the black man's peculiar condition within it. [2]

If the written and spoken word on the subject can be construed as being true, library educators apparently subscribe to the first and second "fallacies." On the other hand, actions and results don't seem to bear out professed intentions. Much ado is made of the effort to seek out qualified and even sub-qualified blacks and other minorities for graduate librarianship education. For, as Paul Wasserman suggests,

> If the field is ultimately to enjoy a better congruence with elements in the culture which now feel disenfranchised, the proportions of librarians drawn from the black population must somehow be dramatically increased.... Yet when the most thoughtful Negroes are turning to roles of advocacy, perhaps the appeal of librarianship is in its identification with information which libraries control. If information is knowledge and if knowledge is power, the library may be seen to be a powerful advocate of advanced opportunity for people. [3]

The barriers are many and complex. I believe that all or most of the problems can be approached from a cultural base. The thesis is that if library education (or any other discipline) is truly to accommodate minority cultures, it must necessarily inculcate the needs, concerns, and indeed, some of the traits of these cultures. The alternative is well supported <u>autonomy</u>. Several of these "barriers" have become apparent, particularly within the context of my experience in library education.

> If I were you --
> but you know
> I am not you,
> yet you will not
> let me be <u>me.</u>

Elitism, be it educational or professional, is the least justifiable but perhaps the most formidable barrier toward realization of racial equity in professional disciplines. Maintaining the professional status quo is the name of the game. The "game plan" is coached by the professional schools.

As long as librarianship continues grasping to establish itself as a true profession, its stake in the game will obviously be Gargantuan. From this point of view, the traditional gate-keeping strategies of professional librarianship would make the medical profession appear as flaming liberals in comparison.

This is not to say that there is not need for academic excellence and the capabilities which allegedly accompany it. It is, however, obvious that the majority of librarians (and other professionals, for that matter), regardless of the emerging trends in library education, will never attempt serious research or teach in graduate programs. Nor is there any evidence of need or justification for such a profession composed solely of scholars and researchers. There is, on the other hand, a glaring need for doers and accomplishers among our decaying communities.

The University of Maryland may be typical, in many ways, in its approach to the problems. In other ways it is not. Here is what could be construed as a major university which houses a library school, and it is understood that the attitudes of the parent institution will influence the actions of the library school.

This university accommodates a community of some 35,000 students, about 7,200 of whom are enrolled in graduate programs. Two hundred and ninety-seven (297) of the graduate students are black. The administration gives constant lip service to racial parity among its ante-bellum architecture. The graduate school points out, with satisfaction, that it is fairly on a par with other universities in its percentage of registered minorities. The bench mark noted is a study of 80 public colleges and universities. Somehow this administration sees no need to point out that over 20% of the state's population is black and that the university is located directly in the Baltimore-Washington, D.C. urban corridor with a combined black population of over one million. Not one cent of the state money has been specifically earmarked for black recruitment or support. Where does this leave the argument that <u>traditionally</u> qualified black applicants cannot be found? There has been no mandate or strong urging that black faculty be attracted. In short, the University is announcing, "We represent the dominant (understood, superior) culture; 'love it or leave it'."

The University's library school faculty is composed of some of the most concerned and eminent thinkers in librarianship today. Consequently the school was quite receptive to a black recruitment program that produced more black graduates than any accredited library school with exception, of course, of Atlanta University. A black recruiter/ counselor was hired and all went well as long as blacks were found who did not seriously question the status quo and were quite able to negotiate it.

A federally funded program to train "urban information specialists" was initiated. Its goal was to produce information specialists with the abilities to enter an urban community by any means (i.e. not necessarily through the library institution) and interpret problematic situations from the economic, social, legal and political perspectives. These professionals would be able to produce <u>effective</u> information as advocates for their client groups

The mere existence of such a program, whose curriculum was developed in recognition of the needs of a different culture, was enough to activate the panic button. There was an almost immediate attempt to evaluate a program (which had little opportunity to demonstrate its intentions, much less its results) in existence for a few months, whereas the "regular" program, in existence for a few years, had not itself been very thoroughly and totally evaluated. Perhaps the almost inevitable death of the urban information project was due to the belated recognition of the second alternative-- <u>autonomy</u> (or self-determination).

> ...You meddle, interfere
> in my affairs
> as if they were yours
> and you were me...

The opportunity should be taken here to point out the problems that are precipitated by federal funding of so-called "minority help programs" without attendant directives to recipient schools for continuation and administration of such programs. Given the present dearth of outside funding, it can be expected that there will be an attempt to "rip off" whatever funding is available, through whatever means are available.

It seems derelict on the part of a funding agency to award grants for the training of "educationally and economically disadvantaged" minorities to an institution which has virtually no history of an attempt to deal with such a sensitive problem. Furthermore, it would seem that the funding agency was purposely closing its eyes to intended misuse of funds by institutions which were not legally and morally committed, beforehand or afterwards, to accommodating the "bastard" program when it did not happen to be among the priorities of the federal agency (or when outside funds run out). In such instances, federal agencies are clearly (even if unintentionally) conspiring against the interest or the civil rights of minorities, despite their claims of concern.

To add insult to injury, the American Library Association, in its latest draft proposal for library education accreditation guidelines, more than suggests that "special" programs will not be recognized as equivalent to regular Master of Library Science degree programs.

If, indeed, there is to be a bridge over this gap (I think I'm still a believer) the solution needs to be approached from several aspects. Up to this point, recognition of the problem has been the main emphasis. The hopeful solution would logically begin with recruitment and proceed then to admission, counseling, curriculum and faculty.

The subject of recruitment will not be treated here. James Welbourne has fairly well covered that subject in The Black Librarian in America.

If it can be argued that the mere existence (over a period of time) of an institution, tradition, etc., is not proof, in and of itself, that its practices are infallible, then a reassessment of the relevance of admissions criteria is in order. Academic disadvantagement, according to traditional criteria, does exist in fact. One only needs read the latest edition of an educational or scientific journal to resurrect the argument concerning the basis of the academic-readiness gap. Is it cultural, inflicted by society, or genetic? The difference, based on testing measurement between the means of the two races, is "X" times the standard deviation of the Caucasian distribution.

With the next journal issue comes a report from a successful program, such as Cornell University's, where the pessimism about the achievements of black students with below average test scores does not exist. This protagonist points out that its entering students with low test scores and grade point averages were selected for evidence of environmental circumstances that might account for low scores and might evidence, indirectly, high motivation for achievement in college.

Regardless of which of the foregoing "notions" is the more valid, the indicting evidence is that none of these "negative" aspects was considered or researched when de jure segregation was an accepted way of life.

Reparative obligation, due to past crimes against blacks and other minorities, legally and morally dictates that institutions of higher learning exhaust their resources in the quest toward bridging whatever "gap" they perceive to exist. Remedial training is, in some cases, a necessary ingredient. However, too often we find that university faculty are more inclined to assign grades (in racially mixed classes) on the basis of ethnic origin rather than reasonable performance, and little inclined to utilize their alleged ability to diagnose student deficiencies and prescribe compensatory measures (devised by the faculty member or by the school as a whole).

"Cultural Shock," as imprecisely defined as it may be, is used to describe a real and ongoing situation when students suddenly find themselves thrust into a different experience among an unfamiliar and distrusted culture. It is mandatory to establish the most effective ongoing counseling program possible. This is best accomplished by persons who possess an empathy and understanding for the student's difficulties. The obvious persons to fill this role are the students themselves and, more importantly, faculty from the same minority culture.

> You are unfair, unwise,
> foolish to think
> that I can be you,
> talk, act
> and think like you.

In schools with any claim to progressive thought, curricula changes are effected according to the needs of its students. Assessment of such needed change is ideally the responsibility of faculty and students. This obviates the need to have faculty representatives from the same minority culture as the recruited students. Ironically, with this realization has emerged the sudden need, it seems, to upgrade the academic qualifications of library school faculties. If the Ph.D. degree were not needed, before the "black invasion," to teach in library schools, there must be at least a few faculty positions that could still be filled with less than this coveted degree. This new criterion for appointment to library school faculties lends itself to serious scrutiny. The obvious course of action, if indeed "qualified" black faculty can't be found on the market, is to grow some. To do otherwise is a conspiracy to maintain institutional racism.

In calling upon graduate schools to face up to their responsibility, it must be noted that they have apparently not done so well with their own qualified majority. Quite often, it has been the refusal of black students to accept the status quo which has precipitated changes long sought by white students before them. Is it simply irony that those whom some thoughtful librarians have characterized as the most informationally deprived groups (namely, inner city dwellers and college students) are those who are most noticeably in conflict with society?

Generations of experience through the school of hard knocks, on the one hand, and newly found knowledge linked with the inability to relate it to life's experiences, on the other, seem to be perfect diametric formulae for conflict.

>God made me _me_
>He made you _you_
>For God's sake
>Let me be _me_.

Notes

1. Dempster, Roland Tombekai, "Africa's Plea," a Liberian poem. (Intermittent passages throughout essay).

2. Welbourne, James C., Jr., "Black Recruitment: The Issue and the Approach," in E.J. Josey, The Black Librarian in America. Metuchen, New Jersey: Scarecrow Press, 1970.

3. Wasserman, Paul, speech delivered at the Conference of the Southwestern Library Association, Oct. 7, 1968, Tulsa, Oklahoma.

PART VI

Organizing for Professional Action

THE PROFESSIONAL LIBRARIAN AS UNIONIST

by Oliver Kirkpatrick

A dispassionate examination of unionism and its advantages and disadvantages for professional librarians will clearly indicate the need for it. In the most basic area, that of salaries, librarians are well below the level of other professionals.

Nevertheless, sentiment opposed to unionism runs deep outside the major cities of the United States, most of which, including New York, Chicago, Detroit, Minneapolis and Los Angeles, are unionized. The arguments against unionism for librarians too often reveal an embarrassing ignorance on the part of librarians of the history of the labor movement in the United States, and an emotional reaction too often based on newspaper headlines during strikes.

Underlying most of these protestations, one can, after some experience in union organizing, detect the real reason for the opposition: an unwillingness on the part of librarians to ally themselves or be associated with the laboring class or blue collar worker. There is the mistaken notion that social cachet is derived from, and some status acquired by, being a librarian. Nothing could be further from the truth. Professionals in other fields regard us with an amused tolerance, and the public by and large thinks of us as "people who stamp out books."

In spite of this some anti-union professionals have openly stated that professional white collar workers demean themselves by becoming unionists.

Following an address by this writer on unionism to a class of graduate students at the Graduate School of Library and Information Sciences of the University of Pittsburgh, two anonymous statements and one signed one were delivered to the office of the instructor. They are worth quoting from, as they represent diverse views.

"A professional person, no matter what the field, considers his job and doing it as well as he can of utmost importance," states one of the anonymous students. He goes on to say,

> There are abuses, slights and a vague lack of respect for librarians out in the real world. The way to cure this is not to give the real world reason to believe that it was right in the first place. After days and years of study to enter a profession, we would do that very profession a harm to equate it in a business association with janitors, steel workers and truck drivers whose necessary and respected jobs require no study or particular effort to learn. A professional needs no contract to tell him how long to work--he will work until the job is done and rest when there is not much going on.

The snobbery and condescension is quite explicit but uneasiness about the views expressed may be the reason that the author of them had to hide behind the shield of anonymity.

The author of the preceding statements had also stated that I was misguided in promoting unionism among professional librarians. In a reply to the above, the second student said, in part: "I don't know where the author has been living but the 'lack of respect' is hardly 'vague'." He says, further,

> A basic facet of any profession is being able to set your own fees. Wouldn't a union really help the librarians to acquire at least this one facet of professionalism? The only harm I can see is that librarians might begin to receive compensation on a par with steel workers and truck drivers.

The third student observed,

> Librarians are underpaid and often overworked, especially if one proportionately assesses the time, money, and effort necessary to be adequately prepared, and then compares this assessment to the conditions found in the 'other' professions. The totally self-sacrificing book lover who works solely for the appreciation of others or because no other

acceptable job is available should be as extinct as the jolly country doctor who took a quart of chicken soup as payment for a house call. Again, this should be clearly evident simply because the time in which we are living will not support people like this at any level but the subordinate.

These views are substantially representative of the feelings of librarians throughout the United States, with the largest number represented by those who reject unionism for snobbish reasons.

The contemporary librarian is heir to a most unfortunate and unhappy past. For a number of years, women were in the majority of the library profession and still are, even today. They were ferociously exploited by boards of trustees and by the comparatively few male librarians. Boards of trustees were then invariably all male.

Most of the women were single, with little hope of being married, and were limited in their choice of occupations to those which were regarded as respectable and acceptable for women. Many were the sole support of widowed mothers. With so bleak an outlook they had little choice but to accept the pittance they were paid. They lived in terror of losing their jobs and became submissive and passive, creating the opportunity for the exercise of callous and harsh treatment against them by their supervisors who often exhibited an arbitrary and feudalistic indifference to their dignity as human beings and their security in their jobs.

Favoritism and nepotism, not merit, became--and remains still, in too many places--the only way to advancement. And this in turn made sycophants of them.

This traditionally low wage scale has hung like an albatross around the necks of succeeding generations of librarians, so that catching up to the prevailing salaries in the other professions has, except through union activity, become a hard, unremitting, and mostly unsuccessful task.

To compound the problem, the profession is still largely manned by women who either bring in a second income to the family or else are single and have no responsibility except to themselves, and are therefore willing to accept the low salaries paid. For the male librarian it

Organizing for Professional Action

presents a practically insoluble economic problem.

During the thirties a group of young, bright and articulate librarians in New York, moved by the parlous economic conditions of the time and barely able to subsist on their wretched salaries, attempted to organize their colleagues into a union. They failed ultimately, and those who remained in the system were systematically excluded from promotion in spite of the fact that their capabilities were substantially superior to those of others who had not participated, and who were advanced rapidly.

Union actitivy was a perilous road to take. Succeed or be damned have always been the only two alternatives in organizing in any field. Failure has always been met by uncompromising reprisal by administrators. This reaction is also characteristic of our national organization, the American Library Association, as witnessed by the recent high-handed dismissal of Peter Doiron, former editor of Choice.

What administrations will tolerate is a Staff Association, a toothless, powerless organization, more accurately known in labor circles as a company union. The representatives of the Staff Association are allowed to air their views and sometimes the administration listens. More often than not they sit and let the drone of words slip by their ears unheard. And, of course, little or nothing is ever done to meet the legitimate requests of the staff. It is the application of the time-tested British technique of providing a Hyde Park forum to let off steam.

Another effort at organizing was made in the early fifties, and that also failed. All the leaders of that effort moved on shortly to other places, unwilling to repeat the experience of their predecessors in labor union activity.

Other attempts were made from time to time, without success. That they continued to be made in the full awareness of the consequences of failure was due less to courage than to the intolerable working conditions and low salaries that existed. Librarians had in fact almost nothing to lose.

Finally, in 1966, after more than a year of intensive organizing, Local 1482 of the American Federation of State, County, and Municipal Employees, AFL-CIO of the Brooklyn

Public Library became the first New York City library to be recognized by election certification as the bargaining agent for its employees.

Once the ice had been broken the other two library systems of New York City, the New York Public Library and the Queens Borough Public Library were also recognized as bargaining agents for their respective employees. Administration by ukase was over in the New York City libraries.

There are those who question the advisability of having a single union representing professional, clerical and blue collar workers. This is natural since in most instances non-professional (clerical, custodial, motor vehicle operators and maintenance) staff outnumber the professionals by at least two to one, and it is feared that by sheer power of numbers they will control their locals and press for their particular goals rather than those of the employees as a whole.

This has not been the experience of any library local. Good unionism is accompanied by education in labor union history and labor union practice. The interrelatedness and interdependence of all library workers is emphasized.

Without a clean and well kept library neither the clerk nor the professional can function effectively, nor can the public make use of the library properly. Nor can the professional function efficiently without the supporting services provided by the clerical staff. Emphasis is placed on the many common needs and goals shared by all library workers, rather than those which are unique to each group.

Others have expressed concern that unionism would take precedence over professionalism, to the detriment of the professional's performance.

Associations of engineers, architects, and doctors, among other professionals, are organized in very similar fashion to unions. The American Medical Association has almost totalitarian control of its members, a characteristic not common among unions.

As the Officers of Local 1482 of the Brooklyn Public Library wrote in reply to a news item in <u>Library Journal</u> covering unionization of Brooklyn librarians:

Organizing for Professional Action

We would like to suggest that, despite the fears of some, unionism does not preclude professionalism. Since a comparison was made between the librarian and the physician, it should be said that the physician does not work 50 to 60 hours a week without adequate compensation, and it is more than unfair to suggest that it is unprofessional or unethical for librarians to seek comparable conditions within the context of our profession....

Unionization will mean more to librarianship than just higher salaries. It is our hope that the total program of the union will enhance the attractiveness of librarianship as a profession, and hence attract more and better qualified people. Its natural result will be an overall advancement of library service and thus complement the aims of the library administration.

Truck drivers, of course, remain truck drivers, and we will continue to be librarians with unlimited possibilities for increasing excellence.[1]

Each occupation has its special needs and special methods of satisfying those needs. White collar unionists have adopted and adapted union practice to meet their special needs, always keeping in mind that one of the principle goals of unionization for them is the enhancement of their profession and of professionalism.

Working conditions contracts are negotiated for all types of library workers and contain both general items which concern all library workers and specific items related to the needs of each type as they affect the nature of the occupation.

The existence of a union local serves to change radically the nature of the relationship between administration and the library employees. Arbitrary and dictatorial behavior is no longer possible on the part of administrations in those libraries which are unionized, because of the existence of grievance machinery for the resolution of differences between administrator and employee, the final step being a hearing before an impartial arbitrator. The resulting sense of security and the maintenance of the individual's dignity as a human being has had a most desirable effect, especially on the professional. Creative energies, previously congealed, have been released and the quality of service in every area has been enhanced.

Considerable improvement in salaries and fringe benefits has resulted from unionization. Insurance covering dental fees, eyeglasses, drug prescriptions and other such benefits have served to increase in a tangible way the remuneration which librarians receive. In addition, night work between six o'clock and closing time is compensated for by payment in cash, and for holidays there is compensating time off and pay at half rate of salary per hour.

There is also a death benefit of $2,500 paid to heirs of the employee. Extremes of weather, either hot or cold, are dealt with, either by closing the unit and transferring staff to a more tolerable location in the case of cold weather, or, in the case of heat and humidity conditions above an agreed upon level, by closing the location and allowing the staff to go home with no loss of pay.

These humanitarian improvements achieved through unionization could in many instances have been implemented by an administration with sufficient human decency to give the matter its serious concern.

The history of the American Library Association shows clearly its antipathy to the organization of people for any purpose other than to provide funds to support their specific and narrow ends. It is an Association devoted to institutions, not to librarians as human beings, and this has been the paradigm by which administrators of libraries have functioned in the treatment of their staff.

In addition snobbery with regard to unionization is many times as virulent among the administrators who control ALA as it is among the rank and file; it is second only to the covert but more important reason for their antipathy: the fear that if unionization becomes widespread among librarians they will no longer be able to exercise the highhandedness with which they now treat the Association's members.

If ever a change were to take place in the attitudes of the majority of the members of ALA, the ideal means would be at hand to create a national organization within the ALA, affiliated with an organization with the size and power of the American Federation of State, County, and Municipal Employees, AFL-CIO.

Such a nationally unionized organization of librarians would solve the problem of the library in the small community which has few professionals. Of the 7,190 public libraries in the United States the vast majority are single units with too few employees to have any power whatever to achieve salary and other improvements from boards of trustees or governmental jurisdictions.

In small communities boards of trustees are part of the social and political establishment. They can hardly be expected to fight city hall on behalf of library workers, since they would essentially be fighting themselves.

An ALA favorable to unionization could bring pressure to bear by boycott, by refusing to allow professionals to accept employment in these libraries until they met certain stipulated standards of salary and working conditions.

There is little hope of this, however, in the foreseeable future. The most promising direction is the present road, organizing under the aegis of AFSCME, which is national and which, as more and more libraries are unionized, will have the power to determine throughout the United States under what conditions professional librarians and other library workers will work.

That there is a pressing need to ameliorate and rectify the rather deplorable conditions under which professionals work is underscored by a statement made by Russell Peterson, the conservative governor of a conservative state, Delaware, to his fellow Republican governors at a meeting early in 1971 of the Republican Governors' Association:

> I think the most important thing for us to pay attention to is not so much that the laws are about strikes and so on, but what we as managers are doing to provide the right kind of working conditions, and salaries, and benefits for our public employees.
>
> As we well know, the only reason we have the union movement in America is because management and industry did a horrible job. History shows us very effectively that they did not pay attention to the rights and proper treatment of employees.

> It seems to me that maybe in another session we would discuss how we would treat state employees, how we compare salary-wise, fringe benefits-wise, how we are managing and so on; be more constructive in solving the kind of problems we are talking about today.
>
> It is certainly going to cost us a lot of money to get the public employees treated equitably. We haven't done the job right and that's why we are having this discussion today. That's going to mean more taxes. We have a great problem. I'm opposed to the referendum, opposed to studying such issues because I don't think they'll get to the heart of the problem. It's hard for me to see the majority of the people deciding to vote money out of their own pocket to raise the wages of public employees.
>
> So, I think it's up to management, the Governors in this case, to have the guts to go to bat, to get the money and better treatment for public employees. Maybe it's a mark of great accomplishment when a Governor gets out of office in so doing. It wouldn't be too bad if we all served just one term, if we did a good management assignment. 2

Most librarians are public employees of one kind or another, and the Governor, obviously not pro-union, has given an accurate evaluation of the plight of the librarian. None, except the naive, will have any faith that governors have either the will of "the guts to go to bat, to get the money and the better treatment for public employees." Nor that heads of libraries will show any more fortitude than the governors in making the fight on behalf of librarians.

The fight must come from the librarians themselves. They must be educated to recognize that by comparison they are the poor relations of the professions, the worst paid and with the worst working conditions.

Perhaps the first step in the educational process is the recognition by librarians that the members of the American Library Association are the Association; that ALA is not the elected officers; that it is their right to govern themselves and not be subject to the often arbitrary and highhanded behavior of these officers of the Association.

Notes

1. Brandwein, Lawrence, and others. "Unions and Professionalism," (letter). Library Journal, 92: 508, 510, February 1, 1967.

2. "A Governor Tells it Like It Is," The Public Employee, 36: No. 1, 9, January-February, 1971.

AS A BLACK LIBRARIAN, I AM ASKING, WHAT'S NEXT?

by James E. Crayton

We have talked of the injustices, but for some reason "the man" does not hear nor comprehend. Books have been written, speeches have been given, and still very little has been accomplished. Yet we continue to write and speak in hope that "the man" will lose his fear, so that he will see all men as equals.

We have revealed our innermost feelings and have taken "the man" back into history through Clark D. Moore and Ann Dunbar's <u>Africa Yesterday and Today</u> and Roland Oliver and J.D. Fage's <u>A Short History of Africa</u>; and Melville Herskovits' <u>Myth of the Negro Past</u> tried to eliminate the myth of my people. Does "the man" believe what he wants to believe? John Hope Franklin's <u>From Slavery to Freedom: a History of Negro America</u> took him back and revealed our past glories, kingdoms, and a civilization that ranked among the greatest in the history of mankind.

How long must we write of our past and try to communicate with "the man"? Maybe just one more historical book will do the trick? Lerone Bennett, Jr. tried with <u>Before the Mayflower, a History of the Negro in America, 1619-1962</u>, as did David Brian Davis' <u>Problem of Slavery in Western Culture</u>. Daniel P. Mannix told of how we got here in <u>Black Cargoes: a History of the Atlantic Slave Trade, 1815-1865</u>.

We helped make America great ... Benjamin Quarles painted this picture of our contributions when he visited the dwelling place of our profession: the Library. When he left he came out with <u>The Negro in the American Revolution</u> and <u>The Negro in the Making of America</u>. Carter G. Woodson had to use a separate entrance to libraries in his day, but in spite of obstacles he told of <u>The Negro in Our History</u> and tried once more to communicate to "the man" in <u>The Story of the Negro Retold</u>.

Organizing for Professional Action

What Next?

We have marched, we have had sit-ins, all to little avail. We have obeyed the laws when they were unjust. We have also disobeyed the laws when they were unjust. Are we to seek changes within the established order? Let's see what James Baldwin, Malcolm X, Martin Luther King, Jr. and Kenneth Clark have to say to "the man" in The Negro Protest. Robert Goldstone's The Negro Revolution puts it all under one roof, and so does Bradford Chambers' Chronicles of Black Protest.

We are still angry because our past has been destroyed. We have been made lower than "the man's" prize pets. What shall we do? Dorothy Sterling's Tear Down the Walls and John H. William's Beyond the Angry Black answered questions raised by lack of racial communication in all phases of life, thereby cooling our anger for the time being.

Is it time for us to Lay My Burden Down (A. B. Botkin)? "No--Hell, No." The marks of our suffering and humiliation have been shown by many: W. E. B. DuBois in The Souls of Black Folks; John A. Williams in The Man Who Cried I Am; Malcolm X in his Autobiography; Claude Brown in Manchild in the Promised Land; Arna Bontemps in 100 Years of Negro Freedom; Margaret Butcher in The Negro in American Culture and Seymour Gross in Images of the Negro in America tell it like it is. But "the man" has not read these books and has not listened to the cry. "The man" does not yet understand that the marching, protesting, etc. have awakened the nation's conscience to the intolerable situation of: poverty, crises in housing, education, employment, economic development, the urban chaotic condition, and the denial of fundamental rights of black folks.

Is "the man" listening now? For there is a revolution. So says Louis E. Lomax in The Negro Revolt, though his may not be the same Choice of Weapons as those of Gordon Parks. James Baldwin speaks of this in The Fire Next Time. Is that the answer to "the man"? Of all things, he has overlooked our abilities according to Eli Ginzburg's In the Negro Potential and Sam Greenlee's The Spook Who Sat by the Door. "The man" has only begun to recognize that our gifts go far beyond the arena of music, dancing, singing, and sports. Yet to be considered equal is still beyond his understanding, according to the late Whitney Young, Jr. in To Be Equal. He has buried our arts, poetry, statesmanship, and contributions and kept them out of the textbooks of his own children as well as ours. For <u>I Am the Darker Brothers</u> of this world and who cares what we can do? Should we continue to write, march, protest, etc., or shall we <u>Burn Baby Burn</u>? Are we in agreement with Dr. King as describes <u>Why We Can't Wait</u>?

Just as our race has suffered, we as professional librarians have suffered because of the prejudices of "the man." He sees us as black first, with all of his bias and bigotry, and cannot see us as professionals. This enables him to assign us to non-decision making positions. He continues to refuse to allow us to be in charge of predominantly white community libraries. Why? If we are considered for any administrative position, it is only to fulfill a quota or because no one else is willing to accept. How long must this practice continue? Will the day ever come when we will be judged on our merit and not on our blackness?

Just as "the man" robbed us of our history, pride and dignity, he now robs us of our professional pride and dignity. As the evil practices of "the man" permeate our profession, they leave behind destruction of the soul and mind. Our ability to write, guide, and lead are hampered by "the man." He is afraid of our potential. We have tried to advance but "the man" consciously or unconsciously blocks our path. Due to ignorance or fear, he does whatever he can to prevent us from moving forward. When we question him about his actions, we are given excuses a child could realize are lies. He echoes the same old phrases: "not now," "maybe tomorrow," "this is not the time," or "it is not politically feasible." He values our opinion only when it suits his needs. We are nothing more than mannequins which he uses to dress his window. He has not read and does not understand our past. He refuses to allow us to be equals.

Where are we to go? We seek help from other sources within and without. We find no answers. Should we be condemned to the lowest rung, robbed of our pride as a race as well as the loss of our professional dignity? Fighting for our professional dignity, we do whatever we can to seek equality. So, once again, we resort to making our discontent known.

After gathering together as much information as possible, and with the cooperation of the County Personnel

Department staff members, the American Civil Liberties Union, the Urban League, and the County Human Relationship Department, we proceed.

On March 4, 1971, concerned minority librarians, with added support from the Mexican American Affirmative Action Committee, formally filed charged with the California Fair Employment Practices Commission, alleging that the Los Angeles County Public Library "has not fulfilled its obligation of non-discrimination" against minorities in its hiring, promotion and placement practices.

In support of our request for an investigation we acquired the support of U.S. Senator John V. Tunney, Rep. Augustus F. Hawkins, other elected officials, the NAACP, and the ALA Black Caucus.

Of the thirteen black and five "other white" librarians, none held administrative positions, even though a number had been with the library for ten years or more. Some had even been with the system as long as 19 years. In addition, many came to the library with experience at other institutions. Verbal promises were made that in one or two years, appointments to higher position would be forthcoming. For years these promises have been broken, just as "the man" has done throughout history.

In spite of having the required qualifications and years of service, the majority of the complainants had watched non-minority librarians with less experience and training rise to administrative positions. For years we had shared our knowledge and skills within the system by training others in the art of librarianship. If we are not wanted for administrative positions, why are we requested to train and instruct? Why are we permitted and, at times, even encouraged to take promotional examinations, when our administrators seem to have no intentions of promoting us?

Once again "the man" has demonstrated that he feeds on others for his own benefits, even if it means genocide to all minorities. Do we have a choice? According to Samuel F. Yette, in The Choice: The Issue Of Black Survival In America, "Black Americans are obsolete" in the minds of a substantial number of Americans. It is my opinion that many high administrative officials within the L.A. County Library feel that minorities are "obsolete" as administrators. In order to keep us at the lower level positions, they surround any opportunity for advancement in bureaucratic red tape and politics.

For years we made our discontent known, only to be told that they know there are problems. As one librarian told the commission, "I want something to happen NOW." We have grown weary of broken promises. We will not continue to behave as children of Job, for we have had patience and failed to reach "the man." We will protect our rights through the ballot, through organized State and Local caucuses, through strategy and tactics, through unity of action, and by all other necessary means. In this battle for professional dignity, we cannot remain quiet and scramble for the crumbs that "the man" is willing to scatter.

For twelve years, one black librarian has continued to bring honor to the library through her participation in local, state and national organizations and writing professional articles. She even received one of the highest awards given to county employees for outstanding services. In spite of this, she has not received a promotion. Other non-minority librarians with far less experience and training now hold higher positions. Yet "the man" tells her to remain silent and wait.

The backbone of any library system is often its sub-professional and clerical staff. These are the positions which most of the minority members hold, and they are the ones who suffer the most. Though non-minority members may be employed at this level, they often leave this classification in less than a year. This is not achieved solely because of ability or qualifications; it is a result of "the man's" attitudes and it is at the expense of blacks and browns. Somehow, non-minority staff score high on the exams and are therefore given the higher level positions in the sub-professional and clerical categories. Statistics reveal that these individuals never fail--not even one out of ten. And so we wonder why minority staff do not move out of this classification. "The man," nevertheless, continues to say that he is fulfilling his obligation of non-discrimination and that every effort is being made to provide for equal employment.

Findings by the Human Relation Department and the Department of Personnel's Affirmative Action Program also support our allegations. According to the County Employee Newsletter, October 1, 1971,

Progress has one meaning for county management and quite another for employees and potential employees of minority groups. With minorities making up 35 per cent of the county work force, only about 3 per cent of the total have reached the schedule 60 pay scale ($1,048 per month).

"The man" appears unwilling to believe his own figures and it seems that little can be done to change his attitude.

Since facts and figures have been presented, he now proceeds to put the blame on someone else in order to evade his responsibilities. Now the problem exists "primarily because of external factors" over which "the man" says he has no control. Although he will continue to provide excuses, we will no longer accept them. The time has now come for our dreams to become a reality, as in Dr. King's most notable speech, "I Have A Dream." We want recognition for our service now.

If pride and honor are to become a part of the library profession, we must all join hands--blacks, browns and whites. We can, and must, overthrow the evils of discrimination and racism wherever they may exist within our profession. Then, and only then, can we begin to develop an affirmative action program that will allow all librarians equality and creativity. This is the task before us in the years ahead.

THE BLACK CAUCUS:
A MEANINGFUL COURSE OF ACTION

by John A. Axam

The year 1946 brought the end of one horrendous struggle and almost simultaneously signaled the beginning of another--the epic struggle of the black man in Africa to shake loose from the enslaving shackles of colonialism so that he might stand, finally, shoulder to shoulder with other men on a basis of equality. Here in the United States the black man, entrapped in this country's own brand of colonialism, is also battling to win complete and unconditional equality, fighting to acquire those rights guaranteed him by the constitution more than 100 years ago. He is engaged in a battle for rights that are assumed by others as soon as they are born or receive citizenship papers. Black librarians must seize every opportunity to involve themselves in this titanic struggle.

In order to participate effectively in this struggle the black librarian must attain the positions of power that will enable him to influence or make decisions that will ultimately benefit the black community. Power is the name of the game. Black people are represented in reasonably large numbers in many fields of endeavor. Yet advancement of the black community in areas related to those fields has been retarded for one basic reason. The black people in those fields, whether professional or non-professional, have failed to use their potential power in order to hasten that advance or to effectuate rapid change. As a matter of fact, many have not realized that they have this power. Black professional and non-professional library employees are just beginning to realize the power that unity can give them in the attempt to attain desired goals in their respective institutions and in the profession as a whole.

There are various methods used by black people to mobilize the power necessary for their advancement. Some have been highly successful, others less so, and some have failed completely.

Organizing for Professional Action

One method now being employed by black librarians belonging to national and local organizations and by some groups employed by institutions, to mobilize the power necessary to ensure that the fullest and most relevant library service is made available to black people, is the use of the black caucus. Black librarians, trustees, and others involved in the field of library and information science need to make even more widespread use of this approach as a means of furthering black liberation.

Black caucuses should be conspicuous by their presence and action in every national, state or local organization that has even the most minute bearing on library service to black people. Even if the organization has only two or three members who are black, these two or three ought to band themselves into a caucus, ever alert to ensure that the organization's activities and goals will aid black progress or, at the very least, that those activities and goals will not be inimical to such progress.

Black caucuses can and have served effectively as pressure groups within the larger organizations. They can also fulfill a glaring need by sensitizing other members of the organization concerning black feelings, black experiences, black frustrations, black desires and aspirations. They can provide the organizations with meaningful insight into the needs of the black community. Programs suggested or designed by black caucus members can be submitted to organizations for their implementation. An example of this might be a plan for a workshop on library service to black people living in public housing projects, submitted to an office of work with the disadvantaged. There are numerous other ways in which black caucuses can impart the ideas and provide the intellectual input that will enable the organizations concerned to better understand and more fully meet the needs of the black community.

Although its primary objective will be to induce the library organization of which it is a part to be responsive to the needs of black people, the black caucus will probably from time to time find it necessary to by-pass the organizational hierarchy and promote its own programs independently, using its own resources and providing its own know-how. Thus, if the organization is slow in setting up the mechanics needed for the recruitment of minorities, the black caucus might decide to set its own machinery in motion to recruit black librarians. It would not, however, discontinue its efforts to persuade the larger body to incorporate this project.

The black caucus has an obligation to scrutinize all facets of the parent organization's internal and external operations. The organization's policies, aims and objectives, on-going and new programs, plans for the future, etc. should all be placed beneath the microscope. All vestiges of racism must be exposed for what they are and obliterated. The overall objective of such an examination, however, should be to determine the potential for aiding the black community of the policy, program or other aspect being examined. Plans of action should be developed that will culminate in the realization of all aspects with positive potential.

Except in very unusual circumstances black librarians will be a decided minority in most professional organizations. Proportionately, even a smaller percentage of black librarians are able to attend the organization meetings where policies are hammered out and where programs are approved. For instance, perhaps as few as three to four hundred black librarians, out of a total registration of 9,000 librarians, can be expected to attend an American Library Association annual conference. By what means, then, is a black caucus going to exercise the power required to bring about decisions beneficial to black people?

It is true that in any organization where black people are numerically outnumbered, they cannot hope to win any issue where the vote is strictly along racial lines. For this reason black caucuses should never let situations deteriorate to the point where the issues to be decided by voting are viewed on a black vs. white basis. Issues put forth by black caucuses should be potentially good for all people, or at least for great masses of people of all races, creeds and colors. This tactic is far from being deceptive, for in truth what is good for the black man is good for society as a whole. So, although the black caucus will, correctly, be considered to be working primarily for the good of the black community, what benefits the black disadvantaged, or the black undereducated adult, or the black college student will also in the long run benefit white persons or persons of other minority groups who fit into those categories.

Aside from the obvious numerical disadvantage that

Organizing for Professional Action

will be encountered by all black caucuses, there is another very important factor that must be dealt with in order to utilize the power necessary to promote black advancement. This is the fact that decisions on issues, whether major and minor, are often made by a few persons who belong to that part of the establishment commonly known as the power structure.

Two strategies can be effectively used by the black caucus in order to overcome the numerical disadvantage. They are coalition and infiltration. For issues that are likely to prove unpopular or controversial as far as the membership or ruling body of the organization is concerned, it is almost mandatory to form a coalition with other groups or units that share a common interest in the issue. It will also often be necessary to form coalitions with groups outside the parent organization in order to attain a goal that is deemed unpopular. It does not matter if the black caucus and the body with which the coalition is formed have disagreed on other issues. It only matters that they agree on the issue being dealt with currently. After the issue is decided, the two groups will often go their separate ways again. They should not hesitate, however, to coalesce in the future around another common cause.

Coalition means that the groups can combine their resources and talents in order to achieve a desired goal. Each group will have its own realm of influence, but the combined pressure that can be brought to bear will far outstrip that which can be achieved by each group individually. Hence the chances of victory will be greatly enhanced.

Coalition may not be necessary for causes that are popular with both the general body and the power structure. The caucus may quite easily push these through without the help of other groups. Generally though, the more support the caucus can garner from other units the easier the job will be. Coalition, even for those causes with general support, is advisable.

There will be times when the caucus will wish to battle for a vital but highly unpopular cause, a cause so unpopular that a group cannot be found within the organization which is willing to align itself with the cause. Hopefully, this kind of situation will arise infrequently. If prosecution through regular channels has failed, or if it is determined that such prosecution has very little chance of success, then more militant tactics must be adopted. These might include boycotting and mass picketing of the organization's activities and programs, withholding of dues, or any number of other devices used separately or in conjunction with each other.

The selection of the tactic to be used is governed by the caucus's estimate of the change it has of victory in the final showdown. If the caucus thinks it has a reasonable chance, it must choose its tactics carefully so that, as mentioned before, the issue does not seem to be primarily a black vs. white confrontation. If the caucus realizes at any point that it has no chance of winning a particular issue, the campaign can become a protest which uses whatever tactics, short of violence, that will convey the caucus's feelings and views in the most effective manner. This might mean a formal protest by a caucus member on the floor of a business meeting of the organization, walking out of a business meeting en masse, or again, picketing, withholding dues or holding protest meetings.

A word of warning should be injected here. The caucus should be absolutely certain that the issue at stake is worth the amount of energy to be spent upon it. The end result should at all times justify the means used to accomplish that result. There is absolutely no sense in winning one minor battle and placing the ultimate victory in jeopardy.

While the black caucus will often work quite closely with other units, it must remain a completely independent entity, becoming a part of no other unit, and in fact remaining an unofficial part of the parent organization. Members of the caucus will, however, become active members of as many other units of the organization as is possible. They will be especially prominent in "pressure group" units with aims similar to those of the black caucus and in those units that may have a great bearing on library service to black people.

Thus the black caucus will be in a position to influence the actions of other units both from the outside as a separate body, and from the inside via members of the caucus serving as bona fide members of those units. Because black caucus members are members of the parent organization they are entitled to join any unit of the organization and can in no sense be termed outsiders. But from the point of view

Organizing for Professional Action

of the black caucus, they are participating in an infiltration operation. Their main objective is to enable the black caucus to reach its goals and hence to advance the cause of all black people. This means, of course, that the caucus must define its goals and objectives so that they will be understood by all of its members. The caucus must also achieve a unity of purpose among its members so that its goals will not be subverted.

As was noted before, most decisions on issues are made by that relatively small portion of the organization known as the power structure. Even while exerting pressure from without, the black caucus should never forget that the most propitious positions to achieve, in order to influence or make decisions that will aid in the progress of black people, are within the power structure itself.

The black caucus must work diligently and continually to get black people in as many of the top administrative and decision making positions as possible. This includes positions on library boards of trustees as well as upper echelon library administrative positions and decision and policy making positions within the professional organizations. Black people can then act from positions of strength on the inside, rather than forever being placed in the position of applying pressure from without.

What can be accomplished by a black person who gains an influential position within a power structure is aptly illustrated by the Reverend Leon Sullivan's appointment to the Board of Directors of General Motors. Within a year of his appointment to the board, the Rev. Mr. Sullivan persuaded GM to give $250 million of its group insurance to two black-owned insurance companies. He also extracted a promise from GM to train 1,000 black people annually as auto body repairmen and mechanics. General Motors will also open a branch of its automotive training center in Philadelphia's Opportunities Industrialization Center (O.I.C.), an organization founded by Rev. Sullivan.

Until black people are in these policy and decision making positions the fight for black progress will be much more difficult. The placing of black people in these positions should, then, become one of the very top priorities of any black caucus.

Persons endorsed and backed by the black caucus for

positions within the power structure must be persons who wholeheartedly believe in the ideals and philosophy set forth by the black caucus and who have the courage and determination to speak out or to take the action necessary to promote the goals and objectives of the caucus. Obviously, these persons must also have the ability to handle the positions. Persons succeeding in acquiring those positions will want to remain a part of the black caucus, working with its members in order to develop new programs or courses of action, and certainly remaining attuned to their thoughts and desires.

Although the foregoing has concerned itself primarily with the black caucus as part of the professional organization, a black caucus composed of employees of specific libraries or library systems is of equal importance. Certainly the impact on a particular community served by a library can be much more tangible, given such an organization. Black library employees, both professional and nonprofessional, can aid library administrators immensely by keeping them aware of the informational and educational needs of the black community.

The institution-connected black caucus will not necessarily strive to improve salaries or working conditions, although these are certainly legitimate concerns. These black employees will be working together primarily to ensure that needs of the black communities are made known to the administration, and to see that those needs are met.

Black caucuses composed of employees of institutions will undoubtedly be the most difficult to establish. Many employees will be timid and will fear repression or retribution in some form from the administration. But library employees who are committed can advance the causes of black people and of librarianship by being courageous.

This type of caucus must maintain sound, positive and productive relations with the administration concerned. Its members must communicate the fact that they are working for the good of the library as well as the good of the black community. The caucus must make clear that it is willing to do its share of the work needed to provide superior library service to the community. Proposals and suggestions must be well thought out, realistic and definitely within long or short-term reach. Criticism must be constructive and not designed merely to antagonize.

Organizing for Professional Action

This is not to say that potentially controversial proposals or suggestions should be avoided. To the contrary, many of the caucus proposals may be designed to turn administration programs completely around. Caucus views will often be in direct conflict with those of the administration. The caucus, however, should always convey to the administration that it has the community's and the library's best interest at heart.

It is extremely important that non-professional and paraprofessional library employees be included in the black caucus. In many libraries, and perhaps in most public libraries, black non-professionals will greatly outnumber the black professional librarians. These non-professional employees will contribute a wealth of ideas, opinions and suggestions. Generally they will have a vast knowledge of the community because they will probably have been residents for many years and may even have been born and raised there. Librarians are likely to have moved to the community from other places, or may not even live in the community. The combination of the non-professional's extensive knowledge of the community and the librarian's expertise will reap the greatest benefits for the community.

The institution-connected black caucus will be in an excellent position to determine community needs accurately, and to transmit and interpret those needs to the administration so that action can be taken. The caucus must not waste its opportunity by allowing itself the luxury of sitting back and theorizing. Pet theories often differ from actualities. Times change, and so do needs and desires. In order to keep pace with the changing needs of the community, caucus members must become functional parts of the community. They must be so attuned to the needs and interests that there will be no need to consult others to find out what those needs and interests are; those needs and interests will be a part of their constitution.

Not only will the black caucus be involved in persuading library administrators to take actions beneficial to the black community, but it must generate action by the community itself that will result in increasing or continuing top-level service. For instance, the community can be of inestimable value in bringing pressure to bear on local legislators to provide adequate revenues to support the many library services so vitally needed by the community. Community groups will also be highly useful in making their needs known to library administrators and boards of trustees.

A word should be said here about community control of libraries. Community control of any public agency will be sought only if the community recognizes the importance of that agency to its well-being, and understands something of the agency's potential to affect its life style either positively or adversely. By and large, most black communities do not fully recognize the great potential that libraries have for aiding black progress. This is evidenced by the fact that most community advisory boards strive only for traditional library services. They want the same things other communities have, and they want them served up in the same way.

Most of the seekers of change in library services are in the library profession. There is very little community clamor for community control of libraries. This is not necessarily a harmful situation. Conscientious librarians, cognizant of and attuned to the needs of the community, can direct library services in such a way that the community actually receives and is aware that it is receiving high quality service tailored to fit its specific needs. In such a case there is no need for community control. However, where such service is not being given, the black caucus must step in to alert the community to the library's real potential and, where the situation dictates, must work for community control.

Because terms like black advancement, black progress, and meeting the needs of black people have been mentioned throughout this essay, it seems appropriate that at least a portion of the black caucus's overall responsibility to the black community should be cited.

In order for black people to deal with the problems which exist, they must have the most factual and up-to-date information available. It is one of the responsibilities of the black caucus to ensure that this information is provided when and where it is needed, and in the necessary quantity. There is a great need in the black community for information that will place the black man in correct historical perspective. Information that will enable black people to cope with their social problems is also among the urgent needs.

The black caucus is responsible for ensuring that libraries continually find and use the most effective ways of bringing this information to the black community. They must see that organizations stand ready to give professional help to individual institutions serving black populations. At times, the black caucus must act as a lobbying unit, either within the organization or with national, state or local legislative bodies. It must keep its eye on censorship problems and take appropriate action.

In short, the black caucus must do all that it can to ensure that the professional organization or individual institution of which it is a part does all that it can to make the American dream a reality for the black man.

PART VII

Toward Better Public Library Service for Black People

THE PUBLIC LIBRARY AND THE BLACK EXPERIENCE

by James R. Wright

The life experience of blacks is significantly different from that of any other race of people in this country. Their background is basically different, because of the enslavement of blacks in this country. While lawful slavery existed over one hundred years ago, its aftermath and repercussions are strongly visible today among both blacks and whites. It is obvious that many white Americans still consider themselves superior to blacks, and as a result of these superior attitudes, blacks today do not yet fully share in the "American Dream." Blacks who have worked hard during their entire existence in this country, trying to be accepted by other races and to cooperate on a non-racial basis, have now decided to develop pride, "Black Pride," in themselves. We have virtually forgotten about acceptance by other ethnic groups and have begun to move out in a grand style toward liberating ourselves. It is also obvious that many blacks are very bitter because of their situation in this country. It is almost impossible for many blacks to refrain from such bitterness toward white Americans in light of the racial situation today. This statement is not to be interpreted as meaning that all blacks hate whites, but that there is a clear consciousness in blacks of their past American experiences, as well as of what they are experiencing today.

Blacks have traveled from South to North, from East to West, South to West, South to East, East to West--in every possible direction. They have come by car and by truck, by bus and by train; rarely do they come by plane. They have said good-bye to a little town in the Delta, good-bye to Alabama's "Black Belt" or to those towns in South Georgia just north of the Okefenokee Swamp, or to the lowlands of South Carolina. Perhaps they have left one of Louisiana's parishes. Perhaps they once lived in Arkansas, near Little Rock or Pine Bluff. Maybe they are not from the deep South. Maybe they are from Appalachia, from eastern Kentucky, or western North Carolina, or north central Tennessee, or any part of West Virginia. Maybe they are from no single place; that is, they have been migrant farm workers, who wander and wander, who may once have lived here or there, but now consider no town, no county, no state or region their "home."[1]

It is true that we moved with little education, no money, no job, with no real home of our own to go to, but we moved with hope. Hope that things would be better when we got to Chicago, with cousin I Baby, or to New York with Aunt Lillie Mae, or to Baltimore with Uncle Big Buddy, or Los Angeles with big brother Munk, or to Detroit with Susie B, or to Washington--where we just knew justice prevailed--to live with Willie Lee. We moved one after the other to many large urban areas in hope of finding a better life. We only met with despair and broken promises from a "liberal White" in the North who's heart had little or no relationship with what he said, unlike the segregated southern White, who's heart was always with what he said when it came to the issue of race. Because of our false hopes and false dreams of a better life, America now is experiencing disastrous results. Black hate groups are organizing one after the other. The failure of America to deal fairly with blacks is discussed today, as never before, on our street corners, and in our bars, where they are saying, "There is no hope for the black man in this country, Jack." This belief and lack of hope is prevalent among blacks for many justifiable reasons. Blacks are still the last hired and the first fired. Blacks with an equal amount of education have an earning power far less than that of their white counterparts. Private segregated schools are growing at an enormous rate in many areas, faster in the liberal North than in the South. With a black population in this country of about 10 per cent of the total, about 75 per cent of our prisoners are blacks and other minorities, while the work force that keeps them there is almost 99 per cent white. There is yet a dual system of justice in America. Many blacks are railroaded into prisons for no reason at all, while many others commit violations because of a life of deprivation.

These kinds of experience must be eliminated and not allowed to continue to shatter the hopes and dreams of young black Americans. The lack of hope and faith is no less prevalent in public libraries, where blacks for the most part are in the most menial jobs; where very few are professional librarians; and where in some cases, there are few or no blacks on the staff at all. Many young, and a growing number of older, blacks who come into the library believe strongly that there is a conspiracy by white Americans to exterminate the black race. Situations like Attica lead many with hope in America to wonder if there is truth in the belief that all men are entitled to life, liberty and the pursuit of happiness in America.

The problems faced by blacks today are numerous and varied; they are as large as the right to exist in America and as small as having the garbage picked up on Monday morning. They are political, social, and educational. The black experience in America has caused a lack of confidence in most of our institutions, including the library.

The first tax-supported public library was established around the middle of the 19th century. Since that time the public library had made many changes. Few of these changes, however, have led to more meaningful library service to the minority members of our society. The public library, like many institutions in this country that had their beginning around this period, is basically a racist institution. Several of our founding fathers of the American Library Association were well known for their strong opposition to non-whites. Melvil Dewey, one of the organizers of the American Library Association, organized the Lake Placid Club in Lake Placid, New York, which restricted its membership to whites only and excluded Jewish citizens. Even today, the Lake Placid Club does not permit blacks or Jews as members. Dewey also organized a similar club in Florida. With this kind of racist background, it is not difficult to understand why even the few blacks who could read had little or no relationship with the public library. The public library from its beginning, and even today in most cases, selects, plans and organizes its materials and services for a middle class public.

In a book published some time ago, when a large number of blacks were still in the South, a writer reported: "among the Negroes of the thirteen southern states the situation is even more serious. Library service is available to only 25.2 per cent of the Negro population in these states, as compared with 56.4 per cent of their total population. Moreover, service is available to only 7.7 per cent of the Negroes living in rural areas."[2] Blacks, before leaving the South, had very little library service available to them and, therefore, had little or no relationship with libraries to bring to their new homes in other parts of the country.

Better Public Library Service

A friend of mine stated that one of his instructors in library school said that his first job in a Georgia public library was to keep the blacks out of the library. He was told when he was employed that no "niggers" were allowed to come to the library, and if any came, to send them away. This instructor's experience is not too surprising when one remembers that there were laws in some parts of the country that made it unlawful for blacks to use a public library. I grew up in Fayette, a small town in northwest Alabama. Fayette was a hot bed, at that time, of racism. It was only 43 miles from Tuscaloosa, Alabama, the home of the national headquarters of the Ku Klux Klan. As a very young boy in elementary school, I had no library experience, school or public. I do remember the development of our school library, when the county school supervisor brought over the old books from the white school to establish our first library. Being eager to escape formal class sessions, I volunteered to help bring the books into the library. This was a memorable experience for me. While I had no access to a library, as a young boy I read every book my parents could afford to buy me from V.J. Elmore's and our local drug store.

When I reached the age of about sixteen, I can remember a county library being erected. Before that time I had no knowledge of any public library. It was a lovely building, and this small town took great pride in it. One afternoon after school, while working at my uncle's cab company, having read everything worth reading in our school library, I thought I would call the new county library and ask if I could come and check out books. I called because I was too afraid to go in person. I explained that I was a "Negro" and wanted to know if I could use the library. This difficult and unusual question was immediately referred to the librarian. I remember, as if it were yesterday, her reply, in a very soft and mild voice: "I am sorry, we can not allow Negroes to come here."

One year later, I graduated from high school and went away to college in Montgomery, Alabama. Montgomery being the capital of the old Confederacy, libraries were segregated there as well as in Fayette. So it was not until after I had graduated from college, at the age of 21, that I ever had the privilege of really visiting a public library. I had a minor in library science and had consequently studied the development and organization of public libraries to some degree, but had never been able to use one, simply because I was born black in America.

I related this personal experience because it is typical of the experience black people have had with public libraries. Reflect for a moment on the black boy who did not have a strong family, parents to buy him books and to encourage him; the boy who never completed high school, not to mention graduating from college; who never had any desire or felt any need to go to a public library. This is the type of individual that many urban libraries today are trying to serve. Some libraries have tried giving away books, and cannot understand why blacks don't just run in to get them. The library will have to be more than a book-centered institution to reach this segment of our public. This should not be interpreted to mean that all blacks need a special type of library service. The type of individual I have described will best be served by a library that is concerned with his informational needs.

The public library can and must serve blacks as well as other minorities. It can change and become as vital in serving disadvantaged blacks as it is in serving middle class whites and blacks. It can only do this, however, if we seriously want it to, if we have an honest desire to make libraries relevant to all Americans. We will need to overhaul the entire public library structure and redesign it to meet present-day needs. This is, of course, a complex problem, and many of us who are interested in improving library service, or society in general, never quite come to grips with the complex and technical processes by which change can be brought about. The public library is not alone in its neglect of the processes necessary for change; the departments in the federal government and the educational system are just as lacking in ability to change and meet pressing needs. We need a public library structure that provides for continuous renewal, for variety and alternatives.

The public library has failed in its service to minorities, basically because it holds fast to its past and conventional ideas. Today we need a public library which will provide for pluralism; which welcomes new ideas and approaches to the problem of service to minorities; which is aware that information deprivation, for this segment of its public, is a serious matter. The library should recruit a new and different kind of librarian, who sees his role as an information specialist. It should let library education know clearly the type of person that is needed to do the job in the field. Most library schools are producing the same type of librarian they graduated fifteen or twenty years ago, and such persons are unable to function effectively today. Those potential recruits who are socially committed can find few, if any, library programs of great interest to them. Most of them enter library school socially committed and come out frustrated and with cramped spirits.

The University of Maryland's library school designed a program "to equip professionals as information specialists to work particularly with the informationally deprived in the urban environment. The primary work role for which the student will prepare is that of Information Interpreter, the essential link between a client with a need for information and the information resources--human and recorded--which exist to satisfy that need. The program is instructed to provide this professional with the range of client, community and information understanding and skills he needs to function in this capacity."[3] A program such as this will provide the public library with the kind of librarian needed to work in the urban areas. The public library should seek staff from minority groups who are best able to relate to other members of minority groups. "As it stands, most white librarians who are trained today lack sufficient knowledge of black people's aspirations, music, food, humor, joys, sorrows, and their total life style, which prevents such librarians from planning and administering meaningful library service."[4] Some public libraries that are really concerned about their relevance in the black community are designing their own programs for the recruitment of blacks and other minorities. They are no longer looking to professional library associations for guidance and leadership in this direction.

The public library attempting to be vital in the black community must be willing to accept failures as well as successes. It must be adventurous and bold in its development of meaningful programs. There is no clear-cut pattern for successful programs in the black community. What works in Baltimore may be a failure in Chicago. Blacks are not all the same, and problems in black communities differ from one area to another.

The day has also arrived for libraries to get away from the obsession with storefront library service to blacks and other minorities. As the black community in almost every urban area is under redevelopment, with new and exciting buildings being erected, the public library should also look and work for new and different types of library buildings in the black community. Blacks and other minorities have had too much of the storefront approach. This does not mean, however, that where it is not possible to build a new building, no library service should be maintained.

The public library still faces the great challenge of serving a people who greatly need its services. In the past five or six years many libraries have accepted that challenge, and have become more meaningful institutions in the black community. One only needs check library literature to see how many action programs and services to the black community have been inaugurated. Far too many libraries, however, have yet to find their role and place in providing informational services to the black community--not just as short-term, special projects but as a part of their regular service to the public.

We can only look to the future optimistically and hope that America and the public library will act in a more democratic manner toward black people and other American minorities.

Notes

1. Coles, Robert. "The South Goes North!" Children in Crisis, Vol. 3. Boston: Little, 1971.

2. Joeckel, Carlton B. and Winslow, Amy. A National Plan for Public Library Service. Chicago: American Library Association, 1948.

3. "A Proposal for an Educational Program to Prepare Information Specialists to Work with the Informationally Deprived." School of Library and Information Services, College Park, University of Maryland, 1970.

4. Wright, James R. "Staffing Inner-City Libraries: Black or White, or Black and White," Wilson Library Bulletin, 45:987, June, 1971.

THINKING OUT LOUD

by Doreitha R. Madden

Each of us must respond to and change attitudes, prejudgments and misconceptions about the black man in his own way and from a base of operations he has appropriated as his own. My base of operation is the library profession.

Today, there is tremendous emphasis on reaching out to the disadvantaged. These efforts, in our country, may be likened to the symbolic celebration of the Chinese New Year: The Year of the Dog, The Year of the Tiger, The Year of the Rat, and so on. It appears that the Year of the Disadvantaged is slowly being nosed out by the Year of Ecology. This phenomenon comes as no great surprise to the black community; many of us who applauded positive efforts of the American society to correct generations of neglect, did so with a stoic recognition that these efforts might be transitory and short lived. However, many of us recognized something else: that this country's continuous denial of basic rights to its minorities has created a deeply imbedded guilt-fear syndrome within our society that gnaws and destroys like a cancer. We recognized also that every member of the black community must respond with the deftness of a skilled surgeon, cutting away this social illness with the sharp scalpel of consistent assertion and positive action.

How can the day-to-day actions of one person make a difference? Use whatever tools are at hand!

In November 1969 there was established within the New Jersey State Library the Office of Library Services to the Disadvantaged. This office was given, by the Administration of the State Library, freedom to change, to modify, to make different patterns of library services as they affect the lives of disadvantaged citizens in New Jersey. One needs no support from the vast number of studies produced during the past decade to recognize that in large part the disadvantaged are comprised of the community of Blacks. With its new responsibility the office was given two instruments for change: 1) Library Services and Construction Act funds for program development, and 2) administrative authority to make decisions.

In today's climate of economic stringency one would think that librarians, long given to the rhetoric of "serving the total community," would have inundated this new office with plans for positive action. But many librarians, like other decision makers, seemed to believe that commitments voiced on convention hall floors and in professional journals were satisfactory avenues by which their responsibility to all the taxpayers of their communities could be discharged. There were other librarians who moved to correct the service imbalance; these librarians recognized that, like other institutions, libraries must change or risk oblivion.

A practical Statement of Action of the New Jersey State Library demonstrated the kind of leadership that is absolutely necessary if an Outreach Program is to have any meaning and purpose. The introduction to the guidelines for the Library Services to the Disadvantaged Grant Program underlined the kind of commitment that was required:

> To encourage public libraries to respond to the needs of that portion of its citizenry alienated from society and its institutions because of severe economic deprivations, cultural, social and minority group isolation and lack of awareness of the library potential for continuing education, the New Jersey State Library has established a grant program for Library Services to the Disadvantaged. This program, made possible by the use of Library Services and Construction Act funds, is designed to help libraries initiate 'outreach' programs. It should be clearly understood that the intent of funds under this program is to help libraries initiate and operate projects which may not be presently fundable from local sources. It is expected that a local library will, within two or three years, be able to incorporate the financing and operation of any project funded under this grant program, out of local funds.[1]

Several libraries in New Jersey began to explore possibilities and soon became aware of the enormity of the task that was before them. One basic criterion which governs the programs of outreach services in New Jersey is that the community of citizens to be served <u>must</u> be involved in the planning, implementation and evaluation of any program designed to serve them. The world of the disadvantaged can be strange and frightening for those who have ignored it or who believe that to serve the poor one must assume the role of benevolent provider. However, the program's criteria also indicate that one must identify goals. If service is to be a goal, it is necessary to determine the needs of those to be served. Many librarians in New Jersey, honestly desiring to provide creative and meaningful services, began to talk and listen to "the folks in the ghetto"; to practice rather than verbalize cooperation; to forget their mistrust of CAP Agencies, Model Cities Agencies and other such agencies which serve the disadvantaged; and to ask "How can your library serve you better?"

Out of this attempt to identify needs came some discoveries which may have seemed revolutionary to those who cherish the traditional ways of doing things. Librarians discovered that bricks and mortar, precise circulation routines, accepted book selection lists meant little to this segment of their community. Some librarians learned and responded to the fact that a child can not be interested in a Caldecott Award book if he is hungry--and they fed him; that people are not overly impressed by an institution which ignores, in its holdings, the contributions of their people; that the theory that libraries need to be where people are is just as true in the ghetto as it is in the more affluent or white segments of the community. The process of communication, re-evaluation and redirection was often difficult and many first steps were floundering ones. However, some very positive programs have evolved and, equally importantly, librarians have come to recognize that this learning process will be continuing and necessary for quite some time in the future.

The program is a little over two years old and there seem to be some ripples of change. New Jersey libraries seem to be aware of and are willing to try different patterns of library services; they have tried diverse approaches to staffing in order to reach the alienated; they have risked the incisive consequences of eyeball-to-eyeball communication; they have taken the library to the people--in community centers, on the streets, in the home, in nursing homes, in prisons--and many are excited by the results. Some of these programs are near the end of eligibility for receiving funds from the State Library and are facing up to the need to incorporate the program financially as a part of their normal library operations. This may mean temporary trauma or panic for some, for others it will demonstrate proof of commitment.

Hopefully some of the actions in the world of librarianship in New Jersey will serve to underline some very basic truths. The pigmentation of a person's skin never has and never will indicate his abilities to achieve, his desire to think, his capacity to enjoy, love and hate, or his right to be recognized and accepted as a human being. Although I am encouraged by the efforts of libraries in my own State and throughout the country to give more than lip service to serving the total community, I am not deluded into believing that we have done much more than scratch the surface of "outreach services" in their fullest dimensions. As an optimistic cynic I am not convinced that our American society is willing to accept that to be an American means to be black, white, red, or yellow; that to develop American culture is to develop a tapestry of culture woven with the variegated threads of the cultures of many people; that the components of education (in its broadest sense) must encompass the diversities of the many backgrounds of peoples; that no decisions affecting the minorities in this country will last unless the minorities are included in the decision making process.

While I am critical and wary of much that is attempted by the white majority to stamp out racism, I believe that each of us in the black community must clearly identify and operate on the basis of a priority of challenges and that each of us must define those priorities for himself. Hopefully, we will not allow the superficial trappings of the black awareness syndrome to deter us from the important task ahead. The Afros, the Dashikis, the slogans are fine, but beyond these lies the need for important action. We must insist on quality and diversified education. We must continue to challenge the local and national political philosophies of the community and must exercise our voting privileges to the maximum. We must replace meaningless rhetoric with involved and positive action, especially in the decision making process.

Note

1. Library Services to the Disadvantaged Grant Program Guidelines, Criteria, Evaluation.

THOUGHTS ON PUBLIC LIBRARIES AND LIBRARIANSHIP

by Thomas Alford

We are entering an era of change and urgency. The problems of this decade and the ones to come demand new solutions, new ingenuity, new boldness, and new imagination. The challenge is monumental.

The sense of urgency must permeate every corner of America. There is a need for Americans, both young and old, black and white, to address themselves to the priorities of ending the war in Vietnam, poverty, inequity in education, oppression, racism, and exhorbitant taxes. Rhetoric must be turned into constructive action.

There is no question but that changing times have left librarianship ill-situated to meet the challenges that face it. However, we in the profession believe that librarians are inherently capable of meeting the most demanding challenges of our day if we are permitted to exercise creativity in the administration of libraries and utilize some of the philosophy with which we have been endowed by the library schools, and if we try to meet the demands of all of the citizens in our public library service areas. We believe that this concerned dedication is necessary to provide the kind of library service the people must have and that the people want.

Our preparation must begin in the library schools and must lead to real service to the community from public libraries. There are three problems that librarianship must respond to. The first is the need for book and material selection that provides a true picture of the black man's contribution to the history of our country. Secondly, librarianship must grapple with the lack of justice and equality for black and other minority librarians. Thirdly, librarianship must address itself to outreach services to children and young adults who have been underserved by the community, the nation and the library.

Let us look at the first of these problems facing our public libraries in the 1970's: the necessity of providing books that give a true picture of the black man's contributions to the history of our country. Too many books have appeared on the market and on library shelves which either contain distortions and misinformation or delete important facts regarding the history of black people.

Today, more than ever before, the selection of books is an important factor in determining how well America is educated. For one hundred years boys and girls have been given a distorted picture of their own image. The books in public libraries showed no black faces among children playing or involved in other activity. The history book painted a picture of happy slaves which had little or nothing to do with the development and progress of our country. The writers chose whom they wanted to set up as black heroes for the black people. This token recognition was sparsely sprinkled on the pages of American history.

The temper of these times has produced a demand that books be revised to include a true appraisal of the black man's contribution to America's growth and development. Realizing the injustice done to the American minorities affected by such books, librarians, community organizations, educators, publishers and interested citizens have begun a concerted effort to right the wrongs that have been done. We must support this movement in selecting our children's, young adult and adult books.

If the library hasn't brought its books and material selection up-to-date with the demand for information on blacks and the Black Experience, it must do so. Some principles that should be adhered to in the selection of materials on blacks are the following:

1. Books, fiction and non-fiction, should be chosen which throw new light on both the history and the present situation of blacks and on black thought.

2. Books should be selected bearing in mind the manner of their presentation of the black man's struggle to enhance his own worth and importance in the evolution of American democracy.

3. The collection should be as versatile as possible.

4. Books selected should protect the dignity of the black man and demonstrate the nature and power of prejudice as a social force.

5. Books should be selected which explore the various dimensions, types, and results of segregation and other forms of discrimination, and which present them in their true perspective.

6. Books and other materials should be used to fill a serious gap in linking the past with contemporary black thought.

Application of such principles to book selection in the 70's would make a real contribution toward the retelling of the story of America's growth and development and the black man's contribution to it as it actually happened; and also toward broader recognition of the black man as an integral part of American life.

The second of the priorities facing librarianship and libraries in the 70's is justice and equality for black librarians as new leadership is developed in the profession.

Black people in general and black librarians in particular can no longer claim that our progress is being impeded by bigotry and discrimination. This is not enough. Though bigotry and discrimination still exist in America, doors of opportunity are open today that have never been opened before, even though some only permit token admission. Black faces are in almost every situation, and not always as fugitives from justice. Black librarians are serving in many capacities in public libraries, but there are not nearly enough blacks to do effectively the job that needs to be done. To say that the problem is less now than it was two or three years ago is like saying that there are now more high ranking black officers in the Armed Forces. Racism still exists in libraries and librarianship. The race of any librarian is not the problem or the issue. The issue is that we cannot allow race to separate librarianship from the mission that must be accomplished. Librarianship needs librarians who identify with the needs of the poor and with blacks and the Black Freedom Movement, and who desire to bring more and better library services to poor people.

For the black librarian to remain true to his heritage and, at the same time, continue as a dynamic force in the struggle of a racially oppressed people for freedom, dignity, and equal opportunity, it is of paramount importance that he be in the vanguard, pushing the public library to reaffirm its commitment to provide quality library services to blacks and all underserved people.

The black librarian's participation in local public library affairs has increased awareness of the scope of urban problems and the complexities that must be unravelled to solve them. Their most significant accomplishment may be their stimulation of local public libraries to approach new problems in new ways. Many directors, through their involvement with black librarians, have learned the importance of sharing responsibilities with the staff, of trying new programs, of developing a total community service pattern, and of providing leadership toward change. Library administrators in the past have been interested, too often, only in those activities for which they were legally responsible: to raise revenues, and to manage. Improvement of public libraries depends on a more highly visible concept of service, and on librarians willing to put the concept to work.

Many library schools do not prepare students adequately for work in the public library. Students emerge from such schools prepared only for the ideal library situation and not for the realities that they will soon face. Having been a part of the public library scene, I have formed ideas and impressions which are far removed from those impressed upon me in library school.

Although a good education in librarianship is basic, there are human factors which are equally important. The librarian without the imagination and patience to work with children, the energy to keep up with young adults, the intelligence and the compassion to understand adults, will be neither successful nor happy in the public library.

There is need for library staffs to be concerned with all of the problems facing society if the library is to respond adequately to these problems. Student unrest, the infiltration of drugs and alcohol on school campuses, private and public immorality, and man's inhumanity to man, in crime or war, have made it mandatory that our public libraries reflect these societal ills in programs and in library resources.

Turning to personnel problems, personnel officers

often claim that they need a complete report on the physical, mental, and personality qualities of each applicant in order to make fair decisions. If there are more qualified applicants than positions, other questions loom larger than fairness. One such is whether the library should not provide opportunities for persons who have been denied professional positions because of their race.

Black librarians do not object to transcripts which give grades and test scores and the kinds of descriptions requested on application forms. They do object, however, to academic ratings which place the student in one of five categories of promise among some mythical group of students. They object to character and personality ratings, knowing that character and personality are not easy to measure and that these qualities will change as a person matures and adapts to new situations. They object to predictions about how a librarian will perform in a library whose cultural and intellectual community is unknown.

Personal observation strongly indicates that a librarian's first job in the profession often determines what kind of a librarian he will be, and, in fact, how good he will be. Acknowledging that it is difficult to change a person after he has been in the profession a number of years, it becomes vital to get new members off to a good start. The best way to do this is with a well-planned and effective orientation program for new librarians.

Timing is of the greatest importance. Waiting too long will cause a program of this kind to lose its impact. The program should be an ongoing activity of the library, and attendance by new staff members should be mandatory. The administrator of the library should be in attendance at these sessions to lend moral support and, incidentally, his presence will help make for good staff relations.

The program can, and should, be geared to the community, its traditions, and the role that the library plays in the community. The program should cover many aspects of librarianship in a fast-moving, informative and, above all, interesting manner. In the 70's sound personnel policies should become increasingly a part of the total program of the public library, coupled with a genuine concern of staff as human beings. Library directors and supervisors should bear in mind the following factors in personnel relations:

(a) The supreme importance of the individual personality;

(b) Each person should feel responsible for the consequences of his own conduct;

(c) Mutual understanding is better than confrontation and poor staff morale;

(d) Excellence in work performance and creative ability should be fostered;

(e) All persons should be judged by the same humanitarian standards. This value calls for the repudiation of discrimination based upon family, race, nationality, religion or economic status;

(f) The concept of brotherhood should take precedence over selfish interest.

Library staff should be encouraged to view all library patrons as people who are entitled to full opportunity for the pursuit of happiness, provided that their activities do not interfere with the similar opportunities of others. Each user should be offered humanitarian and educational experiences which transcend the materialistic aspects of life. These values come from many sources: from the creative artistic expression of the human spirit, from noble monuments of architecture, from the memory of heroic men and women who have served humanity, from contemplation of the stars or a blade of grass, from the smile of a well-loved companion, from poetry and music, from sincere human experiences and hope. The individual who lacks such experiences remains an incomplete person. It is hoped that the public libraries of the 70's will extend full recognition to the arts as a means for expressing and evoking the inner life of man.

To have good staff relations, it is important to keep lines of communication completely open at all times. This means much more than mere conversational freedom and candor; it means a radical, complete sharing of all the important and unimportant areas of work in libraries. To be sure, each librarian in a library will have areas of emphasis and interest his administrator does not share but the administrator must be prepared to discuss programs and interests of staff members without disdain and without turning off enthusiasm.

Another humanitarian issue is the attitude of old-line staff. Attitude has been a trouble spot in American libraries for a long time. Some of the problems in this area result from the fear that equally educated blacks will become competitive and a threat to whites in the profession. Few blacks, if any, in this profession have any desire to destroy the white librarian. All of us are an important part of a vital profession. But the old-line staff needs to be aware that there is grave concern about library services to black people and the treatment of blacks in the profession.

Both black and white librarians have been guilty of providing poor library services to people in the black community, and although there are certain white librarians who may provide the black community with better services than a black librarian, it would certainly increase use of public libraries if more black librarians were assigned to black areas. The black librarian is, ipso facto, a specialist.

Perhaps fewer, but certainly better experimental programs are needed. If public libraries are to attract non-users to their services, they must have viable programs that black citizens view as being relevant to their needs. In a large number of instances, relevant programs require black professional staff.

In the large cities, especially in the solidly black areas, it is puzzling why there is such a predominance of white librarians. It has been demonstrated over the years that a black librarian relates to black people much better. When there is a large percentage of white librarians working in black neighborhoods service is often unrelated to real needs, and is shunned by a community long suspicious of the white establishment.

Another problem is the motivation of black young people to learn. In the predominantly black community the general point of view which should be clearly communicated is that students of a minority group must study harder and learn more if they are to improve their chances for success in later life. In many segregated schools minority students are neither expected nor required to meet standards as rigorous as those demanded of other young people.

This lack of standards in the segregated minority community can be attributed first to the leadership from outside the community. Attitudes that say, "We don't care what happens to you; you are inferior and not worth our concern; it makes no difference whether you achieve well or poorly, as long as you stay in your place," are all too often accepted by the minority child himself. Also, young people tend to use segregation as a crutch to justify lack of effort in the learning situation. Some white librarians in predominantly black communities tend to be over-protective of their patrons for fear of being accused of discrimination by angry parents.

Therefore, librarianship in the 1970's will have to produce in-service training dealing with methods and techniques for motivating brainwashed minority children and young adults, to help them develop a sense of self and a desire to achieve their utmost. These in-service training sessions should be conducted by minority librarians who are familiar with the problem.

Support for the minority librarian from his supervisors and co-workers does not imply complete approval of all of his attitudes and techniques, but the black librarian does expect other librarians to at least show empathy. Black librarians want those in the field of librarianship to be continually interested in their activities and to know them first-hand; they feel that their plans should receive more backing in the profession. On the other hand, the black librarian expects and welcomes professional constructive criticism. All librarians are highly interested in, and influenced by, peer concerns, interests, and attitudes. Other librarians, therefore, should accept this as a challenge to always be worthy examples. Each person must be himself and attain his own stature as a librarian, and those who have been in the profession the longest must serve as strong and positive influences. Black librarians need, and justifiably expect encouragement as well as the respect which should be accorded an adult and a professional within the personnel program of any good, healthy and flexible library.

In the public library there are no "second-class" members, but sometimes the black librarian in the library is given this impression. The black librarians in the profession have not been permitted to share fully in such matters as policy-making. Too often their opinions are not sought or are ignored on matters that are vital to the total library program. Black librarians must be given more than token responsibilities. They must be given a purpose to which they can commit themselves and an opportunity to become involved in a way that will permit them to exercise professional commitment. It is incumbent upon us all to realize that the black librarian has been more exposed to meeting life's basic needs and dealing with the hard facts of poverty and destitution than most other librarians. This exposure has brought about a kind of maturity and sophistication that has forced the black librarian to realize and assume his responsibilities. He knows that if he is to share fully in the responsibilities of the library, then he must be willing to pay the price, must contribute time, talent, money and effort--wherever and whenever needed. In short, as a debtor to his profession, he must be active in professional organizations and contribute money and effort in recruiting more blacks to the profession.

The black librarian is not so naive as to assume that every M. L. S. degree person will become a library administrator, but he does expect responsibilities commensurate with his development and experience. We all learn best by doing. This doing-training process, to prepare the black librarian for the responsibilities he wants to share and eventually bear, will be time-consuming and patience-trying, but the professional growth that will be derived will far outweigh the hard work involved. Such an experience provides not only an exercise in democracy but assures the development of well-informed librarians for future leadership. The black librarian is begging not to be underestimated; his energies and capabilities develop as rapidly as anyone else's.

Another opportunity that the public library must assume is a greater responsibility in its own budget when Federal funding ceases to support outreach programs. With the cities becoming centers of black population, it is imperative that outreach programs do not diminish; they must be increased. The poor and the dispossessed need vital information services from libraries.

It is perhaps most important that the public library extend itself beyond its clean, beautifully appointed glass and brick buildings, out into the dirty, littered, ragged, physically and culturally hungry areas of the community. We must get our feet wet and our hands dirty through involvement with the many problems facing the urban poor. The Library must grapple with the pollution of our minds by stereotypes, prejudice and distorted information, the pollution of bodies by drugs, and the pollution of our land, rivers, lakes, oceans and the air. The eyes of the black librarian and his white counterpart must see things that those blinded by the complacency of less tumultuous times refuse to recognize and deal with.

I mentioned earlier the possibility that many public libraries may have to cease library outreach operations because of the drying up of Federal funds. If Federal funds cease, then, local resources must be found for these vital programs. Urban public libraries without outreach services make no sense; the need was never greater than now. It is underlined daily in the streets of our cities and throughout the pages of the nation's press. Our cities and counties must be forced to face, and to change, the fact that library services are completely bypassing a large percentage of their citizens.

Our profession has produced, and still manages to come up with, new programs for the underserved, but the funds available for their management and maintenance are totally inadequate, and usually much less than is allowed for library services to middle and upper income level people. As much as library services to the underserved are affected by lack of funds, and as great as the need is for increased financial support of the public library, the most pressing need is for a re-ordering of the public library's priorities of concern; the need to end the "hang-up" of continuing the same old programs as usual.

Until our nation recognizes outreach services as vital and makes adequate appropriations and sets realistic policies and guidelines, library programs for the underserved are destined for failure. The objective of a service-oriented library with materials for all Americans will continue to elude us. Many measures have been taken to improve library administration, technical services, and research capabilities, but more librarians are needed to take the lead in the attack on inefficient, indifferent and insensitive library services.

The public library today must provide meaningful services, expand its services to educationally unserved children, young adults, and adults, and help construct new strategies to tackle new problems. The modern library must accept a responsibility to experiment in building new institutions where old ones have proven inadequate. We must teach--through votes, pressure, voiced protest, demonstration, concern and involvement--that good public library service is essential.

COMMUNITY AND OUTREACH LIBRARIANS:
CHALLENGE AND CHANGE

by Ella Gaines Yates

> It is not too much to say that we stand at a crisis in library affairs. There is on us a very real conflict between quality and quantity, between loyalty to our professional ideals, what we know to be good service, and the pressure of an ever-increasing demand. Never have we seen so many things to be done, or felt so keenly our own call to serve. There is a disquieting disposition to spread our energies over too great a number of things, to take on too much work, and to advertise far beyond our ability to perform. It is a very insidious temptation, and I believe it assails the heads of small libraries even more subtly than their colleagues with greater and heavier demands and resources.
>
> If I were disposed to play the role of an unfriendly critic--which I am not--I think I should have to say that as a profession we have not successfully resisted this temptation, this pressure to expand beyond our powers of faithful and efficient performance. In one sense mediocrity may be said to be the key to the library situation in America at the present day. We have few really strong libraries, few very fine collections, few wonderfully expert librarians. We have numbers--large numbers--of fair buildings, fairly good collections, moderately successful librarians and assistants...
> --Wilson Warner Bishop
> "Changing Ideals in Librarianship."

For many years, libraries have offered services outside their hallowed walls, involving community organizations and segments of the population who did not enter the portals. In recent years we have witnessed continued interest and expanded efforts described as community and/or outreach services. We hear more and more talk about community and outreach programs, but in spite of the rhetoric and the accolades, only a few librarians are in the field. How much of this is only talk? How much is really valid? Who are the librarians who are too busy with their involvements to write about them in our journals? And how many directors and staff members make significant contributions to these efforts as back-up personnel within the structure when outreach and community programs are successful?

Libraries offering a great many services are continually faced with demands for more. They seem to sense, or have a greater awareness of, the need for more and expanded services, but face the question of why the already overburdened librarian or librarians should consider additional drains on resources and personnel? The justification rests on the development of new concepts of the library in the community: Are the library's services relevant? Does it meet the needs of all the population, or of the majority of the population? And is it making progress toward meeting the needs of those segments of the community which were previously unserved?

Today we are faced with decreasing circulation statistics, escalating costs of books, equipment, and maintenance, inadequacies in personnel, and tight budgets. The profession is also faced with demands for services far removed from the established structural patterns of libraries and librarianship. Just what type of librarian is best suited to fill the new role, wearing many hats, working many days almost around the clock, with little or no assistance? What type of dedication is required? What type of personality is required? And who really cares within the library structure?

The new trend calls for "people orientation," "media orientation," as well as our traditional literary standards of "book orientation." Book-oriented librarians are not difficult to find in the current flooded job market. Excellent media-oriented librarians are becoming more and more available as our library schools re-vamp courses of instruction in order to meet today's needs. But where do we find excellent personnel with a combined background of book orientation and people orientation? What makes this type of librarian: training, background, human resources, acquired or inbred human empathy, a combination of all four, or something else? Through trial and error, librarians have come to realize, as community and outreach programs have developed, that if they are to succeed in our urban communities, this special type of librarian--people oriented, book oriented, and possessing a deep regard for the human rights and dignity of man, must be found to do the job.

A very large percentage of the librarians working in community and outreach services to the "disadvantaged" are black. Nationwide emphasis is being placed on the recruitment of blacks and other minorities to the profession. The "minority" librarian seems to be the one who can best function and offer the most relevance to our "disadvantaged" population. Yet the librarians delegated to this type of service are far too often among the lower echelon of staff in terms of status, rank, and title, and too often rank among the lower paid. If the need is so acute, if this librarian must be so well equipped, should we not give more than lip service in terms of status and pay? How do we expect to recruit such special personnel when the trend seems to be to lock them into specific job situations without chances for advancement, big promotions, and top pay?

The great vacuum between the library and the black community is unfortunate. But even more disturbing is the great gulf within the profession between black librarians and the established library structure. The capability and professionalism of the black librarian have been evinced over the years. They establish roots in the communities and can deliver effective services with an efficiency and credibility which are hard to match.

One of the mandatory ingredients for successful programming is knowledge and dedication. The black librarian has been proven to possess this ingredient. Librarians must know what they are doing and do it well; yet the library profession still finds it difficult to accept the black librarian as a professional of substance and merit. Community and outreach services are extremely relevant, noteworthy, and essential. Within professional circles, however, we rarely see the directors and assistant directors with direct involvement in these services. Because of the dearth of executive participation, these programs, while they may still be viewed as important, are not considered the jobs that really count.

For the jobs that really count, the jobs that develop assistant directors and directors, few black librarians ever get to know enough about actual administration to reach the competitive slots. Some black librarians acquire "cosmetic" positions but have little or no knowledge of the actual administration. Because of the "black stigma" attached to outreach services and the fear of being locked in and categorized, many young, dynamic, inventive black librarians are avoiding community involvement; they are interested in making it to the top.

The librarians working in the ghetto with the disadvantaged deal with the problems of people faced with urban renewal (commonly termed by the disadvantaged as urban removal): slum housing, unemployment, many aspects of environmental pollution, and manifold personal tragedies caused by poverty and discrimination. These librarians are not interested in speculating about solutions in the distant future. They know, from daily experience, that the survival of human beings is at stake. They are impatient for changes in our total society, and particularly in our established library structure, and want more than "tokenism" services.

These librarians are attempting to achieve equal rights and equal opportunities for minority people. They work with people trapped in the ghetto, and they enlist the help of concerned non-paternalistic community people. They symbiotically confront the business community and established agencies in an attempt to create an atmosphere in which all human beings can turn their potential into accomplishment.

Many more people are needed for this type of service, if it is to be considered quality service rather than a diffusion of efforts and energies signifying nothing. Good librarians in the field, dedicated boards of trustees, dynamic directors, assistant directors, and a dedicated back-up staff of professional and non-professional personnel are mandatory. There must be greater cooperation between the established library institution and the field librarian in working with the community and its problems. The bitterness as well as the unique energies, desires, and expectations of the non-served must be harnessed to constructive channels, and the librarian in the field can't do it alone. Directors receive the commendations for the excellent jobs their libraries are doing, but they have limited knowledge of the frustrations, the disappointments, the day and night involvement, or the feelings of joy and satisfaction experienced by the librarian in the field.

Community and outreach programs are highly demanding, exhausting, and often very frustrating. The black librarian is not the panacea, only one response to a host of urgent needs. An effective outreach program or excellent community relations will not replace or obviate the need for continued efforts within the established library structure to deal with problems of the community. The problems facing us today mandate a wide assortment of creative programs and services. Community and outreach services are only two efforts among many, but they are two strategic ones if given the necessary support.

The role of the librarian in initiating long-range programs for better service to all the community and for better human relations is to become involved with the community. The librarian or librarians assigned or designated for community services must not only attend meetings, but must accept the responsibility of committee work and offices. The only way the librarian can thoroughly understand the workings of a group, its objectives, its needs, and how the library can play a viable role, is to get appointed to offices, committees, and particularly planning committees. This is an excellent means for promoting respect and good-will between the library and the community. Effective community work cannot be a reality unless the librarian involved attends meetings and actively participates; an occasionally attending figurehead serving as a passive auditor is not enough. When librarians carry their wares to the public which supports the library, positive reactions from these prospective borrowers do pay off.

The librarian rendering these community services must have the freedom and autonomy to function as situations and circumstances dictate. The librarian must have the full confidence and backing of the library director and the library board. All situations will not be pleasant ones; many community functions will be somewhat controversial, but the librarian accepting the responsibility to do the job must be prepared to face the unpleasantness as well as the pleasantness. The commitment must be to deal in truths, regardless of personal biases. The director must be as committed as the librarian in the field. Here, again, is the crucial question: is the total community responsibility left on the librarian in the field, or is it shared by other staff members and the director?

It is true that all librarians are not equipped with

that "certain something" that works successfully with outreach programs or community organizations. But all too often the "one librarian" is hired, given the opportunity to work in the field, and left totally alone at all times to sell the library and its services to the public at large. In larger communities, with larger library systems and branches, there are staff members, particularly on the executive level, who from time to time can serve some function with public appearances. In the smaller libraries, where there is less personnel to draw upon, there is a responsibility placed on the library director to participate in some fashion with these community services. It is a very valuable experience for the library director and the other staff members to mix and mingle with the citizenry, learn their likes, dislikes, concerns, and their needs. For the community service librarian who is also involved in book selection and purchases, the community experience provides excellent guidelines in making relevant and sound purchases of books, in adding new titles, making replacements, filling in gaps in the collection, and generally building a stronger collection which meets the needs of the community being served.

In taking the library outside its structured walls, in attempting to relate the library to the total community, are we overcoming the apathy and disinterest of the public? Another very serious question is, are we overcoming the apathy and disinterest of fellow librarians on the job? How many staff members are interested in new clientele which is attracted to the library? How many staff members are turned on to this type of outreach service? What is being done _inside_ the building to sustain the interest of new library users _once_ they are drawn in?

Nowhere more than in the area of effective community programming and outreach services, does this question seem more relevant: are our libraries proficiently administered, professionally staffed, and adequately programmed to accommodate the increased service demands of the regular user plus the demands of new clientele who have been "turned on and tuned in" and are seeking the services they have heard about in the community? The best collection of books, pamphlets, pictures, periodicals, and audio-visual aids will serve no useful purpose unless these services are handled by alert, well informed, and empathetic personnel. Professional librarians are too prone to think they are superior beings when dealing with segments of the population they are hired to serve, yet they play a condescending role with "hat-

Better Public Library Service 247

in-hand" when dealing with officials they elect to serve them. Our role is not one of giving the public services it should be grateful to receive, but to spell out what services we have that people are not using, and being prepared to function when they seek these services. These are changing times, times of unrest, growing racial polarization, times of extreme poverty in the midst of extreme wealth, times that question a future for our young people. The young and old, advantaged and disadvantaged, white and black are all facing these problems. The disadvantaged are only asking for a chance to live, to work out their own destiny in peace and decency. We must formulate new structures in accordance with the times.

If libraries are to continue playing the game, to put it bluntly, of selling themselves community-wise, and the game continues to achieve results, then libraries and librarians must face stepping up programs, increasing staff, and reassigning the more relevant, imaginative and innovative staff members to achieve continuity and justify the time, efforts, energy, and program hours expended by liaison community personnel in the field.

Our youth are displaying a heightened moral commitment and awareness that we professionals could well emulate in fomenting change. Librarians must free themselves of their limited, peripheral vision. We must descend from our ivory towers of literary endeavors and re-orient our thinking and our actions. Instead of being prepared just to handle the questions of the researcher, we must know how to provide the answers to the person who needs to know how to provide food, shelter, and medication to meet the needs of hungry and sick children. What information can we supply which will help in eradicating the shame of housing conditions and miseducation in the public schools? Libraries and librarians must grow and expand through senses and thoughts as well as through their perennial methods and procedures, in order to forge ahead and survive with the human race.

The heretofore unserved should not be expected to stand by quietly while the structured library system tells them what they need and should have. The established library system, for the most part, has accepted the challenge of giving people what they want, and has an obligation to produce when the first attempts are put into motion with outreach and community services. Unless the directors and staff are committed to playing a more direct role, put forth more concerted efforts to serve, and develop more positive attitudes, the librarians in the field should intrench, phase out this overwhelmingly demanding job and refuse to be the "instant figurehead" for the establishment which refuses to put its efforts in areas where it opens its mouth. If this is not done, only disaster can result from what could be and should be a most important challenging social service.

Are we fomenters of disastrous ventures, or are we for real, not token service to all?

FAREWELL TRADITIONALISM: A PERSPECTIVE
OF THE INNER CITY LIBRARY

by Robert B. Ford, Jr.

As a black male who has been a practicing librarian for ten years, I am naturally concerned about what happens in the inner city, especially as it relates to libraries and librarianship. In addition to being born and reared in a southern inner city, six years of my career was spent working in inner city public school libraries. I have observed deprived blacks who overcame practically impossible obstacles to achieve their educational goals and ambitions. At the other end of the spectrum, many students had already succumbed to their environment and had no desire or hope of ever rising above it. External motivation of disadvantaged students is extremely difficult. To expect them to develop an interest in books and libraries, in the light of all their other problems, really is quite presumptuous. However, we do exist in a society that cannot function properly without a literate citizenry and, if for no other reason, that explains the necessity for, and the raison d'être of, libraries. Libraries, like schools, should reflect the surrounding neighborhood, and therein lies the problem: often, libraries in the inner city are not responsive enough to their clientele. What must be done to make inner city libraries viable and vibrant institutions.

Before discussing the inner city library, it is necessary to examine the characteristics and problems of the black community that finds itself trapped in the inner city ghetto. The problems are many and as familiar as yesterday's newspaper headlines: high unemployment, little or no marketable skills, low level of educational achievement, substandard housing, inferior schools, alcoholic and narcotics addiction, etc. It is not my intention to depict only the seamy side of ghetto life. There are many ghetto residents who are law-abiding citizens valiantly trying to survive, despite the meager resources and circumstances. Some may feel that libraries are superfluous to poor people who must spend the majority of their time just obtaining the staples necessary for survival. Libraries, of course, are not superfluous, even for the ghetto resident, because all people, regardless of their economic status, need to read for informational and intellectual stimulation. But if they are not superfluous, libraries are underused, or don't realize their full potentialities--but that is another matter.

History demonstrates that all immigrant groups that migrated to America first lived in the inner city before moving on to a higher socio-economic level and the coveted life in suburbia. The key difference between blacks and other immigrant groups that managed to escape the ghetto is the high degree of visibility of blacks. There is simply no way for us to escape, in the words of a famous author, the "castle of our skin." The black community is as diverse and multi-faceted as any other in the U.S., ranging from the well-educated, middle-class professional to the sullen, inarticulate and poverty-stricken laborer. The former group, like the middle-class whites, have, for the most part, moved to the suburbs to escape the squalor of the ghetto. Although this essay is concerned with the latter group who cannot escape the misery of a hand-to-mouth existence, it is well to note that all blacks, regardless of their socio-economic level, must cope with the tyrannies of oppression, discrimination and racism in American society today.

New Directions in Service

Today's black community has been miraculously transformed as a result of the civil rights movement and the rhetoric of the black power slogan. We are no longer passively pleading for our rights from the white establishment. The phrases "black self-determinism" and "community control" (or more appropriately, community involvement) are concepts that point to the current status and future direction of the black community.

What role must the inner city library play in the emerging and new black community? First of all, the traditional pattern of library service will not suffice, for the most obvious reasons. Traditional libraries were created to serve the needs of a middle-class, white population. Most librarians who serve this clientele haven't needed to demonstrate or prove the effectiveness of the library as an institution. The inner city library must be the very anti-

thesis of the traditional library. It must "reach out" and
actively pursue its reluctant clients; it must take the library
to where the people are, regardless of how unorthodox that
may seem. In essence, it must be, literally, a "library
without walls."

The potentialities of giving the ghetto black the kind of
sensitive and responsive library service that he needs have
only recently been initiated. Much remains to be done.
With the emergence of "black awareness," there is now a
great demand for library materials on black history and
culture. The inner city library should take the initiative to
see that these materials are widely circulated throughout
the black community. Many black adults, who didn't finish
school, are now involved in furthering their education
through high school equivalency programs. A good opportunity exists for the inner city library to provide resources
and services to this courageous group of people. Adult
education, on a large scale, is one of the most important
avenues to equality for any group of disadvantaged people.
Through cooperation with other institutions, especially the
black church and social welfare agencies like the Y.M.C.A.,
bridges of understanding and concern can be built and the
forces of ignorance and anti-intellectualism challenged and
subdued. If its energies are properly channeled, the inner
city library has the opportunity to truly become "the university of the streets."

However, there are certain pitfalls that the inner
city library must avoid at all costs. It is my major contention, after ten years of working in them, that libraries,
as they are currently managed and operated, are "over-institutionalized." There is a great tendency to blindly follow and adhere to certain rules and regulations, regardless
of their obsolescence or unresponsiveness to the people
they serve. This is not to suggest that all rules and regulations should be rescinded. Inherently, as a librarian, I
believe in being systematic and greatly prefer organization
to chaos (as I am sure most good librarians do). Nevertheless, there is an over-regimentation, an impersonal coldness, a lack of concern and compassion to which all institutions, regardless of size, fall victim. Many librarians
reflect an over-institutionalized mentality and display an
inclination to take the path of least resistance; they function
mainly at the custodial or caretaker level rather than actively serving their patrons. The inner city library must
avoid this over-institutionalization and these caretaker

librarians. Failure to do so could well lead to the library's functions being absorbed by another institution.

Another pitfall lies in the major decisions being made by a central administration that is either unaware or unconcerned about the special needs of the inner city library. This "neo-colonialist" attitude on the part of some library administrators cannot and eventually will not be tolerated by the black community. There should be an advisory group of ghetto residents to provide input to the branch librarian about policy matters as they affect the operation of the library. This advisory group will have to be vocal and articulate in order to be an effective pressure group because most administrators interpret silence as consent.

Qualities of the Inner City Librarian

This now brings us to an issue of major concern: what qualities should the head librarian of an inner city library possess, especially since the library's success depends, in large measure, on the insight and vision of its manager? It would be dogmatic and presumptuous to insist that only a member of a minority group should manage the inner city library. Color and proper credentials alone will not make for success in the job. What is needed is a very special person who will bring the right degree of sensitivity, compassion and commitment to a very difficult task. A person who has never lived in a ghetto situation cannot truly understand the special problems of its residents. Sympathy and observation are helpful, but living in it on a daily basis is quite another thing. Working with disadvantaged people is a complex and emotionally-draining experience. However, when positive results and breakthroughs are achieved, the rewards in terms of personal satisfaction are immense and well worth waiting for. The director of an inner city library must be a tireless worker who can transcend the turmoil, tribulations, and frustrations to which most ordinary people succumb.

Many librarians are so print-oriented that they fail to explore or see the potential of audio-visual materials. Graphic and pictorial materials can significantly increase the impact of the inner city library, especially since many of its patrons are semi-literate. The film, videotape, cassette, or tape cartridge can be wonderful stimuli that will eventually lead to the printed page. This technique has proven successful for the ghetto school and can be used to great advantage in the inner city library.

Future Direction of the Inner City

What about the future of the inner city? The key to its salvation will ultimately rest with the emphasizing of human values over materialistic ones. Dr. Robert C. Weaver, former HUD secretary, in his book, The Urban Complex, noted that:

> it is in terms of people that urban problems must be conceived and their solutions developed ... emphasis is placed upon the buildings in the slums and little attention is paid to the people who inhabit them or to the reaction of the rest of the population to these people ... effective slum clearance and meaningful urban renewal must involve a new attitude toward low-income peoples who constitute the bulk of those now concentrated in slums ... without a coordinated program for human rehabilitation and re-examination of the human values of urban life, demolition of slums and rehabilitation of deteriorating areas will probably result in greater dispersal of blight.

Human values as they relate to the operation of institutions is what this essay is all about. The reader will note that the phrase "a new attitude toward low-income people" is underlined. This is important because many well-intentioned people go into the ghetto with a missionary attitude, unaware that they can also learn something of value from ghetto residents.

What can we black librarians do, either individually or collectively, to help make the inner city library the kind of institution of which we can be proud? We must be sincerely concerned about the quality of life in the ghetto and the quality of the institutions that serve it. We must speak out, individually and collectively, against forces that would exploit and denigrate ghetto residents. For better or worse, these are our people and our posterity. We must put our selfish interests in the background and see the larger goals and visions that will eventually extinguish the flame of oppression. That is why such recent developments as the emergence of local black caucuses, and the work of the Black

Caucus within the American Library Association and other similar professional groups, give us hope and promises much for the future.

The library in the inner city can be a viable and vibrant institution if it avoids over-regimentation and responds imaginatively, sensitively and innovatively to the informational and recreational needs of its residents. At its helm should be a librarian who, in the words of Sterling Tucker in his recent book, <u>For Blacks Only</u>, realizes:

> the necessity of working the system, of using for our own goals the levers it provides, the issues that are current and the temporary coalitions we can form with other groups within it.

Such are the political realities of life in the ghetto, and all institutions therein, including the library, must act accordingly.

PART VIII

Librarians as Perpetrators of Change

THE BLACK LIBRARIAN AS CHANGE AGENT

by Louise Giles

It was good to read The Black Librarian in America,[1] for two reasons. First, it was an effective reminder of how incredibly difficult it has been for blacks to enter the professions over the years. The situation, of course, is not apple-pie perfect now, but it is very easy to forget how bad things were before. Secondly, I could use The Black Librarian as an object lesson for my fifteen-year-old daughter, and for other scornful young blacks who seem to be skeptical of anyone over twenty-five. I could say to them, "This shows how blacks of the older generation paid their dues so that you young ones today can do your thing."

One might comment that The Black Librarian is repetitive, but it is that very trait that makes the book a more valid testimony of the black experience in America. The very fact that a number of black librarians from all over the country, unknown to each other, wrote original essays depicting their professional experiences, most of which turned out to be similar, is an impressive commentary on the ubiquitousness of institutional racism in this country. And the book included some eminent librarians who have made impressive contributions to the library field. Why should a book called The Black Librarian in America exist? Possibly because none of these black librarians have been included in books like The Librarian Speaking, Interviews With University Librarians[2] by Guy R. Lyle. Black librarians are no longer content to remain "invisible."

There were some courageous and determined and talented people in The Black Librarian. We can be proud of them. But older blacks already know these stories; it is whites who should read this book. Perhaps it would increase their understanding and thereby build some bridges where there no longer seem to be any.

We were lucky in many ways, we blacks who graduated from college in the early fifties. And we were starry-eyed. We thought we were going to form a corps of educated blacks who were (in our own genteel way) going to change the world. Unfortunately, our impact either wasn't felt fast enough or wasn't felt at all, and the next wave of black graduates emerging in the early sixties was determined to change the world, or tear it up. Of course, neither group succeeded. But both made gains. And the gains made by the later generation could not have been achieved if the way had not been paved by the earlier generation.

When I graduated from the University of Akron there had not been very many black professionals in the city, except for doctors and lawyers catering to a predominantly black clientele. Things were just beginning to open up for black professionals in Akron in the fifties. Then, graduating from Drexel Institute of Technology (now Drexel University) with a master's degree in Library Science a year later, I found that I was a member of a profession that was energetically recruiting members, regardless of race. I was able to make a selection from job offers in Philadelphia, New York, Chicago, Detroit, and Akron. Of course, there were virtually no blacks then in middle and top management positions in libraries but, then, there weren't many of us who had been around long enough to gain the necessary experience for these positions. What is indefensible is that this dearth of blacks in high administrative positions continued for so long. Things are much better now, but there is still much work to be done in assuring that qualified people get top jobs, regardless of race.

In a country that has pioneered as many technological and scientific advances as ours has, it is downright embarrassing that only in the late 1960's have the first black persons become members of the boards of directors of IBM and General Motors; or that the first black has been appointed president of a predominantly white university; or that the first black has been named director of a predominantly white university library; or that the first black has become the director of the public library system of a major U.S. city. Yes, the situation is improving considerably, but we cannot forget that those improvements are long overdue.

Even if opportunities have been improving for blacks in educational careers since the 1950's, there still have been restrictions which kept us from many other professions. And, worse yet, even today, blacks face discouraging and bitter opposition in attempting to enter the skilled and semi-skilled trades. The lag in progress in the skilled trades, in relation to the comparative amount of progress in educational careers, can be viewed as the result of a kind of "occupational blockbusting." That is, since educational careers opened up in the 1950's, the bulk of blacks flooded into those careers, taking the easiest entrance into the professions when, probably, what we should have been doing is concentrating on gaining entry into as wide a variety of occupations as possible.

The foregoing comments, however, are hindsight. Whatever the solution to that old problem, new ones now present themselves for our consideration.

If library school graduates of the fifties and sixties could select from several job offers, the situation is almost the exact opposite today. The job outlook is bleak for those entering the profession. Not only librarians, but teachers, scientists and many other professional people are affected by this employment situation.

In addition to the tight job market, other ills now plague the library profession. The "knowledge explosion," which began by crowding the market with printed materials, has fast turned into the "media explosion," which has converted information into all kinds of new and unfamiliar non-print formats. Worse still, as the cost of both the print and nonprint materials are rising, the financial resources available to the nation's libraries are shrinking.

And the emergence of the tight money market has caused governments and institutions to revise their budgetary priorities. As usual, when money is scarce and people start looking around for "unessential" services to pare, libraries are the first to feel it. To judge from the newspapers and the journals, several large, public library systems in the country are on the verge of folding; certainly, crucial reductions of budgets, resources, and personnel have been effected. Likewise, schools and colleges that feel the money pinch have started to economize by reducing their libraries' budgets and staffs.

On top of it all, the winds of revolution (racial, social, and moral), which have been buffeting society for the last few years, have finally begun to be felt in the library profession. In our professional meetings and

Librarians as Perpetrators of Change

journals the previously unrepresented elements have begun to speak out, thus shaking some of us out of our heretofore staid and comfortable middle-class isolation.

Yet, in spite of all of the changes and challenges that face our profession, there are still those librarians who persist in clinging to tradition. There are still those librarians who persist in thinking that their primary duty is amassing and preserving a collection of books and printed materials. In the face of economic and other crises, there are still those librarians who seem convinced that their main problems are lagging circulation and public apathy; that if only they could just go out and beat the bushes and urge people to come in and read more books, these problems would simply fade away. Like an outdated book, these librarians have been left up on the shelf too long.

It could be that some of those librarians don't even know that they are on the shelf. For twelve years, I worked in various positions in the Detroit Public Library system. I was interested in my work. I worked hard. And I learned a lot, but eventually I got into a rut. I realized this only subconsciously because my hands were always very full and I always stayed as busy as I could; so I didn't have too much time to think about the fact that I was just going through the motions of being a librarian and that I had really been running along on a mental plateau for years.

But this subconscious feeling of being in a rut led me to keep making various attempts to get more challenging assignments. These attempts, however, were mostly failures--mainly because I naively believed at that time (and I'm still rather fond of the idea) that honesty is the best policy, and I persisted in speaking and writing exactly what was on my mind. I have changed only slightly: I'm a little older.

The point I wish to make is that, without realizing it, I was bored with my work and my attempts at getting into something more interesting only got me into hot water. But, don't get me wrong: the Detroit Public Library is a fine system, with the potential to be even finer, and I am proud and appreciative of my years there. I admit, ruefully, that a good part of my eventual frustration there was due to my own lack of, shall we say, sophistication?

However, all of that changed abruptly at the ALA convention of 1965. I was attending one of those crowded publishers' cocktail parties, and an old friend walked up to me and said, "Are you happy in your job?" Without even thinking about it, I said, "Hell, no!" It was the first time I had admitted it to myself. Because he'd always known me as a very gung-ho DPL'er, he was surprised--but, then, so was I. Thereupon, he invited me to apply for a position which involved setting up and supervising a campus Learning Resource Center at Oakland Community College in Union Lake, Michigan, about 30 miles outside of Detroit. I am proud to have been a charter member of the staff of OCC; I started to work there on September 1, 1965. That was also the day the college opened. And that was the day that I learned--not so very subconsciously--that I really had been in a rut. Much of the planning and ordering had been done by others in the months before the college opened and so my task was to find out where they had left off and complete the job, which was not nearly as simply as it sounds.

Oakland Community College was an innovative, multi-campus institution which utilized the "systems approach" in instruction throughout the curriculum. The systems approach had been adapted from Dr. Sam Postlethwaite's "audio-tutorial" method and, rather than the traditional three-meetings-a-week lecture, most courses featured a once-a-week General Assembly Session and students were free the rest of the time to do their work in a variety of learning laboratories, which were equipped with wet carrels and a multitude of media. It was the Learning Resource Center's role to manage all of this media and to provide satellite libraries for all of the learning laboratories on campus.

In 1965, OCC opened two campuses: Highland Lakes in Union Lake and Auburn Heights in Auburn Hills. The Central Administrative offices were moved from Union Lake to Bloomfield Hills in 1966 and the third campus, Orchard Ridge, was opened up in Farmington in 1967. OCC grew fast and became, in only a couple of years, one of the three largest community colleges in Michigan.

In the Detroit Public Library, when someone said "audiovisual" we would think "16mm film"; the word didn't conjure up many other images. Picture me, now, in an instant Community College whose whole concept was built around an instructional mode called "the systems approach."

Librarians as Perpetrators of Change

Picture me in this college where, in order to implement the systems approach, the faculty had to utilize practically all of the media and equipment available on the market. Picture me being responsible for coordinating the selection, ordering and processing, utilization and maintenance of all of this media and equipment when, prior to September 1, 1965, I had not even heard of most of it!

My first impulse was to turn tail and run, but I've never been much of a quitter, so I determined to master the situation and then decide whether or not to abandon ship. Perhaps I didn't master the situation, but I feel I must have successfully assimilated into it because, since 1965, I have participated in the establishment and administration of three community college library/learning resource centers and, each time, I think I have been able to function a little more effectively.

My "initiation" at Oakland Community College was often painful, because I had to stretch my mind to its utmost: I had to create procedures and systems to implement and facilitate practices that I had not known of before; I had to make decisions, many of them financial, regarding situations that were new and unfamiliar. It was at times painful but it was a beautiful experience because, that year, I started to grow again--I learned something new every day. I learned about library materials that I never knew existed, about a dimension of library service that I never knew existed. I developed a wider and more flexible philosophy of librarianship. And, formerly a gentle, lady-like, proper librarian, I learned to "make it" in the hard world of educational politics. Most importantly, I began to re-evaluate my role as a librarian and as a person. I shall be eternally grateful to the friend who came up to me at that cocktail party and "made me a better offer." Today, I am still learning and growing and developing.

John Gardner was right: self-renewal is vital--not only for individuals, but for groups also. Perhaps this is the time for librarians, collectively, to re-examine the role of the profession. Self-renewal at this time within the library field could mean self-preservation. For, I submit that librarians have not done anything to make themselves indispensable to society. Forward-thinking librarians should have been and should now be revising the role of the library in society. We should be revising our objectives and adjusting them to fit the needs of the contemporary world.

Paul Wasserman and Mary Lee Bundy put it very aptly in
<u>Reader in Library Administration:</u>

> The administration of libraries now and in the
> decade ahead will be conducted amidst pressures
> and stresses unparalleled in library history. The
> stakes are high: the issue is whether the conven-
> tional library will perpetuate itself at the center
> or on the fringes of the culture's information
> activity.[3]

Furthermore, forward-thinking black librarians, who are now aggressively seeking to make library services more adequate to the needs of black people and the library profession more responsive to the talents of black librarians, can take note: if society finds the library profession irrelevant, even obsolete, for its needs, what advantage will it be for blacks to have found a place in a dying profession? In other words, it seems obvious that black librarians should be almost as concerned about the long-range survival of the profession as they are about correcting contemporary inequities. In a time of tight jobs and tight money such as the present, we should be pragmatically adjusting our short and long range goals so that our contribution is linked inseparably and symbiotically with those of some other very vital elements of society.

Certainly, effective education of the masses continues to be one of the most vital concerns of present day society. The schools simply have not come up with any generalized solutions; they can use all the help they can get from any source. Isolated schools in isolated situations have made some breakthroughs, but no large educational systems have implemented any methods or materials to improve effectively the education of the mass of students. And, since most of the country's largest cities now have a school enrollment that is predominantly black and, as Nadine Brown says, "Far too many Black kids are coming out of school with little or no education ... Too many are just trying to get by on their Blackness,"[4] it would seem that improvement of education would be a particularly black concern. Black leaders on all levels should feel compelled to push for innovation and/or revolution in education. It would seem that we should all be demanding the best education possible--even the best compensatory education possible (or perhaps, <u>especially</u> the best compensatory education) at a time when the best and newest methods and materials are available. Since librarians too, are leaders, we have an opportunity--no, a duty--to exercise our leadership here.

Item: I read recently of the establishment of a Community Learning Center in Detroit. Supported by Model Neighborhood funds, the aim of the Center is "to help all participants develop their basic skills through a unique and unusual approach to learning, which would be based upon the abandonment of traditional educational techniques: classrooms, textbooks, teachers, etc."[5] The Center has no teachers, but utilizes learning "triads," which are teams composed of one specialist and two resource assistants. The specialists are residents of the community and former teachers who came from schools "where they were turned off by the system."[6] The Center is open to anyone who lives in that Model Neighborhood, and is including "students who are having a difficult time in public school."[7] I was very pleased to learn of the existence of a center like this, but I couldn't help but think: somebody failed. Someone didn't meet the felt educational needs of the residents of this community. Was it the public library? The public school? Or, both?

If a library is a center of learning, as we often claim it is, why haven't we shown more concern about keeping up with the materials of learning? Librarians too often disown involvement with certain learning materials, announcing that those are the responsibility of the "audiovisual man" or the "media man." Librarians must realize before it is too late that knowledge is knowledge, in whatever format it is found, and that films, filmstrips, slides, videotapes, dial access retrieval systems, computer-assisted instruction, etc. are only additional ways of presenting the ideas and information that we used to find only in printed materials. In addition to acknowledging the existence of the new media (an essential first step), we must finally assume the responsibility for selecting and handling the new media and for cataloging it so that it will be as available and accessible as the printed materials.

William Moore, Jr., a fearless, black leader in the community college field, says: "It is not the rhetoric and villanies of war, poverty, crime, drugs, violence, racism, and their harvest of backlash, law and order, and repression; it is not the report that God is dead, the suppression of academic freedom, or even truth that educators fear. It is change."[8] The need for change is universal in the library world, but how do we achieve it? The role of change agent knows no color bounds and is open to anyone who has the courage to seize it. Anyone, of course, can be a change agent, but, for the purposes of this particular essay, I address myself to black librarians. I'd like to suggest, in fact, that the black librarian could possibly emerge as a natural leader in any movement for change, because, by and large, he doesn't have a vested interest in preserving the status quo. If I were in a position to counsel a person who was about to take on the mission of change agent, I would recommend that he consider the following things:

1. <u>The Newer Media</u>. Don't shirk your responsibility toward it; don't avoid it; don't hide from it. Learn to master it to <u>your</u> best advantage (before it masters you). What about computerized operations in your library: circulation systems; ordering; book catalogs; technical processing; information retrieval? Do you have access or potential access to any of these? And, if they are considering cable television in your locality, is your library considering the feasibility of becoming involved in this system? Better to consider it and turn it down for your own reasons than to be completely ignorant of its potential.

Microforms and miniaturization processes? We must continually seek ways of solving the space problems presented by an ever-increasing volume of printed materials. We must keep an eye on developments in the area of microforms and related apparatus--they could eventually be the solution to our space problems.

And, how do you treat your media? Other than books, that is. Do you have all nonprint materials in some separate but unequal classification? Or, have you attempted to use the same basic principles of selection and arrangement of nonprint materials as you use with print materials, resulting in equal accessibility of <u>all</u> media?

2. <u>The Library as Educator</u>. Consider the library, even the public library (especially the abandoned, inner-city public library), as a potential learning center. Could the library provide tutorial facilities and services? Could it provide a Reading Improvement Program? What about serving as a study center for preparing for GED and/or CLEP tests? That's not "your responsibility"? Well, it sure beats supervising collections of books sitting on the

shelves of empty libraries, and it beats closing down libraries for lack of use.

3. <u>The Library as a Community Facility.</u> Consider the library, even the college library, as a community center. Is there an auditorium or are there meeting rooms? Is your library a well-used center of community activity? Are your librarians well known as a resource to community groups? One large public library allows the local community college to hold classes in rooms in some of its branches. The same public library allows the community college to stock and equip some of its branches to serve as community college libraries, too.

4. <u>Interlibrary Cooperation.</u> At least be familiar with any network systems that exist in your vicinity. Consider the possibility of your library being included in the system. What about sharing facilities with another institution? What about state library extension services--do you make them available to your clientele? What about regional processing systems? What about computer networks?

5. <u>The Role of the Professional.</u> Be willing to revise your concept of professional duties. Aren't some of us really paying professionals some awfully high salaries and bogging them down with numerous insignificant, "picky," little duties? Consider what a paraprofessional could do in your library. What about a Library Technician? An Audiovisual Technician? Or, even a Teacher aide? Don't tell me a person has to have a master's degree in Library Science in order to perform some of those little jobs I see them performing! Furthermore, with budget reductions looming and new staff positions getting harder to justify and unions getting more militant, another chief concern of the library administrator has got to be productivity. How to get more work out of fewer bodies at a lesser cost! Growing libraries are going to be forced to stop trying to solve their problems by just adding librarians to the staff. Certainly, we can find more innovative ways to man our libraries successfully.

6. <u>The Funding of Libraries.</u> The schools are in the process of seeking more stable methods of funding public education. Libraries, too, had better join this search. With libraries all over the country in dire financial troubles, it should go without saying that we need to become involved

in some short and long-range planning to find better methods of funding for libraries. Without it, talk of planning more "relevant" or more "responsive" or more "innovative" libraries is to no avail. Libraries cost money to operate and maintain. We can trim the amount of money by adjustments in the utilization of personnel, elimination of duplication of resources, and by many other means. But the basic operating cost of any library unit is substantial in itself and reductions in budgets usually result inevitably in reductions of services.

It is, of course, not easy to be a change agent. As Robert M. Hutchins says of administrators, "The strain on the character is very great. The administrator who is afraid of anybody or anything is lost. The administrator who cannot stand criticism, including slander and libel, is lost."[9] The same comments would apply to change agents. But, after reading The Black Librarian in America, I am convinced that we have both the talent and the courage.

Notes

1. Josey, E. J. The Black Librarian in America. Metuchen, N.J.: Scarecrow Press, 1970.

2. Lyle, Guy R. The Librarian Speaking; Interviews With University Librarians. Athens: University of Georgia Press, 1970.

3. Wasserman, Paul and Bundy, Mary Lee. Reader in Library Administration. Washington, D.C.: National Cash Register Company, Microcard Editions, 1968. p. 322.

4. Brown, Nadine. "People, Places, and Situations," Michigan Chronicle. Vol. 36, No. 38 (Section D, p. 1), January 1, 1972.

5. Burtney, Arnold. "Learning Center Has Alternative Approach to Learning Process," Michigan Chronicle. Vol. 36, No. 38 (Section A, p. 6), January 1, 1972.

6. Ibid.

7. Ibid.

8. Moore, William, Jr. Blind Man on a Freeway. San Francisco: Jossey-Bass, 1971, p. 1. (Excerpt from a speech; University of Washington, February 13, 1970).

9. Wasserman, p. 328.

SPECIAL LIBRARIES, LIBRARIANS AND THE CONTINUING EDUCATION OF BLACK PEOPLE

by Vivian D. Hewitt

Let me say that I'm a great believer in axioms and adages. One for every occasion. To fit the occasion of putting together a chapter for this book, there is this one: "Everything's been said before." So, if what I say has a familiar ring, you've probably heard it before. Perhaps expressed in more erudite terms than I shall write but, nevertheless, important enough, I think, to bear repeating. So here goes.

There is a general impression that when a librarian isn't issuing books he or she is reading the latest novel. Let me assure you that is not so. An efficient library demands a great amount of hard work on the part of those who run it, and it is work which is never finished, because the field itself is almost unlimited. There is always something which cries out to be done.

Time was when the word "librarian" evoked in everyone's thoughts a middle-aged spinster, hair in a bun at the nape of her neck, walking silently on sensible shoes while peering at a book through thick lenses. Or, if a man, a wizened, bespeckled Casper Milquetoast, fumbling about the stacks or "shushing" people if they dared raise a voice above a whisper. Not so these days. Librarians have shelved their old image and stepped out of their ivory towers into the throbbing, real world. The old-time conception of the librarian as a person who guarded books has long been superseded by the conception that his principal business is to get them used.

One of the duties, and also one of the privileges of a librarian is to help readers. Librarians have other duties, by the way. To be a librarian today is to be a social worker, an "Ann Landers," a public relations specialists, a fund-raiser, not to mention the teacher-writer-reference-bibliographer-lecturer bit. Librarians have been creatively working with people using their imaginations, inside of and beyond library walls, in giving service. Such words as commitment, dedication, social responsibility--words that many librarians have always portrayed in their lives--are accepted, and activities in these areas are encouraged.

Libraries have traditionally considered the needs of "special interest" groups in planning the types of service rendered, and the groups serviced have usually been defined in terms of user demand. Public libraries assist business, children, young adults, students, scholars, housewives, the man in the street. The academic library gears itself toward faculty and student needs. The special library, the kind with which I am most familiar, sets up special collections and maintains materials to service a specific clientele. Most provide some form of current awareness service and all are distinguished to the degree and extent of the really personalized service given to their users. This aspect of special libraries is so important that other kinds of libraries are beginning to move in the same direction; that is, they are giving more service and relying less on patron self-service.

Wide sweeping changes in education--in methods and in the vast numbers seeking education--have direct implications for the library. Now, as never before, many groups in American society are searching for identity, not only on an ethnic and racial level but on a class and cultural level as well.

A term we are beginning to hear more frequently these days in library and education circles is University Without Walls (UWW). Its main thrust is geared to providing education for the disadvantaged and undereducated who would not likely to be in college except for the flexible and innovative program offered by UWW. Either because of financial lack, the formidable challenges of the typical degree program, or an aversion to the "irrelevance" of traditional campus offerings, those drawn to the UWW concept of continuing education did not enroll in college after graduating from high school. Many who have had dreams they've lived with for many years can now fulfill them under the UWW plan. A new development, UWW programs are only participated in by about 20 academic institutions nationwide. UWW strives for flexibility in education, a less rigid curriculum, individual pacing in studies, and use of the community as a resource.

A special library of today, however broadly or narrowly defined, has the opportunity, indeed the duty, to assist wherever it can in the educative process. For anyone is disadvantaged, be he black, white, red or yellow, young, middle-aged or old, if he does not draw on libraries to sustain his life.

Today's turmoil and unrest will not permit those of us who are in special libraries to remain aloof from the poor, the powerless, the under-educated, or the under-utilized on our doorstep. It is necessary and important for librarians to Respond to a Restive World (theme of the 1970 ALA Convention, Dallas, Texas). Several special libraries I know of are involved in and financing (in many cases) and, therefore, in the broadest sense, contributing to the University Without Walls concept.

In New York, a major weekly publication has had in operation a program which allows its employees to take adult education courses in any subject and the company pays most of the fee. As a result, employees of various educational levels can grow in the knowledge and enjoyment of a field of their interest. In a communication-oriented library, such as the one I mention, there are vast holdings in the general reference area plus many specialized materials, so the employee user can find assistance for the courses he is taking.

A burgeoning and sincerely motivated social awareness has also manifested itself in some excellent on-the-job educational programs. These projects are usually government-business ventures. One such experiment tried locally in an advertising agency is called JOBS (Job Opportunities in the Business Sector). This is a joint government-business program in which hard-core unemployed are given a chance to continue their education while working, with private industry and government splitting the tab. At the agency about which I speak, a JOBS class of ten black and Puerto Rican students, ranging from 19 to 43 years of age, are taught the five basics: math, science, social studies, grammar, and literature--subjects they need in order to pass the State's high school equivalency test. They work in various departments of the agency and are paid a basic salary. Part of the day, they attend school, taking the subjects described above. As a result they have gained diplomas and good jobs. Their special library has contributed to the program in providing data and document sources. The teachers are specialists, and are not inclined to need much. But the students have found the library and its librarian extremely helpful. Two of the students have been employed in the library, and are considered a fine addition. Another advantage for the class is constant access to use of the library. A concern of libraries everywhere today is to take unskilled students and turn them into patrons who can use the library effectively.

To open a door into the world of thought and intellectual pleasure--and when you open a library you open such a door--is always a significant event. I think now of three special librarians I know, deeply interested persons who have helped to motivate and train a number of young people in their companies, and others, too, through a directed reading program. These librarians have discovered, in some instances, hidden talents, and have then proceeded to motivate and guide young people toward what they could best be. How lucky these youngsters were to receive such help from librarians who cared enough about them!

Several major banks have initiated training programs for high school graduates, often with emphasis on the disadvantaged groups, which utilize an on-the-job training approach. Their libraries are contributing to the training and educative process by helping familiarize the participants thoroughly with subject fields such as banking, finance and related areas.

A few special libraries known for superb collections are now increasingly involved in letting their facilities be used (usually by word of mouth) to serve a newly educated class or better still, a group that wants to learn and is continually learning--a "want to be educated" class (no age limit here): the small-businessman (often minority enterprises), the middle-aged reader who has gone back to school after many years to catch up on the learning denied him during the Depression, the older, often retired reader with leisure time, and the young social iconoclast who wants to "homestead" or begin his own craft business. All of these people are components of the University Without Walls--not degree seeking in a formal sense but seeking knowledge for their own individual enrichment and eventual contributions toward solving social problems of their country. All have been helped by librarians, some of whom it is my privilege to know.

From the examples I have given, I think it can be concluded that the University Without Walls is an increasing force in American education and that the library, whatever its categorization, but certainly including the special library, will be called upon more and more to participate actively in this welcome revolution.

In all the examples of special libraries and special librarians I have mentioned as contributing to the UWW concept, most of those helped were of a minority group, usually black. All the librarians, without exception, were white. Nothing wrong with that. In each instance, while librarians have extended themselves above and beyond the call of duty to give a helping hand to nudge, push, shove or direct these young minority people to greater heights than they ever imagined they could attain. And they did so without condescension. They helped because they wanted to be <u>involved</u>. In my mind's eye, each of these librarians will always be one of those superior color-blind human beings, who know, even as you and I, that the key words here are to <u>act</u> and to <u>help</u>--particularly <u>help</u>, one of the few things in this world that multiplies the more you use it.

What depresses me, though, is that there are still so few black model images in the field, especially in an area so large as Metropolitan New York with its more than 1500 special libraries of one kind or another.

Is it any wonder, then, that I am one of that number of so-called "got-it-made" librarians who believes that we blacks are really not much better off than we were, say, 25 years ago when I began my career. As far as I'm concerned it's the French proverb: "Plus ça change, plus c'est la même chose." Or, in English: "The more it changes, the more it remains the same."

Undeniably there has been progress. It's hard to miss the "first" black face and often "only" in areas which used to be all-white (library Trustee Boards, Museum, Corporation and Foundation Boards), and in the field, department heads, Library Director, Library Professor, Company Librarian, and so forth. I still cringe, after all these years, as I did so long ago, each time I read or hear the phrase, "The First Black," still used in this presumably enlightened decade of the 20th Century.

The record of Special Libraries Association, itself,

as far as I know, is unblemished. At the highest level of authority, its policy against bias and discrimination is crystal clear.

The absence of more black faces in the Association and, therefore, from libraries whose members are its constituents, is as troubling to many white colleagues as it is to me. In an issue of Special Libraries this year, one librarian wrote movingly on the subject of involvement, suggesting some positive steps that could be taken on minority recruitment and minority employment. I commend to your attention the full text of Robert S. Meyer's article, "Light Your Fire."

When a colleague called me a few weeks ago to fill a fairly senior level position in her library, it was her expressed wish to hire a minority person. At the time, each librarian of color whom I called was already satisfactorily placed in a position of importance and did not wish to move. That is why I believe that each of us can never stop seeking out any interesting likely candidates for the profession.

The article by Meyer and the phone call to me are but two answers to the question, "But what can one person do?" "Beaucoup!" has always been my retort. Badger ... with advice, letters, memos, phone calls. Join a committee. Write articles. Give lectures. Spread the word. Sponsor a library school candidate. Help a student. Direct a career. Recruit minorities. Maybe, in spite of all my misgivings, things will change, if each of us is diligent about equality of opportunity in our particular sphere of influence. I, for one, am glad that there is now a Black Librarians Caucus in this metropolitan community. Had it been in existence at the time I received that call from my colleague, it would have been an obvious and excellent source to turn to for recommendations for a qualified librarian. You see, I am essentially an optimist. Optimism is good.

Notes

1. "Black Librarians Aid Blacks on All Levels," Amsterdam News, Oct. 2, 1971, p. D-4.

2. "University Without Walls Reopens Educational Doors," Christian Science Monitor, July 17, 1971, p. 7.

3. Meyer, Robert S. "Light Your Fire! Operation Involvement: Librarians and Social Issues," Special Libraries, 62(No. 2), Feb. 1971, pp. 100-102.

4. "The Role of Libraries as Information Centers for Persons Pursuing Higher Education in the University Without Walls and the External Degree Programs." A Panel Discussion, The Special Library. Excerpts from unpublished manuscript read by the author at the Fifth Annual Congress of Trustees of the Reference and Research Library Resources Systems, Fordham University, Lincoln Center, New York City, May 14, 1971.

A BLACK LIBRARIAN'S CHALLENGE
TO THE PUBLISHING WORLD

by Bessie R. Grayson

> The men and women who have sustained freedom
> of expression and genuine creation among these
> ramparts ... deserve the gratitude of the world.
> The world will have need of what they have here
> established: genuine creative literature as interpretation of life; boldness in maintaining an open,
> straightforward approach to the minds of children;
> faith in the response of the children themselves
> to honesty, dignity and the demands of the emotional experience which reading as an art exacts
> of its disciples; genuine sharing of all that fires
> the imagination through beauty in pictures and design, nor have humor and the need for laughter
> been forgotten.
>
> These are the forces from which new life shall
> come.
> --Frances Clarke Sayers,
> "Of Memory and Muchness,"
> The Horn Book Magazine, May, 1944.

The publishers, because of their close connection with libraries and/or media centers, set the limits within which librarians and/or media specialists and educators must work. Librarians cannot select media (print and non-print) which has not been published; therefore, the willingness--or lack of it--on the part of publishers to risk producing materials will determine what libraries find available to choose from. Libraries will find a full representation of subjects and a wide range of treatments of subjects only if publishers do not limit the media market.

They must accept the challenge of providing multimedia materials that will serve as supportive data for the school curriculum irrespective of the academic level of the students, be they affluent or below the poverty level. The need for a quality education is immediate, especially for the disadvantaged youth of whatever race, color, or creed in our society. Every youth who is a citizen of the United States of America deserves an opportunity to find, in print and/or non-print form, his identity and history. Up to this point in time, minorities, especially black youth, have not been accorded this privilege. These youth represent a large portion of the silent minorities (Indians, Puerto Ricans, migrant workers, and a larger segment of whites than is realized by the American public). They are faced with the perplexing problem of struggling with curricula designed for their more affluent counterparts. A replacement of irrelevant instructional materials is most necessary if "quality education" is the real goal of educators. Observation of education today reveals the need for materials of the highest quality. This is the task of the publishing world.

The key to life is communication. From antiquity to the present, man has made efforts to assimilate and disseminate knowledge. During the early period of civilization, information was passed from one generation to another by word of mouth. The distribution and preservation of knowledge evolved through several stages during which man used a variety of methods and materials such as the quipus, wampum, knotted stick, and carving on stone and bone. The Chinese people invented paper and the people of India invented ink, and it became possible to keep records more easily. However, the most dramatic of all the inventions in the area of preserving knowledge was the invention of the printing press.

Sargent Shriver, Special Assistant to former President Lyndon B. Johnson, painted a very vivid picture in 1964 of the educational desires of the minorities in our country in his "Message to American Librarians":

> It is commonly believed that the poor, coming out of deprived backgrounds with little culture and learning, are not motivated toward books or learning. This is a myth which you can help to overcome. The poor want to learn, to enjoy and to benefit from the fruits of learning.
>
> A library which does not attract new users becomes merely a symbol of the status quo. You must reach out to the under-educated and give them the kind of help that they need and can use. We have the tools to do this job through new library

techniques and reading methods. It is to you that the educators of this country must turn for these tools in their preschool and school programs and the adult illiteracy program.

American libraries have a key role to play in the war against poverty.[1]

This challenge cannot be taken up by librarians unless publishers accept the responsibility of producing materials that are above reproach in quality and in quantity--materials which reveal the history of mankind as it was, is, and should be, in all forms of media.

One needs only to recall a profile of the literature of early America to get a glimpse of the image which was portrayed in media (print and non-print) of the minorities (especially black Americans). The belligerent omission of the history of a people whose labor helped build America as the "leader" among the nations of the world has caused a crisis in our society which is reflected in our total existence. This problem can only be solved if educators, including librarians, insist that the publishing agencies produce materials that avoid and help to eradicate the stereotypes of the past. The damage done by these stereotyped presentations in books of the past is explained in an article by Dharathula H. Millender, written while she was on a sabbatical leave to study educational media at Purdue University:

> For centuries, literature has been valued for introducing readers to each other. Books describe the physical appearance of other people, explaining customs, modes, and ways of living, and illustrate graphically how others are supposed to look, live, and seem to be.
>
> Tragically, however, books have often planted false images in the minds of readers. Certainly, much is being said today about the damage the early books about Negro life for children have done to foster misunderstanding between the races. With little or no contact between the races in the early 1900's, books were the only medium of introduction. Yet, they often explained customs and modes and ways of living not as they normally were, and too often showed grotesque stereotypes in illustrations portrayed as 'true' representations, but not

genuine. They introduced readers to people, but not real people or normal situations. Unfortunately, authors seldom knew the subject about which they wrote, and those who did know, were seldom allowed to make the introductions. The result was irreparable damage. [2]

Publishers of the past, like authors, had little or no contact with Negroes and knew very little about their way of life. Apparently, they desired materials (stories) that reflected the majority thought patterns of the day. The news media of the period probably played a major role in shaping the opinion of the public and, undoubtedly, they had an impact on the publishing world. In the opinion of Carrie C. Robinsin,

> The role of the Negro in American history, and in the history of other cultures, has been most neglected, misrepresented, and least understood. [3]

Stereotypes continue today in many materials which are still used despite the pleas of educators and librarians to discard those which do not present a true and undiluted picture of the whole society, both past and present.

In the first article of a series dealing with minority publishing, Bradford Chambers, Chairman of the Council on Interracial Books for Children, charges that:

> The book publishing industry has been the least responsive of all the communication media in recruiting minority personnel. In a book world exclusively controlled by the white middle class, can books on minority themes be ethnically 'honest'?
>
> It wasn't long ago that minorities were invisible in books, particularly in books for children. This is changing. A basic problem is that, with increased visibility, conscious and unconscious racism is also coming to the surface, especially commercially-oriented books which exploit the new market represented by minority themes. A superficial analysis might suggest that, in the rush for profits from the so-called minority market, insufficient care is taken in the editorial supervision of the books. That is part of the answer, but a small part only. Books produced with elaborate

editorial care can be just as guilty of racial bias as books that are handled with little editorial care.4

In an effort to present the real history of Black America, an increasing number of black publishing houses are being established throughout the country. Black publishing is a growing industry, but economic forces keep the growth rate slow. There is real need for their white-controlled counterparts to share in this venture by providing money and expertise which they have gained through long years of prosperity. Oswald White has this to say in regard to black publishers of our time:

> Black publishers are in the unique position of being part of both the larger white society and the subculture that is Black America--being educated in the predominantly white universities, living and working among members of the dominant white culture to a degree. But, our frame of reference remains the rich, pulsating, vibrant and exotic-- part English, mostly African black culture. We are, thus, doubly gifted and peculiarly suited to fulfill our role as molders of attitudes and opinions, like referees between two contenders.5

According to Loren B. Katz:

> The restoration of the Negro to his rightful place in history will do much to balance the story of our national development. Although it will serve the cause of justice, it will more importantly serve the cause of truth ... a better understanding of the Negro will provide a greater opportunity to solve our national problems. The march toward truth will bring us closer to the 'Great Society.'6

This statement emphasizes the great need for the publishing world to do its part in the restoration of the history of black America. Print and non-print media are needed which provide opportunities for educators to integrate the black man's contributions into the school curriculum as a whole.

What are the criteria for evaluating materials by and about minorities? Azile Wofford points to the following as basic in evaluating all materials: authority, scope, reliability, treatment, readability, subject interest, special features, and potential use.[7] More specific criteria for the evaluation of materials by and about minorities across the ages, however, have mushroomed in recent years as minorities have pressed to become first-class citizens. "Criteria for the Selection of Textbooks," which appeared as a part of the resolutions adopted by the National NEA-PR&P Conference on Civil and Human Rights in Education, puts the matter in capsule form:

> In developing any criteria for the selection of textbooks, we must consider the audience to whom the material is addressed. Textbooks selected should include all minorities--we list racial, ethnic, religious. Any criteria must be applied in all curricular and content areas.
>
> To establish more specific criteria, we offer a series of questions:
>
> 1. Does the author develop the role of minority groups in a scholarly, factual way?
>
> 2. Does the text meet the basic philosophy of our democratic society, particularly as it relates to civil rights?
>
> 3. Does the text demonstrate consideration for human relationships and respect for the dignity of all?
>
> 4. Does the text depict and illustrate adequately the multi-ethnic character of the United States?
>
> 5. Are stereotypes--racial, ethnic, and religious--avoided?
>
> 6. Is the approach to the subject matter realistic? Are materials about minorities chosen for their relevance? Are they woven into the fabric of the book or included as inserted afterthoughts?
>
> 7. Is the text non-sectarian?
>
> 8. Does the text include the unique contribu-

tions of various minority groups or does it just present general categorical descriptions of these groups?

Selection committees should be representative of all professional, educational personnel; if there are advisory committees, these should also have representatives of the ethnic or other minority groups in the community. 8

Since evaluating literature is one of the chief responsibilities of publishers, they must understand that authors write to achieve a purpose; recognize that different criteria apply to different types of literature; that details are selected to contribute to effect; that form contributes to effect; and that theme, plot, characterization, and style all contribute to a unified whole. 9

The world of tomorrow is shaped as a child reads, views, listens, and learns. Cooperative communication among those whose responsibilities include education, publishing, and coordinating community affairs will make it possible for our society to recite with meaning the following statement:

Today marks not the conclusion of our concern, but the beginning of a new impetus and direction in the channeling of our own energies to promote more equal educational opportunity through the clear recognition of all people who have made America great. 10

As we look toward the twenty-first century, society is still calling upon the publishing world to produce multiethnic materials (print and non-print) which will make it impossible for minorities (especially blacks) to continue to view themselves as invisible people in America. No longer should black Americans see themselves in these words of Ralph Ellison's:

I am an invisible man ... I am a man of substance, of flesh and bone fiber and liquids ... and I might even be said to possess a mind. I am invisible, understand, simply because people refuse to see me. 11

Notes

1. Shriver, Sargent, "A Message to American Librarians," Wilson Library Bulletin, 38:833, June, 1964.

2. Millender, Dharathula H., "Through a Glass, Darkly," Library Journal, 92:4571, December 15, 1967.

3. Robinson, Carrie C., "Negro History Week, February 9-15, 1969," Reprinted from School Library Journal, February, 1968, R. R. Bowker Company, 1968.

4. Chambers, Bradford, "Book Publishing a Racist Club?" Publishers' Weekly, 199:40-41, February 1, 1971.

5. _____, "Why Minority Publishing?" Publishers' Weekly, 199:50, March 15, 1971.

6. Katz, Loren, "Some Guidelines in Teaching American Negro History," The Negro History Bulletin, 28: 190, Special Summer Issue, 1965.

7. Wofford, Azile. Book Selection For School Libraries. New York: H. W. Wilson Company, 1962.

8. Bosma, R. Boyd, "Resolutions Adopted by the Conference," National NEA-PR&R Conference on Civil and Human Rights in Education, Washington: National Education Association, February 10, 1967.

9. Wilson, Wade, "As the Child Reads ... and Learns ... Tomorrow's World Is Shaped," National NEA-PR&R Conference on Civil and Human Rights in Education. Washington: National Education Association, February 10, 1967.

10. Brademas, John, "Integrated Textbooks and the Invisible Negro," National NEA-PR&R Conference on Civil and Human Rights in Education. Washington: National Education Association, February 10, 1967.

11. Huck, Charlotte S. and Kuhn, Doris Young. Children's Literature in the Elementary School. New York: Holt, Rinehart and Winston, Inc., 1961.

CULTURE SHOCK, THE THIRD WORLD,
SOUL POWER AND OTHER THOUGHTS

by Miles M. Jackson

During the past 25 years or so, social scientists have been extremely interested in the chemistry that takes place within individuals who experience a foreign culture. Anthropologists and psychologists, in particular, have led in the probe for understanding the true nature of the impact of Westerners on Non-Westerners, and vice-versa. There are some who believe, and rightly so, that the sensation can never be truly understood and known, unless actually experienced. Several years ago Professor Kalvero Oberg, an anthropologist, defined culture shock as the inability of the individual to adjust to a new culture within a reasonable period of time. He suggested that one could observe noticeable symptoms of this malady, including such bizarre behavior as: excessive washing of the hands; extreme concern with drinking water, food, dishes, and bedding; fear of physical contact with attendants; the tropical stare (absent-minded staring at nothing); fits of anger over delays and other minor frustrations; and suspicion that all shopkeepers were ready to cheat.

The American librarian working abroad, particularly in a Third World country, certainly is not exempt from such mind-blowing effects. Norman Cousins, the former editor of Saturday Review, observed that Americans can be found throughout the Third World countries carrying every kind of pharmaceutical imaginable. The small plastic containers do, in most instances, help combat bacteria. But culture shock strikes its victims so hard that it almost seems to be incurable. The "wonder pills" seem to have little effect against what Cousins calls "compassion fatigue," which he says, can cause retching of the spirit and usually upsets the moral and mental equilibrium of its victims. The only sure cure for such persons appears to be a trip home, either on leave or permanently.

The newcomer in a remote part of Africa will feel

the joy of experiencing a new culture; being caught up in the excitement and drama of a new world is indeed exhilarating. Yet culture shock can make the enchantment short-lived. Something happens. Nothing makes sense anymore. In the very beginning, the people or at least the leaders of the host country seemed ready to move ahead into the twentieth century. Now, they are clearly not ready for technology. They are stupid; natural singers and dancers, but never, never likely to learn computer technology. Suddenly, everything collapses.

It does not take much to shake one's faith in his fellow man under such circumstances, particularly when one witnesses men and women hitched to wagons or plows as mules or oxen. But humans are cheap in a country where the birth rate is among the highest in the world--certainly much cheaper than mules or oxen. Ownership of trucks and tractors is out of the question. Faith in mankind grows feeble in a world that is so uncongenial to human life.

The individual who is convinced that the only true culture is of European origin, and that non-Europeans are incapable of producing worthwile culture, is often found on assignments in Third World countries. The librarian who is unable to cope with the realities of a multi-racial society at home--in his own library--will find it difficult, if not impossible, to accept an African or Asian library executive as an equal. I have heard story after story from African and Asian librarians of how they were treated in a condescending way by an American or British library consultant. While visiting a library school in West Africa in 1969, I received the brush-off by the Director, in this case an expatriate Englishman. In addition to being rude to me, a visitor, he was embarrassingly rude to my African host, who apologized to me as we were leaving the university.

The question arises, whether culture shock or compassion fatigue has the same impact on the black librarian. Is there something in the black experience in this country that prepares a black person to approach an assignment in Africa, Asia or Latin America with more compassion than his white colleague? Does the experience of growing up black in a white world add another dimension to the professional competence that a black librarian can bring to people who have experienced the arrogance of a white with a colonial master mentality? If the black librarian experiences culture shock, will his recovery power be greater than his white colleague's? Is he in a better position to understand the tremendous lesson to be learned from one who has had to unshackle himself from the chains of servitude.

These questions do not negate the fact that many whites have been extremely successful abroad. Nor, for that matter, should one ignore the possibility of a black librarian being so completely disoriented that he is ineffective in a non-white culture. This sociological and historical dilemma has been adequately documented in the research of the late sociologist, E. Franklin Frazier, and the radical black sociologist, Nathan Hare. Frantz Fanon, in his penetrating study, <u>The Wretched of the Earth</u>, recognized the tactic of divide and rule. It is to be hoped that it will not be too many years before blacks in the former colonies of European powers and blacks in this country are completely together in their recognition of the divide and rule tactic. W. E. B. Dubois recognized the color problem as a major issue for the twentieth century more than 50 years ago. And Malcolm X stated that "the worst crime the white man ever committed was to teach black people to hate themselves." When Malcolm visited Africa he recognized the danger of neo-colonialism. In fact, the after effects of colonialism even today, can affect the visiting black librarian.

In a few countries in Africa one will find a black bourgeoisie which is totally insensitive to the plight of its less fortunate brothers. Black Americans tend to be romantic when dealing with the question of Africa. But as John A. Williams observed, they can become quickly disillusioned when meeting educated Africans who do not share their own sensitivity to the "have nots" in the Third World countries. I found, on a recent visit to more than ten African nations, not only the beauty I anticipated but unexpected paradoxes as well. The bond between Africans and their American black brothers is evident, particularly in West Africa. In a country such as Ghana a special welcome awaits the black American. But the black librarian must understand the ironies that exist side by side with the glory of African history. One must understand that libraries and library development have very low priority in many countries of the Third World. I listened for several hours to the woes of West African librarians about the lack of government support for libraries. One librarian indicated that this library had not received a book budget since the coup d'etat in 1966!

This raises an important question about the sincerity of some of the Third World countries: do they really want an educated population? Does a military regime or monarchy want to see peasants informed about their government and the world at large? There are cases where countries have refused to continue financing library programs after successful library development projects have been initiated or assisted by countries of the West. When the period of assistance ceases, the financial support is not continued by the government, and the library programs come to a halt. There are many reasons why a government refuses to support libraries and librarianship. Some do not understand how libraries can be of direct help in the social, educational and economic development of the country. If the choice is between spending $100,000 on a regional library system and building a small textile mill, the textile mill will almost certainly receive the funds. There is a lack of recognition that libraries are a vital part of a nation's system of communication, and that development of communications is of major importance in determining the extent of social development. There are still countries that have not recognized librarianship as a career profession and that have no classification for librarians in the nation's civil service. Recently, one Caribbean nation banned from its libraries the writings of Malcolm X, Eldridge Cleaver, Frantz Fanon and other black writers' works on the freedom struggle throughout the world.

Obviously, the realities of life in the Third World countries can be a shattering experience for the naive librarian. If he does not make connections with the realities and the historical relationships which surround him, he can expect compassion fatigue.

The question remains: are the chances of success greater for a black librarian than for his white counterpart in making the connection with reality in Africa, Asia or Latin America? The black librarian <u>can</u> experience culture shock, and if it happens in Africa it <u>can</u> tear at his deepest emotions. Yet the black librarian does have an extra dimension--the Black Experience in the United States--that cannot be attained by whites. This dimension may be called soul power. As a workable state of being, soul power is a combination of many things: the Black Experience, knowledge of the hardening of institutional racism, the refusal of the United States to come to grips with its racial minorities, the Pan-African legacy of W. E. B. Dubois, Marcus Garvey,

Malcolm X and others. The black librarian does have a greater chance of success if he accepts the following:

(1) The fact that knowledge and information can be power;

(2) Awareness of Pan-Africanism;

(3) An appreciation of the liberation struggles of all Third World peoples, particularly those that have known the yoke of colonialism.

DREAMS, REALITY, AND TAILOR-MADE SERVICE

by Ann Knight Randall

The 1970's promise maturity and fulfillment of professional dreams which, presumably, are nurtured in library school. Among these are: computerization of library activities on a much wider scale; utilization of automatic equipment to meet the individual needs of clientele; a deeper realization of the human potential for meaningful communication; and actualization of a self-determined, life-long plan for intellectual and spiritual growth.

To my mind, the most basic of the above is the third: the desire for meaningful communication at the service interface, between librarian and library user, which can stimulate and motivate major innovations in library service.

One aspect of that dream translates itself into a realistic program of systematic self-education in substantive areas which have high personal priority for the individual librarian. One majority priority for many black librarians, at this point in time, is the extension of high-quality library service to the unserved communities of urban and rural America.

I recognize, of course, that such a fine-sounding, altruistic phrase as "high quality library service to the unserved" needs closer attention. As time goes on, high quality service is more and more likely to encompass the use of computer facilities and automatic, mechanical aids such as improved photoduplication and audio-visual equipment. It is more likely, also, to include not only education in substantive areas but the intake of intangibles, acquired only through human contact. Above all, high quality service demands an attitude of flexibility, to adjust to the times. In this respect, a major challenge of the '70's is the provision of information service that is tailor-made to fit the special needs of groups and individuals. More specifically, it is the question of how to program broad-based professional dreams, to fit black reality, in tailor-made fashion.

Impact of Current Educational Trends

At this point in time, black librarians have an unparalleled opportunity to provide tailor-made service. To begin with, we have increased motivation. We have, so to speak, a captive audience. There are more young black people involved in the educational process, and over a longer period of time, than ever before. Black people are reading more, learning more, enjoying more, and most important, questioning more. This is true not only in the predominantly black colleges and universities, but everywhere in the United States.

A case in point is the Open Admissions program of the City University of New York (CUNY). For the first time, in New York City, a realistic attempt has been made to remove artificial barriers that are culturally biased. I mean such requirements as a specific high school grade point average which fluctuates according to available space, a specified aptitude test grade, and rigidly prescribed academic prerequisites in the form of specified courses. More vital black and Puerto Rican New Yorkers are entering these institutions, free of charge, for the first time. They are getting the step up in life that has been available to white immigrants and working class youngsters since the turn of the century.

Politicians now say we want to change all that; there are too many problems; support of the system is too expensive. An important question to ask ourselves is, what do black librarians say? Do we moan with others about the special problems of overcrowded service, the need for instructional programs and special materials, or do we plunge in committed to do all that our professional training demands? And, do we make every effort to convince non-librarians that such opportunity, regardless of how many drop-outs or failures may be included in the initial group of students, is both a meaningful and necessary experience for all who want it?

A lot of what we might want to do is restricted by current library policy based upon traditional points of view. The powers that be are not black or black-oriented, in many cases. Working for high quality service may mean reeducating and sensitizing both the administration and other faculty and library colleagues.

I equate the disadvantaged college student's quest for information with his personal survival.[1] This personal survival includes the educational, emotional and spiritual capability to deal with a complex and demanding environment. We know that such questions as how to confront social agencies, how to fill leisure time with profit, how to select reading matter to explain a confusing situation (i.e., income tax, home purchase, automobile purchase or repair), or how to study at home for academic credit, can be answered someplace in the literature.

Survival skills, in general, include the ability to understand and to be understood, on a fairly high level. These involve participation in the transference of oral, visual and written ideas. Specialized training and general conceptual inquiry are dependent upon the mastery of these skills. One group of resources that we require encompasses at least three categories of materials:

1. Self-teaching or programmed texts, for individualized learning;

2. Popularized, introductory sources, for easy comprehension of important facts and general subject parameters;

3. Study guides and review books, for concise presentation of basic skills and factual data.

Generally, this type of material has not been purchases for college collections. Review books and texts have been considered the responsibility of students. Popularized introductory sources are to be found in public libraries, primarily. The problem is not so much what the library should buy, but rather how we can fulfill our professional and human responsibility to introduce the student to the full range of materials that he requires. A possible solution to the conflict involves some departure from traditional policy.

At the very least, the college library might offer a representative collection of selected and recommended sources, in the categories outlined above. This representa-

Librarians as Perpetrators of Change

tive collection might be called an interdisciplinary "skills" collection. In talking with several librarians, it has been suggested to me that this is properly the function of a good college bookstore.

I agree that these materials should be conveniently available for purchase. But I feel that the opportunity for examination and comparison, in comfort and leisure, exists more easily in the library environment. The library can offer the additional advantage of providing experienced professionals, prepared to evaluate and interpret these resources in terms of their potential for supporting required course materials.

We ought not to worry about the use of these materials as substitutes. For many inexperienced students, the painless introduction to concepts will stimulate further curiosity. The experienced but lazy student has always been able to find this material. Thus, there is no purpose to being secretive or reluctant about library ownership of handbooks, book review media and review book series. In general, it is our knowledge about many sources and kinds of materials that will inform our students and enhance our educational role.

When we think about programs such as the CUNY Open Admissions program we can relate also to the full range of discovery type programs, all over the country. In this region, familiar names are SEEK, HE-OP, College Discovery, Operation Double Discovery, etc. Private and Ivy League institutions, not only publicly supported institutions, feel the need to respond. The reality challenges us as librarians to be aware of interests and trends among people in the library community. The professional dream requires that we detect individual and group needs accurately, and utilize our knowledge, training and personal attributes to provide appropriate materials and services.

Based upon my experience in public and in college libraries, I would have to admit that a good proportion of the current demand represents the need for course related resources, or for titles otherwise required for some specific purpose. But there is also a steadily growing number of minority group young people who frequent the library in search of information that is relevant to their lives. There is nothing new in the "types" of materials that they want. The challenge for librarians is the application of systematic collection building techniques to the practical requirements for balance, cohesiveness and relevance. Nevertheless, it may be useful to think of these resources by category:

1. <u>Contemporary Sources</u>--pertinent to campus, community, national and international developments. More specifically, factual and interpretive material relevant to social and cultural problems and trends.

2. <u>Ethnic and Regional Materials</u>--emphasis on the history and culture of minority groups, not previously enrolled in colleges in large numbers, particularly Afro-Americans, Puerto Ricans, White Appalachians, Indian and Mexican Americans. Unlike the political tracts and social commentary, which belong to the first category, these would be descriptive works in search of the past, and creative works which bare the soul.

3. <u>Career Guidance Materials</u>--concise, realistic appraisals of job market conditions, entrance and promotional avenues through academic and vocational programs, and regional and national trend analysis. Up-to-date directory information, and referral to and interpretation of special sources, are too frequently lacking in most libraries.

Collection Building Techniques

The reality of current educational trends has its impact on the development of collections in libraries. The major development of the '60's was the widespread experimentation with Black Studies programs, in institutions at all levels. Perhaps the most basic problem has related to definition of scope and purpose. Too frequently, librarians have had secondary involvement in these discussions. On college and university campuses, partisan groups of faculty and students meeting in racial caucus or in discipline coalition have not had the sustained participation of librarians that is needed. This situation is less true on the predominantly black campuses than on the growing number of formerly white campuses with a growing representation of minority students. Perhaps this is true because the libraries on these racially mixed campuses have only recently taken interest in problems related to black studies bibliographic control.

The term itself is not easily defined. Black Studies is an omnibus term which has gained popular currency during the decade of the '60's. It refers to the study of the history and culture of people of African descent. As such, it cuts across many geographic divisions and many linguistic barriers. As a proposal for curriculum change, the subject area is emotionally charged and controversial. It is associated with the slogans of student protest, which have polarized campus and community constituencies.

University administrators and scholars have taken a serious interest in the field only recently. I speak here not of the many distinguished black scholars in our educational history, but of the fact that the general impact of their scholarship was limited until recently. During the past decade, there was a dramatic increase in research projects funded by the U.S. government and private foundations. Heavier demand for this material was felt in most college and university libraries than ever before. In addition, the amount of material available to libraries increased dramatically during this period. A general statement on the trends in publishing, a few years ago, was provided by Mel Watkins of the New York Times Book Review staff, who declared that every major publisher had a black history or culture series of one kind or another, and that outside of the established publishing houses, the ferment in black writing and publishing was perhaps even more notable.[2] Of note for librarians was the joint display of black publishing presses at the recent Washington, D.C. meeting of the Association for the Study of Negro Life and History.[3] The appearance of publications like Africana Library Journal,[4] and Black Books Bulletin[5] should have impact on collection building.

The question which emerges for black librarians is, what body of knowledge and experience can we command from the profession to answer the special needs in this area? Guidance is provided by techniques developed to administer special collections and area study collections. Following their lead, it would seem that a coordinated library effort is required, which suggests the utilization of one or more librarian-bibliographers. Given the vast amount of fugitive items appearing in non-indexed and non-traditional sources, it is probable that enthusiasm for the subject area is of real importance, along with the factors of training and experience.

One important concept which is documented in the literature of librarianship has application to the building of black studies collections; that is, the need for a written selection policy. This should be a clear statement of basic goals, major priorities, and the mechanisms for accomplishing the acquisitions program. This task is not easy; it means relating to the objectives of the institution of which the library is a part, and to the specific community to be served. In our attempt to develop such a policy at a large undergraduate library, it was necessary to specify curriculum areas to be served, and different levels of collecting to reflect strength. Such items as language, region and time period are also important to specify. For example, a sizeable library would want a good working collection capable of supporting at least the preliminary investigations of graduate students and faculty for most subjects related to blacks, while a very small institution or branch public library could afford to maintain only the basic information material for general reading and reference, and for introductory teaching. This level of collecting concept has been discussed at length by Danton.[6] Other useful items in the general library literature are by Wilson and Tauber, Fussler, Skipper, Clapp, and others.

A special literature is available to librarians working with black collections. Ann Shockley's manual,[7] developed for the special institutes in Black Studies Librarianship at Fisk University, is important here. Bibliographies of individual library collections are available, since many institutions have embarked on this worthwhile project. These serve an inventory taking function, as well as providing an integrated approach, when materials are scattered throughout the fields. Those few institutions which are getting out current lists of these materials when received are providing service in the tailor-made fashion.

An additional experience with developing a small departmental collection points out the difficulty of depending upon leads from faculty and other users of the collection. The librarian must have the confidence to evaluate the situation, and to get underway the operations necessary to provide information and resources.

Black librarians must have their antennae into the library community, in order to serve as interpreters in the information gathering process. In dynamic situations, such as the creation of new departments, the problem is complex because major guidelines such as program goals, emphasis and audience are in the formative stage.

Librarians as Perpetrators of Change

Subject Access

The reality of current patterns of thought and the vocabulary of black expression have their impact on the way in which information is sought. Meaningful communication occurs when the librarian successfully translates an inquiry into the subject content of the collection, or the network of information. As experienced practitioners, we know that there are many problems related to subject access. As black librarians, we can put together a list of difficulties which are frequently encountered with respect to black collections.

A serious indictment of American libraries today is that our most valued product, the card catalog, is deficient in its response to contemporary black viewpoints. The familiar phrase for computer failures, which is abbreviated as GIGO (garbage in, garbage out), applies to this manual monument also. If the quality and depth of classification and subject heading work is inadequate, then black librarians must seek solutions to the problem.

For college and university library collections, and for large public libraries, dependence upon the Library of Congress Classification scheme is widespread. Over the past decade, reclassification projects from Dewey to LC have been popular. Many of the newer libraries are committed to LC from the beginning. In the 1966 Institute on the Use of the Library of Congress Classification, the list of libraries using the LC system wholly or in part, compiled by Tauber,[8] includes an impressive number of institutions. Needless to say, that number would be greatly increased if the survey were repeated today.

This widespread use of the LC system means that its classification and subject headings are the means by which a significant number of Black Studies collections are presently organized, and this seem likely to continue in the future.

The largest amount of materials devoted to the history and culture of black people in America appears in schedule E. On the basis of observation, it seems that the number most frequently assigned is E185, "United States - Elements in the population - Negroes." This number is subdivided decimally to one or two places, in order to provide a place for the following kinds of material:

history (by period); status and development since emancipation; studies by region, state, etc.; and biography. If space permitted, some interesting observations could be made about the failure of the schedule to deal with today's information. All librarians who are not catalogers should spend some time examining the tables.

The lack of a general index to all the schedules is a real handicap. It would be difficult to pull together all the relevant classification numbers for black studies materials, at least within a reasonable period of time. The many "see references" under numbers in the E schedule indicate the phenomenon of scattering throughout the tables for fields other than history, such as education, political science, law, ethnology, religion, and arts and letters.

For the most part, users of the collection will rely on the alphabetic subject headings in the card catalog. Appropriate terms of entry are not obvious to users of the catalog. Terms which relate to blacks may be based upon primary identifying elements such as the following: race (Negro, Black, Afro-American); religion (Black Muslim, special divisions of Protestant sects such as, National Baptist Convention, African Methodist Episcopal, etc.); geography (Africa, Haiti, Harlem, Roxbury); language (Black English, Swahili, Ashanti); and socio-economic designnation (slave, urban poor, disadvantaged, etc.). With respect to the socio-economic category, our society has channeled blacks into certain socio-economic classes which become identified with race.

There is another group of headings in which the terms refer not to socio-economic designations for people, but rather to phenomena in society. These include terms such as: "Reconstruction," "Pan-Africanism," "Race Relations": and related terms such as "Segregation" and "Discrimination." For retrieval purposes, the proper term may not come easily to the mind of the library patron or to the librarian. Although these terms do not contain any ethnic identifier, they do discuss problems or movements which relate to black people.

Perhaps a more serious problem is the large number of current concepts which are not yet included in the subject heading list. The difficulty of dealing with dynamic fields is one of the weaknesses of LC headings. In the black studies area, specific concepts such as Busing, Backlash, Neo-colonialism, and Liberation are not represented. This means that a large body of current literature will not be easily accessible under the specific concept that is central to the literature.

As in other subject fields and area studies, heavy reliance must be placed upon reference tools to supplement the subject access provided by the library's catalog. Two major resources for this purpose are retrospective bibliographies and the published catalogs of major collections. Of course, some parts of a few major black collections have been made available through commercial reprint and microform projects.

The published indexing and abstracting services continue to be important for identifying periodical, newspaper and other non-book material. Wide gaps still exist, although new services are appearing. The library can aid its readers by listing and surveying the subject access provided in this area for important sources. It is necessary to list the general and specific bibliographies that are scattered throughout the disciplines.

No large-scale current service exists to announce major materials in all formats. This information is still scattered among more than a dozen sources which must be consulted regularly. A list of those selection sources (as well as publishers and reprint catalogs) which are considered important for the library's collection should be compiled and made accessible to the public. Those services which are browsed regularly could be asterisked. This would help to provide some indication of the nature and level of the collection being assembled, with respect to subject scope.

Past and Present

Our professional tasks cannot be divorced from the reality of social environment. For the black librarian, the past has special meaning, in terms of looking into the background and development of black people, their attitudes and their interests. All of us, despite locale and particular circumstance, have had experience with racial discrimination and resultant personal uncertainty. We are well equipped to understand the mistrust and frustration of library users.

As I look into my own background, I recall that to be born black and female, in the midst of the urban ghetto, has its own educational value. Survival and independence were early learned. Watchfulness and the ability to seize opportunity are prized abilities, but difficult to develop. It was necessary in the course of daily life to communicate at many levels: with revered black professionals in the churches and schools; with mistrusted white professionals in public institutions and with neighborhood entrepreneurs; with street corner gang members and neighborhood children. Where in this communications list did the library belong?

My childhood memories of the library would probably parallel those of many blacks in my age group. Library card ownership was a form of neighborhood status. A visit to the library was something of an expedition, although the physical distance to the neighborhood branch was not far. The architecture of the Carnegie building was awesome. There is no memory of a friendly and influential librarian waiting inside, but rather of a succession of people at the circulation desk who warned of overdue penalties and dirty hands. I must admit that story hours had a special appeal.

Later, when homework assignments became more arduous, the neighborhood branch never seemed to have what was required. After what seemed like a difficult trip across town, the main branch was confusing and frightening.

Looking back, Junior High School instruction now seems like a practical joke. There was a large room lined with books in locked cases. We were marched in lines and given five minutes to make a selection, to be read in the library during a forty-minute period. The foreboding librarian was built and behaved like a virtual battleship.

The college library, although bright and cheerful, had its own restrictions. Many painful hours were spent in the reserve reading room, after a full day of classes and an hour-long commuting trip during the New York City rush hour.

I recall Edward Mapp's[9] discussion of seeking high school part-time work in the public library, and I remember that I too was turned away, discouraged and unsure of why. I remember also the succession of giddy, irresponsible white part-timers in the same system, when I later became a trainee.

Librarians as Perpetrators of Change

It was my first library job, which happened quite by accident, which changed a twenty-year image. The U.S. Army library in Bamberg, Germany was small but busy. It offered an opportunity to be challenged and to provide service with an intensity, at all levels--to rural illiterates, to school children, to college graduates, to recruits seeking self-educating opportunities. Particularly vivid is the memory of candidates for court martials who sought basic legal information which we could not provide.

Although no library experience has been entirely satisfying in terms of offering responsibility, freedom and professional growth, I am convinced that great potential is present in the field.

At this point in time, the black librarian has a weak professional voice, but this too is changing. There is evidence that the situation in the nation's number one library is prejudicial to black personnel. New groups like the A. L. A. Black Librarian's Caucus and the Association of African American Bibliographers offer an opportunity for communication about common professional concerns. As individuals we are active in all types of library positions. As a group, our greatest impact has been on service to blacks and the building of black collections. I have seen several situations in which the service commitment of the Afro-American specialist stimulated new, liberalized policies for the total library.

Service Ramifications

The future of tailor-made library service to blacks must conform to the reality of the black experience, in terms of the development and the environment of black people. It is important to understand not only the physical poverty, if this is the case, but also the uncertainty with which the library is approached. I can remember, a few years back, that when black students came to the reference desk in a predominantly white university, it was assumed that they were members of the disadvantaged program. Their requests for materials were automatically translated into the need for basic level texts and popular magazines. Librarians simply cannot make such assumptions about ability and need; most black librarians know this.

In the library world, in general, many exciting innovations are taking place. A few years ago, an evaluation of active use of innovative practices among 1,193 institutions having liberal arts programs was reported in the literature by Sidney Forman.[10] On the basis of his study, he concluded that the library is moving from a passive role toward being an active instrument in the process of teaching and learning. This report was part of a larger inquiry sponsored by the Institute of Higher Education at Teachers College, Columbia University. Innovation was defined to embrace a range from change to complete novelty. Despite his general impression of progress, Forman found that college librarians are not as responsive to special service possibilities--such as table of contents services, selective dissemination of information, selective bibliography, accession list publication, and technical report coverage--as they are to other kinds of innovation. I suspect that this may be equally true of librarians in other types of institutions.

Implications of technical report coverage, for example, might include the blanket order of a microfiche copy of every research report abstracted in Research In Education, the announcement journal of ERIC (U.S. Educational Resources Information Center). The question of technical report coverage becomes an important consideration for the continuing education of the librarian. The Clearinghouse for Library and Information Sciences (CLIS), which is one of the many clearinghouses of the ERIC network, is located in Washington, D.C. It publishes a newsletter which highlights reports of particular significance to its clientele. In addition, selective listing of significant reports is printed in several of the library-oriented periodicals.

It is probable that individual librarians would profit from taking the SDI approach to their own information. The browsing of abstract journals and other announcement sources can add to their own awareness of what is going on in the field. The librarian might simply compile a list of descriptors or subject headings that would constitute his own profile of interest. By putting himself on a routing list, or by checking at regular intervals, he could systematically browse the items of interest to him. A number of large libraries are experimenting with providing some type of current awareness service for their faculty and library staff.

Even if the librarian is not actively engaged in research, this practice could stimulate his thinking about ways to solve problems in his own library. If he knows the types of projects that are being attempted elsewhere, he is better equipped to adapt such programs to local needs. Equally important, he would know where work related to his problem was being conducted, and, through communication, he might avoid unfruitful duplication of effort. Systematic browsing of abstract journals in education, librarianship and subject areas relevant to the librarian's readers' services activities can be a tremendous help.

It has been said that SDI and current awareness activity have the interesting psychological effect of increasing confidence among consumers of information. A person who thinks that he knows his field tends to act with more authority, and to engage in more creative endeavors. This notion has real application for the stimulation of librarians in all types of library positions to seek better and more varied solutions to their problems.

This notion is related also to the concept of tailor-made service. Too often, librarians are hemmed in by tradition and outmoded policies. Frequently, sparks to the imagination and allies must be found elsewhere. Experimentation and change is in the air. It is the task of librarians to seek out ways to meet the changing needs of their individual clientele. This is the reality and the professional dream. It is especially crucial to black people that we provide easy access to the information that they need to survive, in education, employment and daily life.

We are aware that every library activity affects the service potential. Thus, administrative policies, budgetary priorities, technical services systems, and personnel attitudes are as much involved as the readers' services staff. Black librarians, regardless of their position and professional interest, can exercise a viable role in bringing their insight and educational training to the solution of common problems.

Notes

1. Ann Knight Randall, "Information and Survival for Disadvantaged College Students," unpublished paper presented at the American Library Association Convention, Detroit, 1970.

2. Mel Watkins, "The Black Revolution in Books," New

York Times Book Review, August 10, 1969, pp. 8, 10, 12, 14.

3. Association for the Study of New Life and History, Annual Meeting, Washington, D.C., October 21-24, 1971.

4. Africana Library Journal, Africana Publishing Corp., Vol. 1-, 1970-

5. Black Books Bulletin, Institute of Positive Education, Vol. 1-, 1971-

6. J. Periam Danton, Book Selection and Collections: a comparison of German and American University Libraries. N.Y.: Columbia Univ. Press, 1963. Other citations of interest are the following: Louis Round Wilson and Maurice Tauber, The University Library, 2d ed. N.Y.: Columbia University Press, 1956; Herman Fussler, "Acquisition Policy: a symposium...," CRL, 14:363-67, 1953; James E. Skipper, "The Continuing Program of Book Selection and Acquisition," LRTS, 2:265-71, Fall 1958; Verner Clapp, "Library Resources-- the Professional Responsibility," LRTS, 3:3-11, Winter 1959.

7. Ann Allen Shockley, A Handbook for the Administration of Special Black Collections, rev. ed. Nashville, Tenn.: Fisk University Library, 1971.

8. Maurice Tauber, "A List of Libraries Using the LC System Wholly or in Part." (In Richard H. Schimmelpfeng and C. Donald Cook, The Use of the Library of Congress Classification; Proceedings of the Institute..., 1966. A.L.A., 1968.)

9. Edward Mapp, "From My Perspective: a Social Responsibility" (In: E.J. Josey, The Black Librarian in America, Scarecrow, 1970), pp. 184-190.

10. Sidney Forman, "Innovative Practices in College Libraries," CRL, 29:486-92, November 1968.

NOTES ON CONTRIBUTORS

THOMAS ALFORD is Director, Benton Harbor Public Library and Berrien County Library League (Michigan). Previous positions in various capacities with the Flint Public Library, Flint, Michigan. President-elect of Young Adult Services Division, American Library Association; Past-Chairman, Junior Members Round Table, Michigan Library Association; and Past-Chairman of the ALA Black Caucus Planning and Action Committee.

MOHAMMED M. AMAN, Associate Professor, St. John's University, Department of Library Science. Dr. Aman formerly served on the faculty at Pratt Institute, Graduate School of Library and Information Science, and on the library staff of the Alleghany Community College, Duquesne University, and in several libraries in Cairo, U. A. R. He is the author of articles in several publications and two monographs: <u>Analysis of Terminology, Form and Structure of Subject Headings in Arabic Literature.</u>.., University of Pittsburgh, 1968; and <u>Cataloging Notes with Exemplars,</u> New York, 1971. Active in the American Library Association.

JOHN A. AXAM is Head, Stations Department, The Free Library of Philadelphia. Mr. Axam has served as lecturer at Institutes at library schools at the University of Pittsburgh, Drexel University, University of Maryland, and Wayne State University. He is active in the American Library Association.

ETTA STANTON BULLOCK, Librarian for Community and Cultural Affairs, Samuel Paley Library, Temple University. She has held positions in academic and public libraries. Mrs. Bullock spent the summer of 1971 studying at the University of Ghana, Accra, Ghana.

JAMES E. CRAYTON is Senior Audiovisual Librarian, Los Angeles County Public Library System. Mr. Crayton's former positions were with the Cobb County Board of Education, Marietta, Georgia, and the Atlanta Board of Education.

WILLIAM D. CUNNINGHAM, formerly Library Services Program Officer, U.S. Office of Education, is now Director of Libraries, Howard University. Mr. Cunningham has had extensive experience in public libraries and served as Administrative Assistant, University of Kansas Libraries. He has served as consultant and technical advisor for many Federal Projects dealing with libraries and the disadvantaged. Active in many professional organizations including the American Library Association, he is currently Chairman of the ALA Black Caucus. He is the author of several articles in professional journals.

JEANNE ENGLISH is Librarian, Evanston Township High School, Illinois. Miss English has served as librarian with the Detroit Public Schools, the New York Public Library, and the Detroit Public Library. She is affiliated with the American Library Association, National Education Association, Illinois Education Association, and several civic and community organizations. Having done extensive research on the Angela Davis Case, Miss English's research was recently cited in Why Angela Davis?, published by the United Presbyterian Church in the U.S.A., Division of Race.

ROBERT B. FORD, JR., is Acting Chief Librarian, Medgar Evers College. His professional experience has been in libraries in community colleges, schools, and special libraries. Mr. Ford is the recipient of awards and prizes for playwriting and oratory and is active in numerous professional organizations, including ALA.

WALTER J. FRASER is not only a librarian, he is also a computer specialist. He has worked as a Programmer in Oakland, California, and Supervisor, Statistics Laboratory, Graduate School of Education, University of Chicago. From 1967-70, he was Assistant Professor, Graduate Library School, Kansas State College. Since 1970, he has been System Analyst and Head, Academic Library Services, James Jerome Hill Reference Library, St. Paul, Minnesota.

LOUISE GILES, Dean of Learning Resources, Macomb Community College (Michigan), is formerly of the staffs of the Detroit Public Library and Oakland Community College Library. Author of A Research Project to Determine the Student Acceptability and Learning Effectiveness of Microform Collections in Community Colleges: Phase I, U.S.O.E., 1970, and articles in professional journals. Serves as consultant for professional organizations and for regional accrediting associations.

BESSIE R. GRAYSON is Assistant Professor of Library Media, School of Library Media, Alabama A and M University. Active in a number of educational and library professional associations including the American Library Association. Her publications have appeared in educational journals.

VIVIAN DAVIDSON HEWITT is Librarian, Carnegie Endowment for International Peace. Her former positions include the Carnegie Library (Pittsburgh); Instructor, School of Library Service, Atlanta University; Librarian, Rockefeller Fund; and she has served as a consultant abroad. The recipient of many awards, Mrs. Hewitt was the President of the New York Chapter of the Special Libraries Association in 1971. Author of numerous articles in professional journals.

MILES M. JACKSON is Associate Professor, State University of New York at Geneseo, School of Library and Information Science. Former positions at Free Library of Philadelphia; Librarian, Hampton Institute; Chief Librarian, Atlanta University; Lecturer, School of Library Service, Atlanta University; and Visiting Professor and Consultant, University of Tehran. Awards include Fulbright Senior Lecture Award 1968-69 and Council on Library Resources Fellow, 1970. Books include Bibliography of Negro History and Culture for Young Readers, University of Pittsburgh, 1968; and Comparative and International Librarianship, Greenwood Press, 1970.

CASPER LEROY JORDAN, Assistant Professor, School of Library Service, was formerly Assistant Director, Nioga Library System (New York); Supervisor, Technical Processes, Nioga Library System; and Chief Librarian, Wilberforce University. Professor Jordan has held many consultantships, is a member of numerous professional organizations, and a contributor to many professional publications; co-editor, An Institutional Self-study of Wilberforce University; co-editor, College Preparatory Reading List, 2d ed., New York Library Assn.; A Call to Excellences, A Study of the East St. Louis (Illinois) Public Library, Illinois State Library, 1970.

OLIVER KIRKPATRICK is Supervising Librarian, Brooklyn Public Library and was formerly on the staff of The New York Public Library and New York University Library. A former sports editor and columnist, radio newscaster and commentator, Mr. Kirkpatrick is a poet, and his writings, including articles, short stories and poems, have appeared in

New Republic, Travel, and other magazines. A native of Jamaica, he is widely known for his book, Naja the Snake & Mangus the Mongoose: A Jamaican Folktale, Doubleday, 1970; and for Country Cousin, a collection of Jamaica dialect radio talks. Active in ALA and Library Union affairs.

DOREITHA R. MADDEN is Coordinator, Office of Library Service to the Disadvantaged, New Jersey State Library. Former positions held at Hampton Institute; Enoch Pratt Library; and Library 21, Seattle World's Fair. Active in many community organizations, New Jersey Library Association, and the American Library Association. Serves as Consultant and member of Advisory Committee of Institute for Training in Librarianship, Graduate Library School, Rutgers, the State University.

EDWARD C. MAPP, Professor and Chairman, Library Department, New York City Community College, The City University of New York. Member of State University of New York Chancellor's Advisory Committee on Libraries, 1966-69. Active in American Library Association and other professional organizations. Articles published in several journals. Dr. Mapp's books include Books for Occupational Educational Programs, A List for Community Colleges, Technical Institutes and Vocational Schools, Bowker, 1971; and Blacks in American Films: Today and Yesterday, Scarecrow Press, 1972.

MARGARET PERRY is Education Librarian, the University of Rochester Library. Former positions at The New York Public Library; U.S. Army Library in France and Germany, U.S. and the Military Academy. Author of several articles in learned journals and a book: Bio-Bibliography of Countee P. Cullen 1903-1946, Negro Universities Press, 1971.

ANN KNIGHT RANDALL, Lecturer and Doctoral Fellow, School of Library Service, Columbia University. Mrs. Randall has had varied experiences in professional positions on the library staffs of Brooklyn Public Library; United States Army, Bamberg, Germany; Reference Librarian, Queens College, The City University of New York; Indexer for ERIC Documents; Volunteer Abstractor for Schomburg Collection, The New York Public Library. Member of ALA, SLA, and the Library Association of The City University of New York.

BINNIE L. TATE is a member of the faculty of the School of Library and Information Sciences, University of Wisconsin, Milwaukee. Mrs. Tate was formerly Children's Specialist,

Los Angeles Public Library, and served on the staff of the Schenectady Public Library and Florida Memorial College Library. Active in state and national professional associations, she is widely known for her work with publishers to issue better children's books that will depict minorities more realistically.

HERMAN L. TOTTEN is Assistant Dean and Associate Professor, College of Library Science, University of Kentucky. He was formerly College Librarian and Professor of Library Science, Wiley College and Dean of the College, Wiley College. Dr. Totten has also served on the faculty of the University of Oklahoma during summer sessions. Active in many professional organizations, he is the author of several articles in professional and educational publications. During the 1970-71 academic year, he served as an American Council on Education, Fellow in Academic Administration Internship Program.

MARY DAWSON WALTERS formerly served as Director of the Albany State College Library. Presently, she is Associate Professor of Library Administration and Head of the Acquisitions Department, Ohio State University Libraries. Mrs. Walters is the first black professional to head a department at OSU Libraries. Some of Professor Walters' monographs include The Ohio State University Publications: A Bibliography 1961- , OSU, 1961; The Ohio State University Libraries: A List of Departmental Libraries, OSU, 1944; Black History Holdings of the Ohio State University Libraries, A Partial List, OSU, 1969; and Afro-Americana: A Comprehensive Bibliography of Resource Materials in the Ohio State University Libraries By or About Black Americans, OSU, 1969.

ANN STEWART WATT is an Associate in the Bureau of School Libraries, New York State Education Department. Before assuming her present post, she served as school librarian in the School Systems of Baltimore, Maryland, Westbury, Long Island, and Freeport, Long Island; Assistant Professor of English and Library Science at Winston-Salem State College; Visiting Instructor, School of Library Service, Atlanta University; and Indexer for the H. W. Wilson Publishing Company. Mrs. Stewart has published in professional journals and served as Educational Consultant for G. P. Putnam's Juvenile Books. She is also active in professional and civic organizations.

JAMES C. WELBOURNE, JR., President, Urban Information

Interpreters, Inc., and formerly Director, Urban Information Specialist Program, School of Library and Information Services, University of Maryland. Mr. Welbourne also served as the University of Maryland's first full-time recruiter of minority students for the School of Library and Information Services. Frequently invited to address library school colloquia, he also serves as a consultant on urban information needs.

JAMES R. WRIGHT, Director, Phillis Wheatley Community Library, Rochester, New York. He was formerly Assistant to the Librarian, Alabama State University; Branch Librarian, Gary Public Library; and served on the staff of Saint Jude's Educational Institute, Montgomery; author of articles in professional journals; active in ALA and an officer of the Social Responsibility Round Table.

ROBERT L. WRIGHT is Lecturer and Director of Admissions and Student Affairs, School of Library and Information Services, University of Maryland. Previous positions on staff of the District of Columbia Public Library and Federal City College. Active in several professional associations including the American Library Association, Mr. Wright is also serving as the director of an U.S. Office of Education funded Institute for Retraining of Library Staff to Improve Information Service to the Disadvantaged.

ELLA GAINES YATES, formerly Assistant Director, Montclair Public Library, is now Assistant Director of the Atlanta Public Library. Professional experience includes positions at the Brooklyn Public Library, Orange Public Library, Orange Memorial Hospital Library, and East Orange Public Library. Active in many professional organizations including the American Library Association. In addition, very active with many types of civic and community organizations.

INDEX

Advocacy, 20-3
African Librarians, 283, 285
African Reference Books
    Need for guide to, 159
Africana Library Journal, 293
American Federation of State, County, and Municipal Employees, AFL-CIO, 195, 198, 199
American Library Association, 195, 198, 200, 210, 222, 260, 270
    Accreditation of library schools, 157, 171, 187
    Black Caucus, 111, 156, 205, 209-14, 253-4, 299
    President of organization--no black has ever been elected to this post, 33
Angela Davis Defense Fund, 134
Angela Davis Exhibit, 144
Asian Librarians, 283
Association of African American Bibliographers, 299
Atlanta University, 110, 124
    School of Library Service, 109, 186
Attica, 3, 132-3, 222

Baker, Augusta, 121
Baker, George H., quoted, 113
Banfield, Edward C., 105-6
Bennett, Lerone, 96, 105, 202
Billingsley, Andrew, 153
Bishop, Wilson Warner, quoted, 241
Black Activists, 14
Black Advocates, 35-6, 41
Black Americans, 47
    Attitudes by Caucasians toward, 12
    Declaration of Commitment to Black Liberation, 146-7
    Informational needs, 51
    Repression suffered by, 145, 150, 221-2
Black Books Bulletin, 293
Black Caucuses, 8, 156, 209-17, 253, 273
Black Children, 137-40, 141, 143, 146, 151
Black Colleges and Universities, 107, 289
    Librarians in, 109, 155

Libraries in, 108-10, 122-7
   Studies on, 107
Black Community, 5, 6, 138, 209, 243, 249-51
   Control of educational and cultural institutions, 55, 156, 216
   Information industry analysis of, 53-4
   Informational needs, 51, 56-8, 214, 262
   Planning an information service for, 56
Black Congressional Caucus, 158
Black English, 70
Black Information Network, 127
Black Information Specialist, 57-9, 123, 127-8
Black Liberation, 51, 56, 59, 63, 96, 145
   Declaration of Commitment to, 146-7
The Black Librarian in America, 183, 187, 256, 266
Black Librarians, 5, 6, 8, 9, 15, 23, 29, 46-7, 63, 65, 109, 120, 155, 156, 157, 158, 160, 204, 206, 208-17, 233, 234, 238-40, 243-4, 262, 264, 284, 286, 289, 294, 297
Black Library Resources, 6, 120, 121
   Evaluation of, 128
   Network development of, 122-7
   Production of, 123
   Retrieval of, 122
   Union catalog of materials needed, 121, 125
Black Materials see Black Library Resources
Black Networks of Libraries, 122-7
Black Panthers, 20, 142, 143
Black Power, 1
Black Pride, 84-7, 220
Black Professionals, 13, 24, 35, 46
Black Publishers, 123
Black Studies
   Bibliographic control, 292, 293-4
   Library, 96, 98-102, 105-6, 292-4
   Library of Congress classification inadequate for, 295-7
   Value of, 96-8
Black Youth, 14
Brooklyn
   Black and Puerto Rican population, 79
Brooklyn College, 80
Brooklyn Public Library, 81, 84, 85, 195-6
Brown, Nadine, quoted, 262
Bullock, Bessie L., 81
Bundy, Mary Lee, quoted, 262

COSATI see Committee on Scientific and Technical Information

Calley, Lt. William L., Jr., 3, 43
Camus, Albert, quoted, 5
Carmichael, Stokeley, 1
Case Western Reserve University, 167
Cataloging and Racism, 30-1
Censorship, 30
Chambers, Bradford, quoted, 278
Chisholm, Shirley, 84
Churchill, Winston, quoted, 42
The City University of New York
    Open Admissions Program, 289, 291
Clark, Geraldine, quoted, 81
Cleaver, Eldridge, 145, 286
College Libraries
    Collection Building, 291-2
    Departure from traditional programs needed, 290-1
    Service to disadvantaged students, 290
    Unresponsive to innovative services, 300
Columbia University, 164
Committee on Scientific and Technical Information (COSATI)
    Black Research Libraries, 111
Communist Party, 136
Coon, Carleton C., 30
Cooperative College Library Center, 110
Cornell University, 187
Council on Interracial Books for Children, 278
Cousins, Norman, 283

Davis, Angela, 3, 6, 7, 132-46
Dedijer, Stevan, quoted, 40
Dempster, Roland Tombekai, quoted, 183, 184, 186, 188, 189
Departmental Libraries in Colleges and Universities, 113-5
    Role of librarian in, 115-8
Detroit Public Library, 259, 260
Dewey, Melvil, 222
Discrimination
    In Armed Forces, 3, 135
    In educational programs, 135, 203
    In employment, 158, 204, 206, 207
    In housing, 4, 135, 203
    In promotion, 205, 206, 207, 243-4
    In trade unions, 38
Doiron, Peter, 195
Draft Riots of 1862, 86
Drexel Institute of Technology see Drexel University
Drexel University, 257
DuBois, W.E.B., 23; quoted, 121, 159, 285, 286

ERIC see Educational Resources Information Center
Educational Resources Information Center, 300
Elementary and Secondary Education Act, Title II
    Funding for school libraries, 65
Ellison, Ralph, quoted, 122, 281
Evanston Township High School, 132, 137
        Black faculty, 139, 140-2, 143, 144
        Black Liberation Week celebration, 143
        Black students, 137-40, 141, 143
        Human Relations Department, 139
Evers, Medgar, (Mrs.), 80

Fanon, Frantz, 285, 286
Fisk University, 110-1, 122-3, 124, 128, 294
Franklin, Hardy R., 85
Frazier, E. Franklin, 285

Gardner, John, 261
Garvey, Marcus, 286
Ghetto communities, 50, 52, 58, 60-1, 81, 82, 229, 244, 249, 251, 252, 253

Hampton, Fred, 143
Hare, Nathan, 285
Hawkins, Augustus F., 205
Hayes, Gregory Willard, 5
Health
    Mortality among blacks and whites, 13
Hertz, F.K., 164
Hoffer, Eric, 21
Howard University
    Moorland Collection, 120, 124
Hughes, Langston, quoted, 150
Hutchins, Robert M., quoted, 266

Ichord, Richard
Intellectual Freedom, 6, 132-46

Job Opportunities in the Business Sector, 270
Johnson, Lyndon B., 276
Josey, E.J., 183

Kansas State Teachers College, 164
Kerner Commission Report, 61, 150
King, Martin Luther, 141, 142, 145, 150; quoted, 183, 204, 207

The Librarian Speaking, Interviews with University Librarians, 256

Librarians
- As advocates, 20-3
- As professionals, 19-20, 193
- As unionists, 192-200
- Response to social and political conditions, 50
- Stereotyped, 93

Library Education, 7, 95, 163-72, 225

Library Journal, 196-7

Library Profession
- Elitism in, 154, 184, 193, 246
- Exploitation of women in, 194
- Fail to reflect liberalism, 155
- Ignores needs of blacks, 152, 183-9
- Racism in, 7, 63, 152, 154, 204, 233, 258
- Recruitment of blacks to, 7, 31, 154, 156, 184, 185, 209, 225, 243, 273

Library Schools
- Censure racist library schools, 157
- Failure to recruit black professors and deans, 154, 189
- Failure to respond to black needs, 183-9
- Failure to train for public library work, 234
- Provide scholarship for advanced study, 157
- Research needs for black community, 159
- Teaching about media in, 164-72

Lieberman, Irving, 164, 168

Little Black Sambo, 30, 45, 47, 76

Los Angeles County Public Library, 205

Lyle, Guy R., 256

Machiavelli, Niccoló, quoted, 27

Malcolm X, 143, 145, 285

Mapp, Edward C., 298

Medgar Evers College, 80

Mexican American Affirmative Action Committee, 205

Meyer, Robert S., 273

Moore, William, Jr., quoted, 263

Moorland Collection, Howard University see Howard University, Moorland Collection

NAACP see National Association for the Advancement of Colored People

National Association for the Advancement of Colored People, 23, 205
- Legal Defense and Educational Fund, 1

National Black Political Convention, 4

National Committee of Negro Churchmen, 1

National Education Association, 33

New Jersey State Library, 227, 228, 230

New York City Community College Library, 86
The New York Public Library 164, 196
Niemöller, Martin, quoted, 44
Nigerian Libraries, 160
Nixon, Richard M., 2, 3, 105, 135, 140
Nixon, Richard M., Mrs., 87
Nonprint media, 7, 74-5, 163-72, 252, 261, 263, 264, 288

Oakland Community College
    Learning Resource Center, 260
Oberg, Kalvero, 283
Ohio State University, 6
    Black faculty and students, 6
    Black Studies Division, 96-8
    Black Studies Library, 98-102, 105-6
    Employment of black librarians in, 98
Owens, Major R., 84

Peterson, Russel, quoted, 199-200
Phinazee, Annette, 123
Porter, Dorothy, 121
Pratt Institute, 81
Professionalism, 15-20, 35-9, 46, 196, 265
Project Weeksville, 86
Public Library
    As learning center, 263, 264-5
    Black Caucus organization in, 214-7
    Collections should reflect black experience, 232-3
    Community control of, 156, 216
    Discrimination against black librarians, 204, 206, 207, 221
    Need for black representation on library boards of trustees, 213
    Orientation for new staff, 235
    Personnel policies, 235-6
    Racist institution, 222, 233
Public Library Service to Blacks
    Disadvantaged and Outreach Programs, 227-30, 239, 240, 241-8
    Evaluation, 27-8
    Goals, 25-7
    Information imbalance in black communities, 50, 153, 222
    Insufficient programs and facilities, 153, 224, 225-6, 249
    Materials in libraries that are offensive, 30, 232
    Programs, 28-31, 250-2
    Relevance to problems of blacks, 28, 50, 237

Southern states, 222-4
Workshop on library service to blacks, 209, 238
Publishers
Failure to publish adequate materials on minorities, 276, 277-8
Unresponsive to recruitment of minorities, 278
Purdue University
Department of Audiovisual Instruction, 168

Queens Borough Public Library, 196

Racism, 4, 7, 9, 137, 141, 151, 153, 256
Research in Librarianship
By black librarians for black community, 159
Robinson, Carrie C., quoted, 278
Rockefeller, Nelson, 3

San Jose State College, 169
Sayers, Frances Clarke, quoted, 275
Schomburg Collection of The New York Public Library, 110, 120
Schools
Black history, teaching of in, 74
Black librarians, 76
Book selection, 76
Credo for Libraries, 76-8
Discrimination in, 66
Insensitivity of teachers, 68-9, 71, 137
Integrated Education, 140
Libraries, 72-6
Responsibility for integration of, 66-7
Role of librarians, 72-6
Unresponsive to black children, 262
Seale, Bobby, 145
Semmelweiss, Ignaz Philipp, 18, 23
Shockley, Ann Allen, 294
Shriver, Sargent, quoted, 276
Smith, Betty, 79, 84
Southern Illinois University, 169
Special Libraries, 273
Special Libraries Association, 272-3
Special Library, 269, 270, 271
Standards for School Media Programs, 171
Stone, C. W., 167
Sullivan, Leon H., 213
Supreme Court Decision, 1954, 66

Tate, Binnie, 123
Third World, 283, 284, 285, 286
Totten, Herman L., 165
A Tree Grows in Brooklyn, 79
Tucker, Sterling, quoted, 254
Tunney, John V., 205
Turner, Nat, 23

UNESCO, 160, 164
Unions, Library, 8, 195-200
United Negro College Fund, 110, 111
Universities
    Changes in, 91
    Relations with black communities, 54, 91
University Libraries
    A black librarian's assessment of, 94-5
    Changes needed in urban institutions, 95, 290
    Collection building, 291-2
    Departmental libraries, 113-5
    Governance, 92-3
    Racism in, 93
    Service to disadvantaged student, 290
    Urban institutions' problems, 91-2
University of Akron, 257
University of Maryland
    School of Library and Information Service, 185, 186
    Urban Information Specialist Program, 154, 186, 225
University of Missouri
    College of Education, 170
    School of Library Science, 170
University of Pittsburgh
    Graduate School of Library and Information Sciences, 192
University Without Walls, 269, 271
Urban League, 205

Virginia State College, 5

Wallace, George, 4, 40, 45
Washington, Booker T., 23
Wasserman, Paul, quoted, 184, 262
Watkins, Mel, 293
Weaver, Robert C., quoted, 253
Welbourne, James C., 183, 187
Wendt, P., 169
Western Reserve University *see* Case Western Reserve University
Whitenack, Carolyn, 168

Wright, Frank Lloyd, 18

Yette, Samuel F., quoted, 205

Z
711.9
I65